CONFRONTATION AND COMMITMENT

C. W. E. BIGSBY

Confrontation and Commitment

A Study of
Contemporary American Drama
1959-66

UNIVERSITY OF MISSOURI PRESS

Copyright © 1967 and 1968 by C. W. E. Bigsby
Library of Congress Catalog Card Number 67-23023
Standard Book Number 8262-0064-8
Reprint paper edition, 1969
Manufactured in the United States of America

For my wife Pam – with love

ACKNOWLEDGEMENTS

THIS book owes its final shape, but not its faults, to the generous help and advice of Brian Lee, of the University of Nottingham in England, and Warren French, of the University of Missouri at Kansas City in the United States. Brian Lee, over a period of two years, read each chapter as it was completed and offered suggestions which were invariably helpful and perceptive while Warren French, who long ago fired my enthusiasm for American literature, endured the rigours of a protracted trans-Atlantic correspondence with remarkable good humour.

I also owe a debt to Jordan Miller at Kansas State University who first demonstrated to me the virtues of American drama and to Richard Gilman, drama editor of *Newsweek* magazine, for a healthy note of scepticism which he introduced to my view of that drama at the Salzburg Seminar in 1965.

I would also like to thank the librarians at the University of Nottingham and the University College of Wales at Aberystwyth for their continuing co-operation, and Morfydd Jenkins for her top-speed typing of the revised text. My greatest debt, however, is to my parents and wife for their encouragement and patience.

Portions of this book have appeared in *Modern Drama, Wisconsin Studies in Contemporary Literature, Journal of American Studies* and *Twentieth Century Literature*. I gratefully acknowledge permission to use them here where they appear in revised form.

CONTENTS

CONFRONTATION AND COMMITMENT

It began to seem that one would have to hold in the mind forever two ideas which seemed to be in opposition. The first idea was acceptance, the acceptance, totally without rancour, of life as it is, and men as they are: in the light of this idea, it goes without saying that injustice is a commonplace. But this does not mean that one could be complacent, for the second idea was of equal power: that one must never, in one's life, accept these injustices as commonplace but must fight them with all one's strength.

JAMES BALDWIN: *Notes of a Native Son*

INTRODUCTION

MARY MCCARTHY, writing in 1958 and looking back over the previous twenty years, could say with justification that 'the American theatre was not only bad, it was very bad' and that 'most American plays were horribly badly written.'[1] Certainly those looking for new and vital forms in drama had turned, not to the New World but to a developing European theatre. As they had looked, in the nineteen-twenties, to Kaiser and Pirandello rather than O'Neill so they now turned to Ionesco and Beckett rather than to Miller and Williams. Indeed Arthur Miller's nine-year silence, from 1955 to 1964, served to indicate the extent to which the reputation of American drama had come to rest on the achievement of one man.

Looking for a source of regeneration Mary McCarthy turned to the off-Broadway theatre, to that 'witty theatre found in downtown basements and converted lofts'. Less concerned with economic viability, companies like the *Artists' Theatre* (1953–1956) and *The Living Theatre* (1951–1963) sought to produce the *avant garde* and the contentious; to escape, as Herbert Machiz explains, the middle-class theatre of Hellman, Miller, Laurents, Inge, Rice, etc.[2] Yet significantly these theatres too were menaced by the necessity to achieve financial autonomy and indeed both the *Artists' Theatre* and *The Living Theatre* were forced to close as a result of economic failure. Nevertheless Mary McCarthy was clearly correct in identifying this as the possible source of renewal for it was from this 'non-commercial' theatre in 1959 that there stemmed a genuine renaissance in American drama to match that fostered by the *Royal Court Theatre* in England with John Osborne's *Look Back in Anger* in 1956. This minor revolution arose from a discontent which was at the same time both aesthetic and social for the new writers who came to the fore in the early sixties were dedicated on the one hand to extending the metaphysical scope of drama and on the other to extending its social utility.

Aesthetically playwrights like Gelber, Brown and Albee were concerned with escaping that theatre which had occupied itself with 'dissecting modern life either sociologically or psychoanalytically' and

---

[1] Mary McCarthy, *Sights and Spectacles 1937–1958* (London, 1959) p. xv.
[2] Herbert Machiz, *Artists Theatre: Four Plays* (New York, 1960), p. 8.

with escaping what they saw as an 'exhausted naturalism'.[1] This concern with the form and purpose of drama, inherited from a vital European theatre, could only be pursued in the small non-commercial theatre, however, and thus it is that of the writers considered here most secured their first production off-Broadway. While receiving its impetus from the experiments of the absurdists this drama does not reflect the ironical despair which is the mark of that theatre; neither, however, does it endorse the demand for resolution and reassurance which has largely dictated the form of Broadway's naturalistic plays. Rather it is concerned with testing new structures and with re-examining the implications of realism in a way which is reminiscent of the surrealistic experiments of the nineteen-twenties. To Gelber and Albee realism is to be interpreted as a positive dialectic rather than a style. Indeed they insist that the confrontation of reality should be seen both as the chief function of the dramatist and as the first duty of the individual. Thus the 'drama of confrontation' is a conscious attempt to break away from a theatre which Albee sees as dominated by 'real estate owners and theatre party managements' and which had been dedicated to presenting 'a false picture of ourselves to ourselves.'[2]

Robert Brustein, in his book *The Theatre of Revolt*, has paradoxically identified Albee and Gelber as dramatists protesting against the metaphysical life of man, as concerned with what he identifies as 'existential revolt' (using the term, he explains, not in the sense attributed to it by the school of philosophy but in the neutral sense 'of and pertaining to existence'). To him this sort of revolt is 'impotent and despairing', its characters subhuman, its concern 'human bondage.'[3] Yet while the post-war American drama has been marked by a genuine concern with man's metaphysical situation it has not, with the exception of O'Neill and Williams, recoiled in terror and fear nor does the impotence which emerges as its strongest distinguishing feature derive from the metaphysical life of man but rather from the denial of that life. *The Connection* is devoid of the regenerative presence of women because this microcosmic group is effectively impotent as a result of its retreat from reality, while Nick and Martha, in *Who's Afraid of Virginia Woolf?* (1962), fail in a sexual escapade because they are drunk. The drugs of the former play and the drink of the latter are concrete images of the

[1] Ibid., pp.8–9.
[2] Edward Albee, 'Which Theatre is the Absurd One?' in *Directions in Modern Theatre and Drama* by John Gassner (New York, 1965), pp. 330–4.
[3] Robert Brustein, *The Theatre of Revolt* (Boston, 1965), p. 26.

enervating effect of escapism. Far from protesting against the meta-physical life of man Albee, Gelber and the later Miller insist on the need to embrace it.

The distinction between the theatre of the absurd and the drama of confrontation is a necessary one to make, however, for although the absurdist *technique* is also that of confrontation the absurd lacks the redemptive aspect of the new American drama. Brustein, in linking Gelber and Albee with Beckett and the whole theatre of the absurd, is failing to understand Albee's philosophical standpoint as indeed is Martin Esslin when he similarly includes him in his theatre of the absurd. The faith which Albee proclaims in man at the climax of *The Zoo Story* would be entirely alien to the European absurdists; for man in this play has heroic possibilities. Albee accepts, what Beckett and Ionesco cannot, that martyrdom is possible. When the old couple jump out of the window in Ionesco's *The Chairs* (1951) the result is and must be, nothing. Man's attempt to snatch dignity and stature only results in his becoming more absurd. To Albee, however, dignity is obtainable, neither need man be totally alone. If communication is difficult and even pointless in *The American Dream* (1961) this derives not from the absurdity of existence but rather from man's failure to face the horror of his metaphysical situation. The basic difference between Albee's outlook and that of the theatre of the absurd lies in the fact that he sees man's impotence and absurdity as of his own making. Esslin, in summarising his arguments, strangely contradicts not only much of his own work but, incidentally, Brustein's observa-tions as well. He says that the theatre of the absurd does not reflect despair and urges that the confrontation of reality is an aspect of man's dignity.[1] In doing so, however, he is ignoring the fact that Beckett's vision encompasses not only an awareness of the nature of man's situation but also a proclamation of the impossibility of human dignity. Buried to the neck in sand, lying in a dust-bin, such dignity as there is functions as self-parody. Man's ability to 'carry on' is the final mockery. Brustein is clearly correct in identifying the 'existential revolt' of the theatre of the absurd as 'impotent and despairing' but wrong in extend-ing this definition to the fundamentally different drama of confronta-tion. So that Esslin's final comment becomes, ironically, a better descrip-

[1] Lionel Abel's denial of the very existence of the absurd in his book, *Metatheatre* (New York, 1963), is hardly very helpful but he too notices the inconsistency of Esslin's definition which is so strangely irrelevant to most of the playwrights whom he treats.

tion of Albee's vision than it is of Beckett's or Ionesco's. 'For the dignity of man lies in his ability to face reality in all its senselessness; to accept it freely, without fear, without illusions—and to laugh at it.'[1] No wonder Albee says, 'Amen' to that in an article called 'Which Theatre is the Absurd One?'[2] Indeed of the plays considered here only *The Brig* could be seen as a part of the theatre of the absurd and to my mind even this lacks the irony which Brustein correctly observes as a mark of the absurd and, indeed, of 'the entire existential drama'. *The Connection*, for all its similarities to *Waiting for Godot*, trancends the quietism which emerges as Beckett's idea of a valid response to the apocalyptic vision, while all of these plays, with the possible exception of *The Brig*, reveal a faith in man which is foreign to the basically anti-humanist theatre of the absurd.

Fundamentally opposed as these two groups are in outlook the American dramatists do something to counter-balance that destructiveness which Kenneth Tynan saw as implicit in Ionesco's work, 'The peril arises' he had said in an attack which he launched in *The Observer*, 'when it (Ionesco's personal vision) is held up for general emulation as the gateway to the theatre of the future, that bleak new world from which the humanist heresies of faith in logic and belief in man will forever be banished.'[3] Starting from the same premise as the absurdists, namely that man is born astride the grave in an empty universe, these new American dramatists reconstitute these 'humanist heresies.' This is not that humanism which exalts man as of supreme value, however, but rather that which Sartre identifies with existentialism (using the term now in its philosophical sense) 'There is no other universe except the human universe, the universe of human subjectivity . . . This is humanism, because we remind man that there is no legislator but himself; that he himself, thus abandoned, must decide for himself . . .'[4] To Sartre the solitude and abandonment which can be taken as the human situation constitute not a debilitating force but the confirmation of freedom. Existence, to him, is distinct from the meaning of existence. Since meaning derives from the individual's choice of possibilities it must accordingly vanish with the relinquishment of freedom. Thus the

[1] Martin Esslin, *The Theatre of the Absurd* (New York, 1961), p. 316.

[2] 'Which Theatre is the Absurd One?' p. 333.

[3] Eugène Ionesco, *Notes and Counter Notes*, trans., Donald Watson (London, 1964), p. 92.

[4] Jean-Paul Sartre, *Existentialism and Humanism*, trans., Philip Mairet (London, 1948), pp. 55–6.

absurd, for Sartre and Albee alike, lies not in man's situation but rather in the ridiculous prospect of his surrendering freedom and thus identity to a systematised conformity. Thus to Sartre, and equally to Miller and Albee, the realisation of the emptiness of the universe is the first and necessary step towards understanding the freedom and responsibilities of man. It is for this faith in the need to confront that vision of the world and to accept that freedom that Miller and Albee between them produce the myth and indeed the litany.

Concurrent with this upsurge of experimental, metaphysical drama there arose also a corresponding renewal of social commitment. Just as the English theatre before 1956 had tended to ignore whole areas of society so too the American theatre, reflecting a post-war political disengagement, tended to cut itself off not only from the immediate problems of social inequity but also from the vitality which is an aspect of commitment. Wesker, Pinter, Delaney and Behan, however, forced the English theatre to acknowledge, virtually for the first time, the immediate realities of working-class life, while Hansberry, Duberman, Jones and Baldwin performed the same function for the Negro in the American theatre. Largely ignored or travestied in previous plays the Negro now became the centre of a drama which recalled both the strength and, ironically, the weakness of the nineteen-thirties' committed theatre. If the Negro dramatists have largely lacked the originality of Gelber and Albee, however, they have introduced a remorseless power which has hitherto been largely absent from the American theatre.

While it is impossible to make an assessment of the final value of the writers considered here it is clear that the period from 1959 to 1966 has been of central importance to a developing American theatre. For these new dramatists have largely turned away from the Ibsen/Chekhov traditions and have demonstrated a willingness to experiment which can only serve to extend the potentialities of drama. The powerful metaphors of Jack Gelber and Kenneth Brown, the surrealistic experiments of Edward Albee and Saul Bellow and the increasingly metaphysical foundation of their drama are all signs that the American theatre is beginning to liberate itself from the restrictions of Broadway. Certainly the American theatre has established itself, within these last few years, as capable of making a genuinely original contribution to world drama and, indeed, in many respects has largely surpassed the more limited iconoclasm of Europe.

Section One

CONFRONTATION

People who shut their eyes to reality simply invite their own destruction, and anyone who insists on remaining in a state of innocence long after that innocence is dead turns himself into a monster.

JAMES BALDWIN: *Notes of a Native Son*

I want no weeping. Death must be looked at face to face.

FEDERICO GARCIA LORCA: *The House of Bernarda Alba*

. . . such a momentous enlightenment—an enlightenment that is to be the starting point of a completely new existence—a real companionship, founded on truth and purged of all falsehood . . .

HENRIK IBSEN: *The Wild Duck*

The end of the movement of absurdity, of rebellion, etc., . . . is compassion . . . that is to say, in the last analysis, love . . .

ALBERT CAMUS: *Carnets 1942-1951*

1
An End to Revolt

ALTHOUGH Jack Gelber's *The Connection* (1959) was recognised by a small group of devotees as an important play at the time of its first production its true significance can only really be appreciated in the light of later developments. The strong relationship between Gelber's play and the drama of Samuel Beckett and even that of Jean-Paul Sartre established a European influence which was potentially as important as the European-derived expressionism of the nineteen-thirties. *The Connection*, indeed, functions as a fulcrum between the works of O'Neill and Williams and the dramas of Edward Albee and the later Miller. It confronts and rejects the essential 'optimism' of the former playwrights and yet does not fully adopt the tentative positivism of the latter ones. It is important too in that its basically 'non-linear' development involves a concept of drama which was largely foreign to a theatre which had flourished on social realism and expressionistic satires. New and vital in terms of American drama, however, *The Connection* was merely a reflection of a process of dramatic experimentation which had long typified the European theatre.

The French theatre theoretician Antonin Artaud, writing in 1938, expressed his disgust with a theatre which had become little more than a form of distraction. He wanted to see a theatre whose object was not 'to resolve social and psychological conflicts, to serve as battlefield for moral passions, but to express objectively certain secret truths, to bring into the light of day . . . certain aspects of truth that have been buried under forms in their encounter with Becoming.'[1] While Artaud's own radical solutions to this seemingly enervated theatre were not always workable he did appreciate that a concern with the substance of drama itself was the key to revivification. For, as he says, 'To . . . link the theatre to the expressive possibilities of forms . . . is to restore it to its original direction, to reinstate it in its religious and metaphysical aspect, is to reconcile it with the *universe*.' Writing twenty years later

[1] Antonin Artaud, *The Theatre and its Double*, trans., Mary Caroline Richards (New York, 1958), p. 70.

Ionesco too recognised the need for the theatre to attempt 'a constant rediscovery of self, at each historical moment of time.'[1] If this concern with the nature of drama itself, this effort to reinstate its metaphysical aspect was almost totally absent from American drama until virtually the late nineteen-fifties it was not as remote from the European theatre, however, as Artaud and Ionesco suggest.

The significance of Pirandello's *Six Characters in Search of an Author* (1921) for example, lies not in the originality of its form but rather in the fact that it raises the seemingly simple question, 'what is drama?'. It is a dramatisation of Artaud's own speculation. While there is nothing intrinsically interesting in witnessing a dramatist's analysis of himself and his craft it is equally obvious that through such an examination drama can attempt to renew itself. As Richard Gilman points out, in an article entitled, 'The Drama is Coming Now',[2] it is possible to see this concern with the validity of art itself as a central pre-occupation of every aspect of twentieth-century art from Picasso, Stravinski and Joyce to Kafka, Brecht and Mann. Self-consciousness is often a source of strength for the artist and so it proved with Pirandello who in understanding the deficiencies of dramatic art came also to appreciate its strengths. He realised, for example, what Artaud and later still Ionesco were to stress, that, far from being a means of communication, language is often a barrier. As the Father says in *Six Characters in Search of an Author*, 'How can we understand each other if into the words which I speak I put the sense and the value of things as I understand them within myself . . . While at the same time whoever is listening to them inevitably assumes them to have the sense and value that they have for him . . . We think we understand one another . . . But we never really do'.[3] He recognised too the limitations which are thrust upon the dramatist by the nature of his craft—the need to present as a totality what is merely a fragment and the need to assess character in relation to single events. Pirandello's play is not a cry for naturalism or romanticism, it is a direct insistence on the need for a re-examination of the motives and intentions of drama. This implies an understanding which has been far from the minds of American dramatists, who, if they have been ready to borrow the modes of

[1] *Notes and Counter Notes*, p. 32.

[2] Richard Gilman, 'The Drama is Coming Now', *Tulane Drama Review*, VII, iv (Spring, 1963), pp. 27-42.

[3] Luigi Pirandello, Six Characters in Search of an Author, trans., Frederick May (London, 1954), p. 17.

presentation of a developing European theatre, have all too frequently failed to appreciate the movements of which they were the expression.

Artaud published *The Theatre and its Double* in 1938 while still incarcerated in a mental hospital where he was to remain until 1946. He too felt the inadequacy of language and called for, 'a theatre in which violent physical images crush and hypnotize the sensibility of the spectator seized by the theatre as by a whirlwind of higher forces'.[1] To him dialogue was a mark not of drama but of literature. In saying this he was not unaware that the sort of theatre for which he was calling could not hope to serve the purpose of character analysis, but, as he insisted, 'who ever said the theatre was created to analyze a character, to resolve the conflicts of love and duty, to wrestle with all the problems of a topical and psychological nature that monopolize our contemporary stage?'[2] He wanted to see established a theatre which would challenge the whole moral system rather than investigate the petty concerns of individuals. The theatre for which he called, in other words, was a theatre of metaphysics. While Eric Bentley identifies the chief characteristic of modern drama (which he dates from 1880) as the rise of the playwright as 'thinker', a more significant classification might in fact designate the playwright as metaphysician. For true drama, which Artaud calls poetry, is indeed 'willy nilly, metaphysical and it is just its metaphysical bearing, I should say, the intensity of its metaphysical effect, that comprises its essential worth'.[3] Artaud is here simply taking the iconoclasm of Ibsen, Strindberg and Shaw a stage further. For what he is demanding is simply the destruction of what has hitherto constituted the foundation of all drama; plot, character and language. As long ago as Ibsen's *When we Dead Awaken* (1899) and Strindberg's *A Dream Play* (1902) European dramatists had shown their readiness to re-examine the fundamentals of their craft but none of them were prepared to go as far as Artaud whose desire was to create a *theatre of cruelty*.

The emergence of the playwright-philosopher, which has been the mark of the twentieth century, has not for the most part resulted in esoteric thesis drama, however, but has revealed itself in an intensified perception of the human condition and the human situation. This movement towards metaphysical concerns has been matched by a

[1] *The Theatre and its Double*, pp. 82-83.
[2] *Ibid.*, p. 41.
[3] *Ibid.*, p. 44.

corresponding re-examination of the nature of drama itself so that Beckett's *Waiting for Godot* (1952) can be seen as the apogee of this dual movement. There is no sense of inevitability about this, however, for the work of Sartre and Camus, both metaphysical playwrights, relies less on the highly 'simplified' theatre of Beckett than on Shavian discussion and exemplification. Nevertheless Beckett's play was a demonstration of the prophetic nature of a comment made in 1941 by Jacques Copeau, one of France's greatest directors of the first half of the century. In talking about a new and revivified theatre he stated his belief in the necessity for rediscovering what he saw as the original purity of drama. 'I believe that the more the theatre intends to appeal effectively to a wide public, to remain vivid in its memory, to influence its life on the deepest levels, the more it will have to be simplified and purified, reducing its elements numerically in order to develop their force.'[1] To Copeau this was a return to original purity and indeed he cited Greek drama as his criterion. To his mind drama now lay under the accumulated conventions of centuries and the time had come to shuffle them off. If European drama, starting as Bentley suggests with Wagner and Ibsen, had been concerned with just such a process then the pace of that simplification or renewal was accelerated by an increasing self-analysis. The fusion of emotions with thought—a compound which produced not deadly intellectual exercises but a drama of depth which transcended the trite solipsisms of conventional theatre— proved the source of revivification until almost the middle of the twentieth century. It is notoriously and obviously easy for iconoclasm to harden into convention, however, and by the time of Artaud, and indeed even of Pirandello, Ibsen was as much the enemy as Scribe and the vivid experiments of Strindberg seemed as irrelevant as the jokes of Restoration Comedy. Nevertheless the changes brought about by Ibsen had been no less significant in his time than were the, perhaps more obvious, changes introduced by Samuel Beckett. Where Ibsen was concerned with making intellectual enquiry the animus of his work Beckett was more concerned with the destruction of plot and character and the establishment of a dramatic communication which relied not on intellectual assent but on what one can only call 'visceral' contact.

The changing shape of drama, which is most noticeable with the rise of what Martin Esslin has called the 'theatre of the absurd', is not a

---

[1] Jacques Copeau, 'Once again: Style', trans., Leonard C. Pronko, *Tulane Drama Review*, VII, iv (Summer, 1963), p. 188.

response to the call of theoreticians, however, for changes in drama, as Gilman has pointed out, are never brought about by fiat. Indeed Artaud was not establishing an arbitrary dictum himself. The changes for which he called in drama seemed to him to stem directly from his perception of the world. While the favourite theme of the eighteen-eighties and nineties—the gap between an individual's desires and his attainments, his character and his environment—stemmed from a general spirit of change and disillusionment, Artaud, in rejecting what he called the misdeeds of the psychological theatre (which he traced back to the neo-classicism of Racine) turned to a theatre of cruelty as an expression of his awareness of 'the anguished, catastrophic period we live in'.[1]

One must remember at this stage, however, that drama never falls quite so easily into patterns. For while this main tradition, which Robert Brustein correctly identifies as revolt, was changing the face of drama the *pièce bien fait* still dominated much of European theatre while some playwrights corrupted the new concern with thought into the bastardy of persuasion and propaganda.

In America this sub-tradition has long been dominant. The well-made-play has been and still is greeted with an enthusiasm which is reserved in Europe for the imaginative perception of a Pirandello or a Beckett. Playwrights like Inge and Hellman assume a status which is hardly justifiable by any but the commercial standards which dominate Broadway.

The American theatre has never fully absorbed the lessons of European drama. When Arthur Miller said that he was concerned with the drama of the whole man he came close to understanding what the European tradition from Ibsen to Beckett was about; but his own plays, for the most part, failed to match his intentions. The Ibsen which he captured was the social critic whose emphasis on individual integrity chimed with his own faith in transcendental independence. Yet there is a deeper commitment in Ibsen which is concerned not with man's social relationships but with his metaphysical ones and while Miller is clearly aware of this more fundamental level his own plays never entirely escape the social simplicities of the thirties, unless it be in the unwieldy *After the Fall* (1964).

America has remained strangely insulated not only from the European revolt against the well-made-play but also from its rejection of a drama of resolution and reassurance. Certainly at the very time when

[1] *The Theatre and its Double*, p. 84.

European dramatists were turning away from psychology and sociology the American theatre was producing plays like *Tea and Sympathy* (1953), *Cat on a Hot Tin Roof* (1955) and *A View from the Bridge* (1955). The power of the European theatre lay in its concern with relocating man, with establishing the first task of a dramatist as being a commitment to man and his metaphysical situation. It is this which essentially links Ibsen with Beckett and which, with the exception of a very few plays, represents the division between American and European drama. American drama has tended all too often to capitulate before social and economic pressures and has pleaded necessity as the cause of the un-adventurous nature of its theatre. Even the giants of the American stage tend to be experimenters only within the native context and have largely lacked the European's concern with self-examination. Nevertheless in the final year of the nineteen-fifties it became apparent that American drama, capitalising on the lead of Eugene O'Neill, was beginning not only to realise Artaud's true metaphysical drama but also to investigate seriously the dramatic process itself. In July, 1959, Jack Gelber's *The Connection* played to enthusiastic audiences in New York while in October of the same year at the Reuben Gallery a group of artists began to experiment with a form of 'theatre' which they called 'happenings'. In September Edward Albee's *The Zoo Story* received its first performance in Europe and reached New York in January, 1960. This sudden efflux of activity served at one go to raise the stature of American drama both in America and Europe while it soon became apparent that its principal concerns constituted a challenge to the main tradition of revolt in modern drama.

The Connection did potentially for American drama what Pirandello had done for Italian and indeed European drama as a whole. It dismissed a form which had ceased to serve the theatre and the purposes of drama. When a series of conventions reach the point at which they deny their ostensible objective then the time for change has arrived. When Pirandello's Producer says, 'But what's the truth got to do with it? Acting's what *we're* here for! Truth's all very fine . . . But only up to a point',[1] then it becomes obvious that the time has arrived either for a new form or a new and lesser objective. In America Gelber's play thankfully cleared the ground and Albee, at least in part, filled it. Yet even his lack of understanding of the nature of drama became clear in the intriguing but theatrically gross *Tiny Alice*.

The metaphysical concern of the European theatre had not been

[1] *Six Characters in Search of an Author*, p. 17.

entirely absent from the American scene, however, for the last plays of Eugene O'Neill, plays which are only now beginning to receive their due recognition, are founded on a concern with the relationship of the individual, not to his fellow man, but to his own concept of reality. O'Neill, earlier in his career, had told Joseph Wood Krutch, 'Most modern plays are concerned with the relation of man to man, but this does not concern me at all. I am interested only in the relation of man and God.'[1] Although at this stage in his career he was literally speaking of God whom he constantly attempted to re-define in plays like *The Fountain* (1924), *Marco Millions* (1925), *Strange Interlude* (1928) and *Dynamo* (1929), this precisely defined deity is superceded finally by a generalised sense of man's metaphysical situation. While his earlier work is all too frequently a pastiche of forms and themes culled from the dramatic literature of the world and often lacking both control and credibility, his last plays evidence a power and perception which transcends that of any of his contemporaries.

Soon after completing *The Iceman Cometh* (1946) O'Neill remarked that it constituted 'a denial of any other experience of faith in my plays'.[2] The faith which he had affirmed in those plays, however, had varied from the strictly political to the philosophical and indeed his work had been consciously devoted towards establishing some sort of creed which could satisfactorily fill that void which European dramatists from Ibsen and Strindberg onwards had sought to bridge. In a letter to George Nathan, O'Neill voiced his belief that the 'playwright today must dig at the roots of the sickness of today as he feels it—the death of the Old God and the failure of science and materialism to give any satisfying new One for the surviving primitive religious instinct to find a meaning of life in, and to comfort his fear of death with'.[3] It is ironical that in plays like *The Fountain* and *The Great God Brown* (1926) that faith should transpire to be somewhat older than the Old God, for in these plays he celebrates a pantheistic belief in the goodness of everything. In the latter play Cybel, the earth-mother, voices this faith: 'Always spring comes bearing life! Always again! Always, always forever again!—Spring again!—life again! summer and fall and death and peace again!—but always, always, love and conception and birth and pain again—spring bearing the intolerable chalice of life again!—

[1] *The Theatre of Revolt*, p. 331.

[2] *Ibid.*, p. 339.

[3] Joseph Wood Krutch, *The American Drama Since 1918* (New York, 1957), pp. 92-93.

bearing the glorious, blazing crown of life again!'[1] The justification for suffering and death is thus sought in the reality of the Great Chain of Being. In his final plays, however, he retreats from this grandiose and unconvincing affirmation to the apparently more human stance which Ibsen had adopted before him. *The Iceman Cometh, Long Day's Journey into Night* (1956) and *A Touch of the Poet* (1958) all endorse the validity of revolt against existence which expresses itself in a retreat behind illusions. Human kind, in T. S. Eliot's words, can indeed not stand too much reality. In this final and intensely personal world O'Neill postulates only two kinds of peace; that of existence within the bounds of a subjective reality—a 'pipe dream'—or the final tranquility of a complete withdrawal from life.

The Iceman Cometh is set in a bar, 'Bedrock Bar, The End of the Line Café, The Bottom of the Sea Rathskeller'. Here are gathered together a group of men whose collective illusions constitute not only the sole barrier between themselves and despair but also a dialectic which influences their lives more profoundly than the political faith which is projected in the background as an alternative response. These men have been left behind by the events which had shaped them. They are not 'down-and-outs' in the usual sense of the word for most of them had at one time been a distinguished part of that society which they have now deserted; one of them is a Harvard Law School Alumnus, one a Captain of British Infantry and one an editor of an Anarchist periodical. Now, however, they sit in the back room of the bar and drink. They retain their dignity and identity through their mutual tolerance of each other's illusions. Their faith is expressed in the names of two of the group, Harry Hope, the proprietor of the bar, and Jimmy Tomorrow, a one-time Boer War correspondent. Their philosophy is the Latin one—*mañana*.

Into this group there intrudes the figure of Hickey—a travelling salesman whose previous visits have always been the excuse for drunkenness and riotous parties. On this occasion, however, he brings with him an almost religious fervour for converting the group to a belief in the necessity to face reality. He no longer drinks because, as he says, this is no longer an escape which he needs. He urges them all separately to put their illusions to the test and find out their falsity. To Hickey illusion and guilt are inextricable and the only escape from the latter lies in a destruction of the former. But Hickey carries with him

[1] Eugene O'Neill, *The Plays of Eugene O'Neill* (New York, 1951), pp. 322-3.

'the touch of death'. The religion to which he tries to convert the group is one of callous brutality which stems, we ultimately discover, from his own need to justify the murder of his wife. She had been the epitome of tolerance and forgiveness but her unshakeable belief in the goodness and ultimate redemption of her husband had only chained him to feelings of guilt and inferiority. Her 'pipe-dream' had thrown the burden of compassion and responsibility onto Hickey's shoulders. In the words of Arthur Miller's *After the Fall*, to regain innocence 'you kill most easily'.[1]

The lines of force which connect this play with Ibsen's *The Wild Duck* (1884) have been noted before but are especially important in the context of this study for the stance adopted by both Ibsen and O'Neill is precisely that against which Albee and, eventually, Miller revolt. *The Wild Duck* is based on the belief, expressed through the drunken but compassionate Relling, that if 'you take away make-believe from the average man, you take away his happiness as well'.[2] Gregers Werle, again a man intent on shuffling off his own sense of guilt, is determined to open the eyes of his school friend, Hjalmar Ekdal, whom he believes his father has tricked into marrying his former mistress. Hjalmar has been happily married for fifteen years at the time of the play and is absorbed in his daughter and in an invention which will clearly never become anything but a 'pipe-dream'. Gregers, however, inspired by what Relling calls 'acute rectitudinal fever' tells Hjalmar of his suspicions in order that he and his wife may be able to establish 'a real companionship, founded on truth and purged of all falsehood'. While this has an ironical tone in a play in which the 'momentous enlightenment'[3] leads only to death and disillusionment it is important to realise that this is a precise description of the standpoint later adopted by both Albee and the later Miller. For both Ibsen and O'Neill to destroy a 'life-lie' is ultimately to destroy a life (although he does accept that some illusions are dangerous, see for example, *A Dolls House* 1870 and *Ghosts* 1881). In Ibsen's play Hedvig, Hjalmar's daughter, shoots

[1] Arthur Miller, 'After the Fall', *The Saturday Evening Post*, Feb. 1, 1964, p. 58.

[2] Henrik Ibsen, *Four Great Plays by Ibsen*, trans., R. Farquharson Sharp (New York, 1959), p. 294. Bernard Shaw similarly declared, 'Take away from the activity of mankind that part of it which consists in the pursuit of illusions, and you take out the world's mainspring.' Eric Bentley, *Bernard Shaw* (London, 1950), p. 119.

[3] *Four Great Plays by Ibsen*, p. 277.

herself when her father, unhinged by Gregers' revelations, refuses to see her. So too in O'Neill's play Parritt, an anarchist who has betrayed his own mother, kills himself because he can neither face reality nor create a pipe-dream which can save him. In Ibsen's play there are for-bears of the self-deceiving inhabitants of Harry Hope's bar. Old Ekdal, Hjalmar's father, wanders around a darkened attic believing himself to be in the forest of his youth while Molvik, an ex-student of theology, believes himself to be a demoniac. As the compassionate Relling says, 'That is only a bit of make-believe I invented to keep the life in him. If I hadn't done that, the poor honest wretch would have given way to self-contempt and despair years ago'.[1] The prophet who would force the apocalyptic vision of reality becomes the anti-life force. It is Relling, suitably, who is given the last word for to him 'life would be all right if we could only be rid of these infernal fools who come to poor people's doors presenting their "demands of the ideal".' So in O'Neill's play Hickey, who becomes identified with the iceman of the title, is the equivalent of Gregers and is the anti-life force. In preaching to his twelve 'disciples' he is like his predecessor whose destiny was always to be 'the thirteenth at table'.[2]

When the inhabitants of Harry Hope's bar try to transform their illusions into reality they succeed only in destroying that fragile barrier which had stopped them slipping into self-contempt and despair. Forced into retreat by Hickey's attacks they turn on each other and refuse to accept the putative reality of their fellow sufferers. Even Larry Slade, whose air of cynical disengagement covers a compassion which links him with Ibsen's Relling, is jolted out of his pose and, indeed, with the exception of Parritt, is more radically affected than any of the others. Shaken out of his protective illusion he realises suddenly that, unlike the others, he can never slip back into it. He finds himself face to face with the reality of the apocalyptic vision and realises that his pose of world weariness has been transformed into reality by Hickey's self-justifying meddling. 'Be God, there's no hope! I'll never be a success in the grandstand—or anywhere else! Life is too much for me! I'll be a weak fool looking with pity at the two sides of everything till the day I die! May that day come soon! By God, I'm the only real convert to death Hickey made here. From the bottom of my coward's heart I mean that now!'[3] He thus embodies the only alternative to

[1] *Ibid.*, p. 293.
[2] *Four Great Plays by Ibsen*, p. 305.
[3] *The Plays of Eugene O'Neill*, pp. 726-7

death and illusion and his empty and fearful life is the direct outcome of Hickey's demand of the ideal—a demand ultimately rooted in self-justification. To O'Neill and Ibsen alike, then, the prophet of reality is the unwelcome guest while his creed is callous and ultimately disastrous. So that revolt against the human condition is not only justifiable but essential to meaningful survival.

In *Long Day's Journey into Night* O'Neill transforms the agonies of his own life into a play whose force and intensity lack real parallel. This play, which in moulding art from private fears and frustrations surpasses even Strindberg's drama, takes O'Neill's dialogue between reality and illusion a stage further. Coming to terms with the forces which had torn at his own intellect and emotions he accepts one further response to the fact of existence. In his story of the Tyrone family one son, Edmund, has already attempted suicide while the whole family share the faith in alcohol which the inhabitants of Harry Hope's bar had shown. It is Edmund who defines the third alternative response to life which O'Neill now recognises—a response which is close to Whitmanesque naturalism and his own earlier pantheism. At sea on a sailing ship Edmund had become 'drunk with the beauty and singing rhythm of it, and for a moment I lost myself—actually lost my life. I was set free! I dissolved in the sea, became white sails and flying spray, became beauty and rhythm, became moonlight and the ship and the high dim-starred sky! I belonged, without past or future, within peace and unity and a wild joy, within something greater than my own life, or the life of Man, to Life itself! To God, if you want to put it that way'. Yet this barely attainable vision of peace which confers 'the joy of belonging to a fulfillment beyond men's lousy, pitiful, greedy fears and hopes and dreams' survives itself as scarcely more than a transient pantheistic insight in which 'For a second there is meaning! Then the hand lets the veil fall and you are alone, lost in the fog again, and you stumble on toward nowhere, for no good reason!'[1]

All four of the Tyrones positively writhe in a spiritual joust between illusion and reality. At base all of them are intensely compassionate, aware of the need for tolerance in a world which is unspeakably bleak without it. Yet each character is obsessed with and in part controlled by a guilt which makes him turn, as the inhabitants of Harry Hope's bar had done under Hickey's tortured probing, against the illusions of his fellow sufferers. Indeed the play is structured on the cutting

[1] Eugene O'Neill, *Long Day's Journey into Night* (New Haven, 1956), p. 153.

yet essentially truthful remark which is immediately withdrawn with genuine remorse and understanding. Mary Tyrone, who retreats from life entirely with the aid of morphine, speaks for them all when she says, 'We've loved each other . . . Let's remember only that, and not try to understand what we cannot understand, or help things that cannot be helped—the things life has done to us we cannot excuse or explain'.[1] If Edmund, with his library drawn from Voltaire, Rousseau, Schopenhauer, Nietzsche, Ibsen, Baudelaire, Whitman and Poe, is virtually a professional cynic whose pantheistic insights are subsumed in romantic necrophilia, there is little in the lives of the Tyrones to justify any other attitude. The reality of their situation is horrifying while the curses of drug-addiction, drunkenness and consumption which assail them are all ultimately traceable to inherited characteristics. The play is essentially a recapitulation of the nineteenth century regret over the gap between desire and fulfillment, visionary freedom and actual determinism. So that Edmund (O'Neill's *alter ego*) clearly states O'Neill's own opinion when he asserts the validity of a world of illusion, 'Who wants to see life as it is, if they can help it? It's the three Gorgons in one. You look in their faces and turn to stone. Or it's Pan. You see him and you die—that is, inside you—and have to go on living as a ghost'.[2] Clearly this is the fate which faces the family at the end of the play. If Mary Tyrone finally slips into the protective world of her youthful dreams the others are left to look on in dismay seeing in her retreat an escape which they can never finally achieve themselves. For while she has lost the Catholic faith of her childhood she has sublimated this loss in a drugged world of illusion. Yet even this is described by O'Neill as a 'sad dream'. The others look forward to living as ghosts, subduing their sense of desolation in alcohol and remaining 'a little in love with death'.[3]

O'Neill's last full-length play, *A Touch of the Poet*, is similarly concerned with the need for redeeming illusion to feed a spirit too easily subject to the pressures of the human experience. A lesser play than either *The Iceman Cometh* or *A Long Day's Journey into Night*, *A Touch of the Poet* stresses not only the need for illusion but also the deterministic nature of a world in which the tormenting illogicalities of love and pride project the battle between reality and illusion from

[1] *Ibid.*, p. 85.
[2] Eugene O'Neill, *Long Day's Journey into Night* (New Haven, 1956), p. 131.
[3] *Ibid.*, p. 154.

one generation into the next. Yet for all his failure fully to believe in the victory of illusion (a failure derived from the exigencies of life itself) he never fails in his belief in the necessity for compassion—a compassion which evidences itself in a tolerance for the dreams and hopes not only of his characters but also, in retrospect, for the tortured family at whose hands he suffered.

Any account of American drama must start with Eugene O'Neill and indeed can hardly start any earlier. In spite of his early experimentation, which all too often resulted in hollow and artificial theatre, it is still true that through his sheer power of creative talent he alone was responsible for establishing American drama as a genuine and valid force on the international scene. If the Nobel prize was a recognition of the immensity of that achievement rather than a mark of genuinely outstanding dramatic ability it nonetheless served to place him in a context justified by his later work.

O'Neill was the first American dramatist to establish the validity of a drama in which metaphysical concern was no longer merely an aspect of character but rather the central and motivating force of the whole play.[1] At the heart of these plays was an awareness of the nature of solitude and an acute perception of the failure of life to generate intelligible meaning of itself. Groping for some code to place in the stead of a religion, which to O'Neill had died of pity for man, he flitted from socialism to deism. In the end, however, the only faith to which he could fully subscribe was that of Ibsen's *The Wild Duck*, namely that if you 'take away make-believe from the average man, you take away his happiness as well'. If O'Neill's world is a little darker than Ibsen's and its torments more endemic this grew from his perception of a determinism which emerged from personality and environment and which he had seen operating within the bounds of his own family.

Where O'Neill's drama is fundamentally a protest against the exigencies of existence—a protest which can be seen as an aspect of European revolt—it is followed in the American theatre by a movement to which Ibsen's 'momentous enlightenment' is a serious vision and whose faith is genuinely placed in what Ibsen had ironically referred to

---

[1] It must be pointed out, however, that the plays in which this concern with man's metaphysical situation become fused into a moving and forceful dramatic form were not published until a relatively late date (*The Iceman Cometh*, 1946; *Long Day's Journey into Night*, 1956; *A Touch of the Poet*, 1958). This accounts for the importance of Miller in the development of serious American drama.

as 'a real companionship, founded on truth and purged of all false-hood'. In search of meaning, as O'Neill had been, in a world seemingly lacking in justice, these dramatists profess to find it in an acceptance of the reality of man's metaphysical situation and in a declaration of man's freedom. O'Neill's vision is fatalistic. Given a deterministic universe, retreat into illusion or further into stoicism seems justified. To the 'drama of confrontation', however, there is no determinism and illusion becomes a denial of identity and essential existence. To Hickey, in *The Iceman Cometh*, the destruction of illusion had seemed to imply the destruction of guilt. To both Miller and Albee the reverse is true. Illusion to them becomes an escape from guilt so that Albee's Julian, in *Tiny Alice* (1904) and Miller's Quentin in *After the Fall*, accept responsibility and guilt in accepting reality.

The dialogue between reality and illusion thus continues in a new context. To O'Neill, conscious of the death of the Old God, reality constituted only the undeniable facts of biological determinism seen against an empty universe. While he groped for a supra-reality which could bring some semblance of meaning to this vision he could never fully believe in the fleeting glimpses which he allowed his characters. Neither could he pronounce any affirmation except the validity of illusion. To Arthur Miller, whose own work progresses from an Ibsenesque disavowal of 'rectitudinal fever' to a total embrace of the need for confrontation, reality lies primarily in the admission of human limitations and the recognition of human possibilities. In *Death of a Salesman* (1949) the protagonist's son says, 'I'm just what I am, that's all'[1] while in *After the Fall* the whole crux of the play rests on the protagonist's acceptance not only of his individual limitations but also of the boundary which circumscribes the limit of human possibilities. The facile illusions of success society are rejected as firmly as is the naïvete of perfectable man. Innocence is no longer a credible premise. Equally to Albee reality cannot reside in escapist abstractions but consists rather in a clear vision of metaphysical isolation.

Nevertheless Eugene O'Neill does not mark the end of revolt as a theme in American drama neither is his compassionate justification of illusion the last such plea, for Tennessee Williams, although a lesser artist, is essentially in the same tradition. In a world in which 'We're all of us sentenced to solitary confinement inside our own skins, for life'[2] he places his faith, like O'Neill, in the need for compassion above

[1] Arthur Miller, *Arthur Miller's Collected Plays* (New York, 6157), p. 217.
[2] Tennessee Williams, *Orpheus Descending* (Harmondsworth, 1961), p. 54.

all things and, again like O'Neill, he sees a validity in transcendental withdrawal. While he is critical of the more debilitating illusion of passionless sexuality and wholesale commitment to a decadent society he does endorse Ibsen's rejection of 'rectitudinal fever'. While Brick declaims against mendacity in *Cat on a Hot Tin Roof* it becomes apparent that the truth can be unnecessarily brutal. When he confronts his father with the true facts about his imminent death mendacity becomes associated with compassion. Similarly in *A Streetcar Named Desire* (1947) Blanche's brutal insistence on the truth serves merely to destroy her husband. If there is a sign, in *Night of the Iguana* (1961), of Williams accepting the validity of stoicism as his answer to the need 'to live beyond despair and still live' this reveals itself ultimately as but another version of O'Neill's naturalism enshrined here in the verses of an old man who dies in creating this, his final poem (perhaps in doing so incidentally revealing Williams' sense of artistic martyrdom).

'How calmly does the orange branch
Observe the sky begin to blanch
Without a cry, without a prayer,
With no betrayal of despair.

Sometime when night obscures the tree
The zenith of its life will be
Gone past forever, and from thence
A second history will commence.

A chronicle no longer gold,
A bargaining with mist and mould,
And finally the broken stem
The plummeting to earth; and then

An intercourse not well designed
For beings of a golden kind
Whose native green must arch above
The earth's obscene, corrupting love.

And still the ripe fruit and the branch
Observe the sky begin to blanch
Without a cry, without a prayer,
With no betrayal of despair.'[1]

[1] Tennessee Williams, *The Night of the Iguana* (Harmondsworth, 1964), pp. 114-15.

Yet for all Williams' continued concentration on the plight of the romantic in an unromantic world the dominant theme of contemporary American drama is that embodied in the work of Gelber, Albee and the later Miller. The need to confront reality, expressed either through direct exhortation or through a simple re-enactment, is expressed in all the major drama of the United States since 1959. This movement, which constitutes an end to revolt, has been accompanied by an increasing artistic self-awareness so that these last years have produced a greater and more original re-assessment of the nature of the dramatic process than has ever been the case before in America. The experimentation sparked off by *The Connection* and the first of the 'happenings' in 1959 eventually led to Kenneth Brown's *The Brig* (1963), a work which fulfilled the prophecies of Artaud and Copeau and which went substantially further than the European theatre in refining the dramatic experience. With the exception of this work (and if we are to believe Brown's comments on his own work not even this exception need be made) the primary mood of the drama of confrontation is affirmation. Where society is attacked, where bourgeois standards are ridiculed and where the fierce undercurrents of personal relationships are critically examined this is essentially an aspect of an affirmative response to the human situation. Nevertheless all of these playwrights are careful to avoid the tendency (evidenced in the absolutism of the nineteen-twenties and thirties) of affirmation to congeal into resolution. There is nothing here of the positive and definitive response of O'Neill's pantheism or Williams' 'flight' but rather a tentative affirmation of human possibilities. Their universe lacks the social and psychological determinism of O'Neill (*Mourning Becomes Electra* (1931), *Desire under the Elms* (1924), *Long Day's Journey into Night*) and Williams (*The Glass Menagerie* (1945), *Cat on a Hot Tin Roof*, *Camino Real* (1953)). Metaphysical solitude, however, remains at the core of these works and the physical divisions of society, which Albee identifies in *The Zoo Story*, are of no social significance. They serve merely as images of a more fundamental isolation, as do the cage-like rooms of the West-side apartment houses in the same play. Similarly Miller, in *After the Fall*, is concerned with the ease with which those apparently united by love can become 'separate people'. To Albee it is only through a confrontation of this solitude that its relevance can be destroyed. So too for Miller love, genuine human contact, is an article of faith which only holds plausibility after the violent horror of the concentration camp or the caustic virulence of personal treachery has

revealed the reality of its counterforce. The 'momentous enlightenment' becomes the key to meaningful life.

To Beckett man is a passive victim. To Ionesco the gesture of rebellion is doomed to failure. The absurdity which is the subject of this
European theatre is essentially that defined by Camus which sees man
as the victim of arbitrary and anarchical forces. In *Cross Purpose* (1944),
he indicates what he sees as the only valid response. This profoundly
nihilistic play concerns the murder of a man by his own mother and
sister. Returning from abroad he conceals his identity from them and
they kill him hoping to gain, by his wealth, their desires for happiness
and real identity. The advice which the sister subsequently offers to
the dead man's wife evidently stands as Camus' conscious message for
it is a natural conclusion to the ironical destructiveness of the play's
action. 'Pray your God to harden you to stone. It's the happiness He
has assigned Himself, and the one true happiness. Do as He does, be
deaf to all appeals, and turn your heart to stone while there still is
time'.[1] To Beckett life is a period of waiting in which man degenerates
physically and mentally and during which happiness is little more than
a recurring irony. In essence his response to the absurdity of life is the
same as Camus'. In his *Act Without Words*, I (1957) he presents an
analogue of man's life. A man is thrown onto the stage. A whistle blows
off stage and he responds but to find himself flung back again. After
this has happened several times he ceases to respond. A carafe of water
is then lowered so that it is just out of reach. Several cubes are also
lowered. He climbs onto these only to find that the water has again
risen out of his reach. He tries unsuccessfully to lasso the carafe.
Eventually it becomes apparent that he will never be able to reach it.
At the end of the mime he sits looking at his hands and ignores the
whistles which are blown and the water carafe which now dangles
directly in front of his face. This, then, is the savagely ironical world
of the theatre of the absurd in which man's reason and passions are
directed against him and to which the only valid response is quietism
and complete withdrawal. It is this theatre which Brustein links with
Albee and Gelber as an example of 'existential revolt' against the
metaphysical life of man; it is this theatre, also, which Martin Esslin
sees as the natural home for Albee's *The American Dream* and in part
at least for Gelber's *The Connection*. Camus has claimed that beneath
the pessimism of *Cross Purpose* there is a deeper optimism but, as

[1] Albert Camus, *Caligula* and *Cross Purpose*, trans., Stuart Gilbert
(London, 1965), p. 155.

Cruickshank points out in an introduction to an edition of his plays, such an assertion would necessitate the destruction of the very principle on which the play is based. This is equally true of Beckett's work. In his world of ashes and emptiness the only real possibility is stoicism and in the context even this is transmuted into brutal irony. Any attempt to group together the theatre of the absurd and the works of Albee and Gelber, in anything but style, therefore, is misguided. For, as with Sartre, to Miller, Albee and Gelber alike the reality of the human situation implies total freedom and freedom in turn implies responsibility and guilt. It is uncertainty, then, a fear of facing a world in which the only pattern is that imposed by the individual, which freezes their characters into inaction. They cling as long as they can to their illusions, willing to sacrifice freedom to apparent certainty and finding in inauthentic living a qualified innocence. But both Miller and Albee force the confrontation and their protagonists, in confronting the apocalyptic vision of man's metaphysical situation, discover the anguish of choice but also open the way towards the promise of dignity and meaning. Gelber, too, while not positively affirming this process does indicate a belief in freedom and a subjective reality which anticipates much of Albee and Miller.

Camus, whose intellectual self-examination at times lacks some of the stringent precision of Sartre's, saw, however, that absurdity had implications which were ultimately terrifying. On the physical plane it gave a validity to totalitarianism; on the metaphysical, to despair. It was in this mood that he recognised a progression which had the inexorability of movement and counter-movement. 'The end of the movement of absurdity, rebellion, etc.,' he has said 'is compassion . . . that is to say, in the last analysis, love'.[1] It is this progression which underlies contemporary American drama. The need for compassion arises out of an acute awareness of absurdity. For as he has said 'The greatest intellectual economy is to accept the non-intelligibility of the world—and concern oneself with man'.[2] This is an accurate description of the basis of the drama of confrontation which is concerned with confronting the apocalyptic vision of the human situation and through this 'momentous enlightenment' establishing a genuine basis for a life centred on man and tempered by the affirmative nature of compassion. The terms pessimism and optimism become irrelevent. What we are

[1] Albert Camus, *Carnets 1942-1951*, trans., Philip Thody (London, 1966), p. 103.
[2] *Ibid.*, p. 57.

concerned with is the area of experience which the writer chooses to stress. Where the theatre of the absurd chooses to stare into the darkness of a nihilistic universe the drama of confrontation concentrates on man. The 'non-intelligibility of the world' remains the 'given' but this very fact re-institutes the need for a liberal humanism. The drama of confrontation is indeed the end of both absurdity and rebellion. It is concerned with what Germaine Brée and Margaret Guiton, in *An Age of Fiction* (1958), refer to as a 'return to man'.[1]

Ironically this new movement in American drama answers the question that Bertolt Brecht posed in 1955—ironically because Brecht's answer, not surprisingly, was social action while Albee's and Miller's answer hinged on philosophical recognition. The question, inspired originally by Friedrich Durrenmatt, was, 'Can the present-day world be reproduced by means of theatre?' Brecht's reply, predictably, was that it could only be described 'to present-day people if it is described as capable of transformation'. His reply is of particular interest in so far as it goes on implicitly to attack the work of the absurdists and to describe, in effect, that affirmative drama which finally emerged in America at the end of the decade and which saw the possibility of 'transformation' through confrontation. 'Some years ago' Brecht continues, 'in a paper I saw an advertisement showing the destruction of Tokyo by an earthquake. Most of the houses had collapsed, but a few modern buildings had been spared. The caption ran "Steel stood". Compare this description with the classic account of the eruption of Etna by Pliny the Elder, and you will find that his is a kind of description that the twentieth-century playwright must outgrow.' He continues, 'In an age whose science is in a position to change nature to such an extent as to make the world seem almost habitable, man can no longer describe man as victim, the object of a fixed but unknown environment. It is scarcely possible to conceive of the laws of motion if one looks at them from a tennis ball's point of view'.[2] Albee, Miller and Gelber studiously avoid showing man as a victim of anything but his own fear and myopia. In turning away from the absurdists, who reproduce the present-day as a deterministic and frequently grotesque progress towards a welcome destruction, they see the question of describing the world not as a social one, although they are critical of society, but as a philosophical and even a moral one. They admit to

[1] Margaret Guiton and Germaine Brée, *An Age of Fiction* (London, 1958).
[2] Bertolt Brecht, *Brecht on Theatre*, trans., John Willett (London, 1964), pp. 274-5.

the possibility of transformation but this not in the essential reality of the human situation but rather in the individual response to that situation. It becomes a question, therefore, not of the morality of wealth or war but of the morality of illusion and innocence. To Miller and Albee the former morality is dependent on the latter and Brecht's naïvete represents the sort of superficiality which Miller himself had barely escaped.

Saul Bellow, in assessing the artist's role, has said that: '. . . either we want life to continue or we do not. If we don't want (sic) to continue, why write books? . . . But if we answer yes, we do want it to continue, we are liable to be asked how. In what form shall life be justified? That is the essence of the moral question. We call a writer moral to the degree that his imagination indicates to us how we may answer naturally, without strained arguments, with a spontaneous, mysterious proof that has no need to argue with despair'.[1] The pursuit of affirmation, which is the basis of the drama of confrontation as it is the central tenet of Bellow's novels, relies not on a casual recourse to optimism but on a direct confrontation of the substance of life. The prayer of Albee's and Bellow's protoganists alike becomes, 'for Christ's sake preserve me from unreal things'.[2] But the act of confrontation is not sufficient in itself. For a world confronted in isolation is far from constituting a justification of life. To Albee and Miller as to Bellow, therefore, genuine justification lies in a readiness not only to face the real world but also to re-establish the prime importance of human relationships. Self-indulgent pessimism and the pursuit of success both defer to compassion which Camus had seen as the end of absurdity and rebellion. In the words of Bellow's Henderson, 'I had a voice that said, I want! I want? I? It should have told me *she* wants, *he* wants, *they* want. And moreover, it's love that makes reality reality.[3]

Where Tennessee Williams and Eugene O'Neill had given a qualified blessing to pipe-dreams this new generation of dramatists sees little purpose in pretence. The rose-coloured lights of Williams give way to the harsh lights of *The Connection* and *The Brig*. In a sense realism is here no longer a mode of presentation nor even an attitude of mind; it is an article of faith and a central issue in a drama intent on denying the relevence of social theatre to an audience uncertain of their

[1] Saul Bellow, 'The Writer as Moralist', *Atlantic Monthly* (March, 1963), p. 62.
[2] Saul Bellow, *Henderson the Rain King* (London, 1959), p. 253.
[3] *Ibid.*, p. 286.

own true identity and unaware of the irrelevance of contemporary obsessions. Theirs is not a negative response for in a sense they are fighting against intellectual and spiritual appeasement. They transcend the debilitating determinism of Beckett and propound a positive dialectic which if frightening in its application reconstitutes the possibility of dignity. The obtrusive optimism of American literature is here transmuted into a genuine philosophical stance. As Artaud had predicted, in reinstating the metaphysical they have achieved a reconciliation with the universe.

2
Arthur Miller

THE MOVEMENT, which becomes apparent with Gelber and Albee, towards a consideration of the relationship between man and his metaphysical situation had long been delayed in American drama. The fervour of the ideological drama of the nineteen-twenties and thirties had deflected the creative impulse into the area of politics and sociology while the post-war theatre had re-discovered psychology as a natural extension of its concern with the dialogue between the individual and society. If the light of the intellect was largely absent from pre-war American drama, however, Miller (in the absence of O'Neill's best play, *Long Day's Journey into Night*, which was not released until 1956) is popularly supposed to have brought it to the post-war theatre, and so in a sense he did. Nevertheless his early work is more truthfully characterised by a confusion of purpose than by a clear-sighted attempt to seize on the fundamentals of existence. In *All My Sons* (1947) he is still fighting the battles of the thirties and if he is conscious of more vital issues under the surface it is precisely his failure to develop them which makes the play so unsatisfactory. That it should have been so well received at the time and, indeed, that it should remain so today is a mark of the state of a theatre which shunned the plays of Brecht and Pirandello and yet treated as profound and vital the empty pretentiousness of Macleish's *J.B.* (1956) or Wilder's *The Skin of Our Teeth* (1942).

In a sense, however, Miller could be said to have paved the way for that revival of the American theatre which started in 1959, for like O'Neill before him he was a playwright prepared to confront seriously aspects of the human situation ignored by a theatre obsessed with psychology and sociology. He was not, for the most part, content merely with approaching the theatre as a means of expression but, as Richard Gilman says of the European theatre, 'as a means of *knowing*'.[1] His achievement lies not in his sensitivity to contemporary issues but in his ability to penetrate to the metaphysical implications of those issues. Nevertheless Miller never entirely shakes himself free of the

[1] 'The Drama is Coming Now', p. 30.

26

influence of the commercial theatre while even in theatrical form he has tended towards conservatism. In his introduction to *The Collected Plays* (1957) he disapproves of certain new trends and emphasises that a play 'must end, and end with a climax'[1] and that he aimed at 'a true climax based upon revealed psychological truths'.[2] These, incidentally, are the very principles against which Gelber was to revolt in *The Connection*. In truth Miller is more of an elucidator than a pioneer. Even the 'continuous present' of *Death of a Salesman* is less adventurous when placed beside Strindberg's *A Dream Play* or even Wilder's *Our Town* (1938). If *Death of a Salesman* marked something of a watershed in the development of American drama, however, its achievement was a mark of the victory of sensibility and theatrical power over intellectual and dramatic confusion. As originally conceived the play was to have been a monodrama with a title reflecting its form—*The Inside of his Head*. In abandoning this approach Miller succumbed to what was a potentially debilitating obliqueness of viewpoint. Although he speaks, in his introduction to *The Collected Plays*, of the form of his play as being that of the confession it was not until *After the Fall*, when Gelber and Brown had shown what a fusion of form and theme really implied, that he achieved the confessional structure. In this latter play, however, Miller ironically succumbs to intellectual self-indulgence and demonstrates, after a nine-year silence, a pretension of dialogue and a narcissistic introspection which, perverting Eric Bentley's expression, presents the playwright as *manifest* thinker.

Yet this should not blind us to his importance in deflecting American drama away from its role as dramatised case-book. For his attempts to make man, instead of men, the centre of his work linked him not only with the European tradition of Ibsen and Strindberg but also with the philosophical concerns of Sartre and Camus, whose plays were in process of stimulating the post-war French theatre.

The works of principal interest for the purpose of this study are *Death of a Salesman* and *After the Fall* since it is in these plays that Miller uses the theatre most clearly 'as a means of knowing'. It is in these plays too that Miller expresses his belief in the necessity for confrontation—a belief which takes him outside the main tradition of revolt. For although his plays remain 'social', in that his metaphysical concern is never entirely divorced from his concern with the community of men, the primary mood is one of affirmation built on con-

---

[1] *Arthur Miller's Collected Plays*, p. 13.
[2] *Ibid.*, p. 20.

frontation. *All My Sons*, his first Broadway play, is also significant however both because it acts as a point of departure for the drama of confrontation and because it throws light on the artistic weaknesses which Miller derives in part from his early involvement in the social activism of the *Federal Theatre Project*, in part from a tendency to intellectual diffuseness and in part from a misunderstanding of Ibsen.

Miller's dramatic career started, thematically speaking, where O'Neill's left off for his first Broadway production, *All My Sons*, has parallels in Ibsen's *The Wild Duck* (and not so much in *The Pillars of Society* (1877) as is popularly supposed). While a diffusion of moral purpose together with an obsessional concern with the process of plot leaves the play finally unsatisfactory, Miller does show something of Ibsen's suspicion of the ideal and sentimental attraction for the validity of illusion. The significance of Miller's work, for the purpose of this study, lies in the process whereby he progresses from this tentative affirmation of illusion towards his final belief in confrontation—a process in which the social and psychological become subordinate to the metaphysical. *All My Sons* is a play which suggests immediately both the deficiencies of Miller and the potential which made him for many the chief hope for a vital American drama, for it raises certain issues which, if they are not confronted here, do nevertheless suggest an awareness of concerns beyond the idealistic egalitarianism of a post-war world.

Joe Keller, a small-time industrialist, allows his partner to take the blame for a war-time swindle. His firm had allowed cracked cylinders to be put in aircraft rather than stop the faulty process which was producing them. These aircraft subsequently crashed. Although her own son, Larry, had died in the war Joe's wife, Kate, will not accept his death for if she does so, she feels that Joe must be held responsible for it. He defends himself on the grounds of sound business procedure and the family responsibility which he claims as his motivating force. His other son, Chris, returns from the war having been converted to the principle of brotherhood, partly as a result of the self-sacrifice of men in war and partly as a result of his own culpability for the death of his platoon. Anxious now to marry his dead brother's fiancée Ann, he forces his mother to confront the fact of her son's death and his father to admit to the ideal of brotherhood and thus ultimately his own guilt.

In *The Wild Duck*, similarly, of the two partners in a business venture one was found guilty of fraud while his partner, against whom nothing could be proved, went free and prospered. Like Chris in

Miller's play, Gregers Werle cannot dissociate himself from a sense of guilt derived from participation in his father's firm. In reaction, and in large part to expiate this sense of guilt, he urges the 'demand of the ideal' which leads directly to death and despair. Miller has said that Ibsen's influence on him was 'less his moral and ideological side . . . than the structural one',[1] but it is clear that he also absorbed some of Ibsen's thematic concerns.

So that when an Ibsenesque distrust of the ideal is wedded to nineteen-thirties' idealism the consequence is not ordered ambiguity but moral confusion for Miller does not adopt an objective stance but rather commits himself to both sides at once.

Ostensibly the moral spine of the play is embodied in the title with its overtones of Emersonian transcendentalism or the more recent Marxism of Steinbeck. Joe Keller is brought from his disavowal of ultimate responsibility to his final acceptance of the rest of society as being, 'all my sons'. In the words of Steinbeck's *The Grapes of Wrath* (1939), 'Use' ta be the fambly was fust. It ain't so now. It's anybody'.[2] It is thus not Joe's legal culpability which is of importance but his ability to accept the necessary relationship between self and society which is implied in his acceptance of the ideal of universal brotherhood. Yet if this post-war egalitarianism is indeed the core of Miller's moral purpose he subverts it in part through a failure of craft and in part through an empirical distrust of the ideal. Over-concerned, as Miller has admitted that he was, with 'telling the story' he succumbs to the temptation to over-emphasize the element of intrigue. While Joe's legal guilt should be subordinated to his moral awakening the chief crises of the play are centred on his admission of this legal guilt and on the discovery (through an outmoded theatrical device) of a direct connection between his crime and his son's death. So that his final statement that they were 'all my sons' follows proof of physical causality rather than moral conversion. More fundamentally, however, this victory of the ideal is undercut by the proliferating examples of savage and self-justifying 'idealists' which Miller presents in the persons of Chris, George—his fiancée's brother, and Jim the next-door neighbour.

If Joe Keller represents the immorality of a society which considers people to be less indispensible than an industrial process then Chris surely represents the immorality of the idealist whose motives, like

[1] In an interview with T. G. Rosenthall, *B.B.C. Third Programme*, Feb. 2, 1966.
[2] John Steinbeck, *The Grapes of Wrath* (New York, 1958), p. 606.

Gregers Werle's in *The Wild Duck*, cannot be finally dissociated from individual justification. Gregers had told his father, 'it is you I have to thank for the fact that I am harried and tortured by a guilt-laden conscience,'[1] while Chris is similarly activated in his idealism by a consciousness that 'I was made yellow in this house because I suspected my father and I did nothing about it'.[2] His attempts to destroy his mother's illusions stem from his wish to marry Ann while Joe becomes a scapegoat for his own guilt. When he brutally insists on reading a letter in which his dead brother indicates that his death had been a suicide inspired by knowledge of his father's crime, the ideal of truth becomes suspect while 'justice' is secured only at the expense of compassion. So too George, Ann's brother, arrives at the house determined to secure some semblance of justice for his father, Joe's former partner. In effect, however, he too sees Joe as a scapegoat for his own inhumanity, an inhumanity stemming at base from idealism. On returning from the war he had refused to visit his father who as Joe's assistant had been jailed in his stead. He admits the enormity of his action, 'Annie—we did a terrible thing. We can never be forgiven. Not even to send him a card at Christmas. I didn't see him once since I got home from the war!' (p. 101). Even Jim, a next-door-neighbour, who as a doctor acknowledges a responsibility to man, shows the same disregard for individual men which does little to recommend the validity of his principles.

The play thus becomes a battle between justice and humanity—a battle in which Miller largely abdicates both moral and artistic control. Far from expressing a sense of conflicting principles, the moral confusion serves not as an expression of paradox but as an indication that Miller here lacks Ibsen's clarity of thought and sureness of vision. If his intellectual assent is given to the Marxian ending his sympathies clearly lie with those whose world has collapsed under the impact of truth. In this play, as in *The Wild Duck*, the idealist is left stunned by the destruction which he has caused. Thus the compassionate tolerance of Ibsen and O'Neill brought into conflict with inflexible dogma, survives more as a wistful regret than as a viable philosophy. Nevertheless neither is Miller fully convinced of the wisdom nor the morality of confrontation—a dilemma which recurs in his adaptation of Ibsen's *An Enemy of the People* (1882). Here too his ostensible theme is the

---

[1] *Four Great Plays by Henrik Ibsen*, p. 269.

[2] *Arthur Miller's Collected Plays*, p. 123. All future references will be incorporated into the text.

necessity for integrity and the need to recognise that responsibility operates outside of the immediate family group. Yet like Chris Keller and the other idealists of *All My Sons* there is an inhumanity about the protagonist, Stockman, which threatens to invalidate the ideal which he propounds.

All My Sons is in many ways a compromise. It is a compromise between the social dramatist, eager to endorse the message of brotherhood and integrity, and the empiricist, all too aware of the reality behind the ideal. If his message in this play amounts essentially to an acceptance of Emersonian transcendentalism then the unresolved issues which persist below the surface reveal his flirtation with the oversoul as an uneasy relationship. Even Stockman, depicted as the outstanding example of the individual finding values in his own conscience and shunning the corruption of society, had evidenced a callousness towards his family which is hard to reconcile with his ideals. It is clear that transcendentalism does not incorporate the sense of guilt—a guilt surpassing the mere legal culpability of Joe Keller—which many of his characters feel. Neither does it account for the cruelty which seems a natural corollary of those individuals who are released from the illusions of success society (It is interesting to note that John Arden has created a powerful drama, *Sergeant Musgrave's Dance* (1959), out of the very same paradoxes which Miller senses here). It is not until *After the Fall* however that he finally resolves these issues and begins fully to understand their significance.

All My Sons remains an unsatisfactory play because of its failure to come to terms with the issues which it raises and because, in his desire to master form, Miller has produced an example of Scribe's *pièce bien fait*. Indeed he himself has recognised as much: 'Against my will, *All My Sons* states, and even proclaims, that it is a form and that a writer wrote it and organised it' (p. 25). If its theme owes something to Ibsen so does its style. The painfully symbolic tree which dominates the stage at the beginning of the play is little more than ill-digested Ibsen while the final shot which echoes round the stage had similarly concluded many of the Scandinavian's plays.

Nevertheless while he demonstrates a continued concern with the moral absolutes of the nineteen-thirties he does avoid the immediate simplicities of caricature. Joe Keller is no hard-skinned business-man intent on making a fast buck at the expense of his fellow man. For all its faults *All My Sons* already demonstrates Miller's perception of issues which transcend the immediate social situation. Already his concern with identity, guilt and the need to re-affirm innocence indicate that for him the social and the psychological could ultimately be traced to their source in the metaphysical. Already, too, it is clear that even at the beginning of his career he could not fully endorse O'Neill's and Ibsen's faith in the validity of illusion and that for all his social-consciousness revolt had begun to retreat before affirmation.

In his next play, *Death of a Salesman*, we find much the same schism between ostensibly social drama and what verges on an examination in depth of the human condition. If it carries about it vestiges of the nineteen-thirties, with its implied fear of mechanisation and its apparent concentration on the little man as victim, it becomes apparent that Miller is attempting more here than Rice or Odets in previous decades. He is not concerned with painting the deficiencies of society or calling for a better deal for salesmen. The salesman is for him an image as indeed is the society to which he eventually sacrifices himself. For in this play man's stature and destruction derive from his own failure to perceive the true reality of the human situation. *Death of a Salesman*, like Albee's *The American Dream*, which was to follow it eleven years later, is concerned with highlighting the absurdity of a society which frenetically pursues the goals of dream and illusion in preference to confronting a reality which is cold and unattractive. The salesman is an image, for Miller, of humanity in retreat from reality desperately placing its faith in appearance and accepting as valid and necessary the outworn clichés of Horatio Alger.

Willy Loman is a tired and dispirited salesman who at the age of sixty-three has found himself reduced to living on commission. His physical and mental health have deteriorated and this process is hastened by the return of his son, Biff. At the age of thirty-four Biff still has no regular job, a fact which Willy sees as a standing reproach to himself, since, in a climactic scene earlier in his life, the boy had discovered him with another woman in a hotel room in Boston and apparently as a result of his disillusionment had lost his will to succeed.

Loman, feeling defeated, has suicide on his mind and his wife, Linda, finds a length of gas piping which her husband has presumably bought to end his life. When he tries to get transferred to an office job he is fired. Biff, who had gone to see a former employer on the chance that he might have backed him in a business venture, confesses that he has failed. The two sons leave their father in a restaurant which was to have been the scene of a triumphal meal. When they return home Biff apparently admits his love for his father, a fact which only serves to

confirm Willy in his decision to commit suicide and thus leave the
proceeds of an insurance policy which would enable Biff to succeed.
He kills himself in an automobile but Biff has learnt his lesson and sees
his individual salvation in deliberately rejecting Willy's values and
thus the values of the society which had first frustrated and then
destroyed his father.

In *Death of a Salesman*, then, Miller challenges the process whereby
the individual defers to society. Willy Loman refuses to accept his own
freedom to act. He retreats into a world of illusions and grants as real
and important, 'Only rank, height of power, the sense of having
won . . . the galaxy thrust up into the sky by projectors on the rooftops
of the city he believed were real stars' (p. 30). The society to which
Willy devotes himself is clearly that of the American dream. He feels
that his son must perforce succeed in '. . . the greatest country in the
world' because he is 'a young man with such—personal attractiveness' (p. 134). This society is a rationalisation and an extension of
Willy's search for ecstacy in life. For Willy's self-examination is his
attempt to search out the cause of a far deeper failure than that which is
underlined by his redundancy. In fact it is Miller's failure to make a
clear distinction between Willy's actual failure within the terms of
society and his deeper spiritual and moral failure which accounts for
some of the dramatic confusion of the play. Indeed it might be justifiably argued that Willy's inability to succeed within the terms of society
distracts attention from the play's real concern. If Miller contrived
Willy's situation as an excuse for his introspection he simultaneously
introduced an element which forced a comparison with pre-war social-
protest plays. For while he is careful to avoid the caricatures which
marked that theatre, audiences were not so far removed from the
nineteen-thirties that they could not react to the sight of an employer's
dismissal of an old employee, however human that employer was made
to seem.

Like Chris Keller, in *All My Sons*, Willy is devoted to trying to
'find himself' unaware that, as Miller says, 'he is his past at every
moment' (p. 23). The self-knowledge which he seeks is dependent on
his admitting to himself his culpability for the disillusionment of his
son. For, again as Miller says, man '. . . "is" what he is ashamed of',
he 'becomes "himself" in the act of becoming aware of his sinfulness'.[1]
His failure to build anything worthwhile stems from his inability to

[1] Arthur Miller, 'A Foreword by the Author', *The Saturday Evening Post*,
Feb. 1, 1964, p. 32.

confront reality and his failure to adopt the affirmative stance which his son Biff finally outlines to him at the end, 'I'm just what I am, that's all' (p. 217).

Happy Loman, Miller tells us, had never turned 'his face toward defeat' (p. 136). This necessity is fundamental to *Death of a Salesman*. It is Biff's ability to do this at the end of the play which confirms his understanding of the nature of the human condition. It would not be fanciful here to compare this necessity to face defeat with Sartre's parallel necessity—that of acknowledging despair. To Sartre we as men must 'limit ourselves to a reliance upon that which is within our wills'. He continues, 'When Descartes said, "Conquer yourself rather than the world", what he meant was, at bottom, the same—that we should act without hope'.[1] Miller's insistence on the necessity to face defeat is this ultimately the same as Sartre's acknowledgement of the need to confront despair. It is an acceptance of the fact that an authentic life is that spent not in the conquest of an external world but rather one in which man 'should be without illusion' and act within the boundary of possibilities. As Quentin says in *After the Fall*, 'despair can be a way of life; but you have to believe in it, pick it up, take it to heart, and move on again'.[2] Willy Loman is not the victim of society, if he were intended as such we would expect a much harsher picture of the capitalist world. Willy is a victim of his own failure to accept those basic tenets which can alone define his identity. He will not face the reality of his situation but chooses rather to take refuge in dreams of success and popularity. He will not accept the guilt which united him with his son Biff and he cannot recognise the value of the love which Linda offers but instead buries his failure in the cold sexuality of infidelity. Like Bellow's Henderson, in *Henderson the Rain King* (1959), he hears a voice which says, 'I want, I want' but unlike Henderson his experience never brings him to the affirmation which comes through a confrontation of reality and an acceptance of the value of human contact. His life matches with precision the sad determinism which Henderson sees as the only alternative to that confrontation: '. . . desire, desire, desire, knocking its way out of the breast, and fear, striking and striking. Enough already! Time for a word of truth. Time for something notable to be heard. Otherwise, accelerating like a stone, you fall from life to death. Exactly like a stone, straight into deafness,

[1] *Existentialism and Humanism*, p. 38.
[2] Arthur Miller, *After the Fall* (London, 1965), p. 14.

and till the last repeating *I want I want I want*, then striking the earth and entering it forever!'[1]

In spite of the considerable advance over the confusions of *All My Sons*, *Death of a Salesman* is still not free of the faults which marked that play. In abandoning monodrama as a form for his play Miller succumbs to a debilitating obliqueness of viewpoint; for the drama which was to have been worked out inside Willy's head is now resolved with an inartistic arbitrariness. Biff's final understanding does not emerge from his observation of Willy but from a sudden and unprompted revelation. So that while Miller's whole dramatic attention is thrown on the plight of the enervated Willy Loman, the moral crux of the play is centred on Biff. Had the play been the intended monodrama this split would have been irrelevent since all the characters would have been expressions of Willy's mind. In its present form, however, Biff has an independent existence and the gratuitous manner in which Miller segregates plot from moral focus results in an unsatisfactory diffusion of attention.

Miller tells us that love is the force which is in a race for Willy's soul yet this love never really manifests itself in the play, neither is it clear whether love is the compassion offered by his wife, Linda, or that sense of brotherhood which had driven Joe Keller to his death. Linda herself remains such a profoundly unsatisfactory character that she can hardly be said to represent a real alternative nor is there any indication that her love would serve to turn Willy away from his addiction to false values.

Ironically, therefore, it is Miller's lack of artistic and intellectual control which operates against force and insight in *Death of a Salesman*. Nevertheless it did serve to demonstrate that 'philosophical' drama did not necessarily imply sterile debate. It established in America what had long been accepted in Europe, that serious drama is not that in which thought and philosophical concerns are grafted onto action as aspects of character and mood but rather is that form of drama which finds its animus in metaphysical enquiry. In the words of a letter written by Andreyev in 1914 and quoted by Eric Bentley, 'Neither love nor hunger nor ambition; thought, human thought, with all its sufferings, joys, and struggles—there is the true hero of contemporary life!'[2] If thought was to be the hero, however, it was not to be so in the sense that wit is the hero of Oscar Wilde's plays. If Miller succumbs, in

[1] *Henderson the Rain King*, p. 297.
[2] Eric Bentley, *The Playwright as Thinker* (New York, 1955), p. 67.

After the Fall, to a sad posturing in which the thinker is seen thinking then in *Death of a Salesman* he succeeds in delivering American drama from the mindless passion of previous decades. In the absence of O'Neill's last plays Miller would be justified in claiming, as Pirandello had done in the European theatre of the thirties, that 'One of the novelties that I have given to drama . . . consists in converting the intellect into passion'.[1] Nevertheless the American theatre chose to ignore the possibilities represented by *Death of a Salesman* and continued to applaud the emptiness of Macleish and Inge while Miller's theatrical conservatism together with his continued flirtation with social theatre failed to touch a spark from an experimental theatre in search of a sense of purpose and direction. Attention was diverted into the possibility of the play constituting a modern tragedy—a concern which did more to demonstrate the American theatre's need for added stature than a genuine belief in the arrival of a new age of drama.

After the Fall, written fifteen years after *Death of a Salesman* and five years after *The Connection* and *The Zoo Story,* is concerned with the quest and affirmation of reality. It feels its way painfully towards affirmation through confrontation. Its action is concerned with the 'momentous enlightenment' of its protagonist and its theme with the necessity for a 'real relationship, founded on truth'. In *All My Sons* and *Death of a Salesman* Miller had been concerned with a society which had inverted its values and placed the importance of success in economic and social spheres above the necessity to establish real contact between human beings. In *After the Fall* the pursuit of success becomes merely one aspect of man's egotism—an egotism which leads to cruelty and, in the name of innocence and truth, to a dissociation from fellow man which is itself a source of guilt. The 'truth' which the play's protagonist, Quentin, discovers is the need to concede the inconstancy and violence of man and yet to renew love in the face of this knowledge. He learns, in the course of the play, to accept that the world which he inhabits is a world seen after the Fall. Miller accepts here the vision of the absurdists but denies their pessimistic conclusions. For him this momentous enlightenment represents the necessary foundation for a new life, purged of falsehood. 'Is the knowing all? To know, and even happily, that we meet unblessed; not in some garden of wax fruit and

---

[1] Luigi Pirandello, *Right You Are! (If You Think So). All for the Best. Henry IV.* Introduced and edited by E. Martin Browne (Harmondsworth, 1962), p. 7.

painted trees, that lie of Eden, but after, after the Fall, after many, many deaths. Is the knowing all?'[1]

After the Fall has been hailed as a play stemming so directly from Miller's personal experience as to constitute an affront both to good taste and to the generalised validity which he clearly claims for his drama. While it is true that a critic in full knowledge of the personal parallels (Maggie can be recognised as Marilyn Monroe and Mickey as Elia Kazan) might find it difficult to view the play with the requisite objectivity it is also true to say that the difficulty is no greater than that which faces the critic of Hemingway or Lawrence and is at any rate no more than can be expected of a critic whose duty must always be to the work of art itself. If *After the Fall* fails, its failure does not lie in the intrusion of the personal, any more than it did in Strindberg's *The Father* (1887), but rather in Miller's failure to transmute the personal into art.

The form of the play constitutes a return to the technique which Miller had intended to use for *Death of a Salesman*—a technique which he has identified as a confession. *After the Fall*, however, represents not merely the confession of an individual anxious to resolve the paradox of his life but also man's attempt to catalogue the sins of a generation in a search for comprehension.

Quentin, who has been twice married, is now considering a third marriage but feels a compulsive need to understand himself and the reasons for his past marital failures. He stands in a position where, looking back over his life, he clearly sees the irrelevence of his success. 'His success as an attorney has crumbled in his hands as he sees only his own egotism in it and no wider goal beyond himself'.[2] He is appalled by the potential for violence, particularly in personal relationships, which is constantly realised. He is horrified at his ability to hurt others and, on reflection, to be hurt by others. On the point of marrying again he suddenly becomes aware of the reality of man's situation.

---

[1] *After the Fall*, p. 127. When *After the Fall* was first produced at the Lincoln Centre, *The Saturday Evening Post* published the complete play in what it described as a 'pioneering effort for magazine publishing'. When the final version of the play appeared in book form, however, it became obvious that certain changes had been made. Where reference is made to *The Saturday Evening Post* edition, therefore, this fact will be noted in footnotes. Where reference is to the Secker and Warburg edition the title will be abbreviated to 'A.F.' and incorporated into the text.

[2] Arthur Miller, 'A Foreword by the Author', p. 32.

He realises that he is himself totally responsible for the choices which shape his existence. He recognises the death of the absolutes on which he had previously relied. 'I no longer see some final saving grace! Socialism once, then love; some final hope is gone that always saved before the end!' (A.F. p. 26.) The death of these absolutes throws responsibility directly onto him. 'Whether I open a book or think of marrying again, it's so damn clear I'm choosing what I do—and it cuts the strings between my hands and heaven.' (A.F. p. 33.) It is the fact of power without responsibility, however, which Quentin sees as the unifying element in the individual and corporate violence and cruelty with which he is surrounded and in which he participates. He relives moments of his life which serve to highlight this egotistic foundation of violence.

Two main symbols provide the background for the examples of personal cruelty and love destroyed by egotism which abound in Quentin's past. These images, a tower of a German concentration camp and the Committee on Un-American Activities, are in their own way both personifications and public extensions of these personal failings— the one in a physical and the other in an intellectual sense. The symbols gain their particular effectiveness from the realisation that both institutions derive their power from the ready complicity not only of the 'innocents' who stand by and watch but also of the victims who succumb still naively believing in the folly of opposition and the virtue of inactivity. Miller uses both of these symbols but particularly that of the camp tower literally to highlight these individual acts and thus show that in essence they both have their genesis in the same source. When Quentin's mother, Rose, discovers that her husband has lost all of their money in a stock crash all that she can think about is, 'My *bonds*'. Where human understanding is called for, all that she can do is callously to degrade her husband in front of his son. Quentin looks up at the tower and thus establishes the connection, which Miller is at pains to enforce, between private and public violence. The bond of love, which Quentin as their son imagined to exist between them, is shattered under stress thus contributing to his own distrust of love as a force and to his awareness of the guilt with which an insistence on innocence can be invested. He recalls, too, another incident of personal violence and 'treachery' when Lou, a personal friend, is degraded by his wife. Lou, having been arraigned by the *Committee on Un-American Activities*, wants to publish a book which he has written. His wife feels that this will only serve to draw the Committee's attention to him once again, this time perhaps with more serious results. She exclaims bitterly that if he were thrown out of his academic job he would be incapable of doing any other work. When Lou protests she cuts him down with contempt, 'This is hardly the time for illusions'. (A.F. p. 37.) The generic connection between this and the other instances of cruelty is enforced by the instant recall of Rose's vicious denunciation of Ike and the lighting of the camp tower.

It is this easy and instant recourse to treachery between those who should be united by love which sets Quentin searching for the origin of cruelty in his own life. He realises that at an early age he had been made an accomplice of his mother in her shame at her husband's lack of sophistication. The stress which had been laid on his learning to write well had stood as a reproach to his illiterate father. He remembers too an occasion on which he had been tricked into staying at home while the rest of the family had gone to the sea. Thus he had been introduced to the mechanics of treachery at an early age and the older Quentin is the victim of his own youth just as Maggie, his second wife, is the victim of hers. Nevertheless he is not content with assembling the evidence of cruelty but rather strives to understand its nature and to come to terms with its existence. The paradox which he discovers is that 'innocence' cannot be erected as a goal for which to struggle, as an opposing force to this treachery which is itself a negation of love. For innocence possesses its own guilt which stems from a wish for non-involvement. He realises that to turn one's back is not to escape evil. It is merely to become guilty through a refusal to accept responsibility. In an attempt to remain 'innocent' he had avoided Mickey, another friend who had been called before the Committee, 'I guess I—I didn't want to know any more . . . not to see! To be innocent!' (A.F. p. 43.) He realises that this treachery stems directly from self-interest whether it be Mickey himself who decides to 'name names' in the sacred name of truth but in reality to secure his own peace of mind, or those who built the concentration camp, conscious only of a relief that it was not they who would be killed there. Quentin in his turn links himself to the cruelty which he has, in retrospect, discovered in others by confessing that there was a sense in which he was prepared to allow Maggie, who had taken an overdose of sleeping pills, to die. Recognising the signs of barbituate poisoning he delays taking action, feeling that to do so is to accept responsibility. Similarly he admits to relief on hearing of the suicide of Lou, whom he was to defend before the Committee. Looking back he discovers now the source of this desire for non-involvement—for innocence. He discovers in whose name he has turned his back. 'And the name—yes, the name. In whose name do you ever turn your back . . . but in your own? In Quentin's name! Always in your own blood-covered name you turn your back!' (A.F. p. 126.) He recognises, finally, the source of the personal violence which he has identified and in which he is himself implicated. He finds, in fact, that cruelty and violence can be defined in terms of self. They are a concentration on self to the exclusion and eventually to the extinction of others. And yet, having understood this, he is still faced with the apparently insoluble enigma that he loved those whom he hurt just as Rose had loved her husband, and Elsie, Lou. He recalls that after Elsie had viciously cut her husband down she had been immediately gentle and kind to him, 'How tenderly she lifts him up! . . . Now that he is ruined. Still, that could be a true kiss. Or is there no treason but only man, unblamable . . .'.[1] Reality, as he finds it, is a world of individuals in which the links which ought to exist have long since broken down. Love can temporarily link these 'separate people' but eventually the inborn violence of man operates to fracture this relationship. Man is not capable of absolute love—this is a function which Quentin ascribes only to God. But man is capable of renewing love knowing that defeat is inevitable but knowing also that fear is not and that consciousness of man's double nature does not vitiate the value of that better part.

After the Fall in a sense is a revolt against the simplistic response of the dramatists of the thirties and forties to social questions themselves not fully understood. The absolute answers of socialism and universal love were in fact treatments for the symptoms and not the disease. These cures required a belief in perfectable man—man who with the will might return to his pristine state and secure a balance in society whose justice must be assumed to represent the norm. If men would sink their sectional differences, would ignore the dictates of self-interest and destructive egotism, they suggested, then all might be for the best in the best of all possible worlds. *After the Fall*, like *A Clearing in the Woods* (1957) by Arthur Laurents (see p. 43) and *Who's Afraid of Virginia Woolf?*, is devoted to challenging the basic premise of the social theatre. It declares that man is not perfectable and that it is necessary to accept this fact. In an age of disillusionment and uncertainty absolutes hold a persuasive attractiveness. While it is true that immediate economic and social evils could be cured by this sense

[1] 'After the Fall'. p. 44.

of corporate strength, however, it is equally true that the same panaceas were of no revelence to the underlying problems which had their origin, not in any specific social system but rather in the nature of man. Miller is concerned firstly with identifying this fact and then with the necessity of facing it as a fact of existence. This is man after the Fall, imperfect, self-centred, but with the capacity to renew love even in the face of his imperfection.

Love remains the one possible answer but it is a love aware of its own limitations and prepared to admit to the fact of individual and corporate cruelty as an inescapable legacy of the Fall rather than an inbuilt fault of society. Miller is no longer content with a world-picture which sees man as a victim of a hostile society. To him a genuine optimism lies in a future based on an understanding of the present.

These were facts which he had seen through a glass darkly in his earlier plays but which he had not fully developed nor even, one suspects, fully understood. In *All My Sons* universal love was apparently proffered as the golden hope of the age and yet the cruel selfishness of his characters left the audience painfully aware of some ill-defined insufficiency in that hope. Joe Keller's death, necessary to *All My Sons*, with its insistence on absolutes, which was the legacy of a war situation, would have been unnecessary to the later Miller. To him as we see in *After the Fall* and the later *Incident at Vichy* (1964), the necessity to recognise one's partnership with fellow men, one's 'complicity', is sufficient in itself. Death, in *After the Fall*, becomes, in fact, an alternative to a confrontation of reality. Maggie and Lou both kill themselves rather than face the responsibility for their own actions. Here, too, Miller examines the insufficiency of success—an insufficiency which many did not derive from characters such as Charley and Bernard in *Death of a Salesman*. Quentin is in fact a successful Willy Loman made suddenly aware of the inadequacy of success and made to admit to egotism and to the cruelty which this imposes on those around him. Quentin senses that the pursuit of success is a positive barrier between people. Like Willy Loman his concern with the future had destroyed the human necessities of the present. 'A Future. And I've been carrying it around all my life, like a vase that must never be dropped. So you can't ever touch anybody.' (A.F. p. 91.) Like Bellow's Henderson he becomes aware of a contrast between 'becoming' and 'being'—a contrast which Miller had implicitly made in *Death of a Salesman* between the frantic striving of Willy and the final affirmation of Biff. Here Maggie is changed by success. When Quentin had first met her she was in a state of 'being', she was, he explains, not 'defending anything, upholding anything, or accusing—she was just *there*, like a tree or a cat'. (A.F. p. 67.) In becoming successful as a singer, however, she loses immediate contact with reality and goes beyond that frank acceptance of things which had attracted Quentin. Whereas she had previously said, in Biff's words, 'I know who I am' (A.F. p. 84) she ends her life in a drugged uncertainty which serves to highlight her failure to accept guilt or responsibility.

In Bellow's *Henderson the Rain King* Henderson is taught by his native mentor, Dahfu, of the need for acceptance through confrontation. In the course of his instruction he is forced to enter a lion's cave firstly because 'she is unavoidable' and secondly because she forces 'the present moment on you'.[1] Confronted with this ineluctable reality Henderson becomes 'one huge mass of acceptance'.[2] When Henderson has learnt this lesson Dahfu poses a question to which the only answer is affirmation. 'Well Henderson, what are the generations for, please explain to me? Only to repeat fear and desire without a change? This cannot be what the thing is for, over and over and over. Any good man will try to break the cycle. There is no issue from that cycle for a man who do [sic] not take things into his hands.'[3] This is in essence the lesson learnt by Quentin in *After the Fall*. It is a lesson embodied not only in his own experience but also in the experience of Holga, the girl he is about to marry.

She takes Quentin around a concentration camp and admits that she herself feels guilt for what has taken place there. Although originally unaware of the existence of such places once she has discovered the truth she cannot turn her back. '. . . no one they didn't kill can be innocent again'. (A.F. p. 32.) She tells Quentin of an incident which had occurred during the war—an incident which functions as a parable of the need for confrontation. During this time, she tells him, she had lost her memory in a bombing raid. Wandering around she had shied away from the violence which she saw around her, 'Every day one turned away from people dying on the roads'. She tries to kill herself but an injured soldier pulls her down from the bridge from which she was about to jump and takes her home. Once there she dreams that she has given birth to an idiot child and becomes convinced that the child is an image of her life. She realises that although the child is idiot and

[1] *Henderson the Rain King*, p. 260.
[2] *Ibid.*, p. 223.
[3] *Ibid.*, p. 297.

repulsive yet there remains a need to embrace it. She does so and in future when she has the dream, 'it somehow has the virtue now . . . of being mine'.[1] This is the answer which Quentin eventually discovers. However repulsive life appears to be it is necessary, in Holga's words, to 'take one's life in one's arms' (A.F. p. 33). Holga is not blind to the violence of man. She has learnt to face up to it. She has learnt from the facts of war what Quentin has to discover in the inability of love to overcome the cruelty which springs from egotism. 'What burning cities taught her and the death of love taught me: that we are very dangerous!' (A.F. p. 127.) He accepts the image of the idiot child—a child who if he is bad is so by reason of his very nature and therefore needs all the more a love which does not baulk at the fact of his nature but which renews constantly in the knowledge of its ultimate failure. Quentin walks to Holga at the end of the play and in doing so accepts his responsibility for his past cruelty but recognises also that this stems from the nature of man and that the only crime is to stop trying, '. . . the wish to kill is never killed, but with some gift of courage one may look into its face when it appears, and with a stroke of love—as to an idiot in the house—forgive it; again and again . . . forever?' (A.F. p. 127). The question mark emphasizes Miller's desire to avoid casual resolution but there remains little doubt that his faith rests in a 'real relationship, founded on truth' and sanctified by a love which however fallible remains a genuine consolation, 'No, it's not certainty, I don't feel that. But it does seem feasible . . . not to be afraid. Perhaps it's all one has.' (A.F. p. 128).

This concept of 'acceptance' through confrontation is here clearly defined for the first time in Miller's work. In 1957, however, Arthur Laurents had in part anticipated him with *A Clearing in the Woods*. This play, first presented at the *Belasco Theatre*, New York City, is an expressionistic presentation of the struggle of a young woman against accepting those parts of her character against which she is in rebellion. Her refusal to accept at first erects a barrier between her and those to whom she is naturally drawn. She refuses to accept that reality which does not correspond to her own dreams and wishes. In the end, however, Virginia, the protagonist, comes to accept the cruelty in her character and the limitations which life forces on her. She comes to accept dreams as dreams and reality as the only base for a life lived with integrity and without fear. This is a play, too, which stands as a forerunner to *Who's Afraid of Virginia Woolf?* where Virginia—in this

[1] *After the Fall*, p. 40.

case Virginia Woolf—again stands for an abandonment of dreams which is not an abandonment of hope. In that play, as in this, impotence is a function of the unreal world in which the characters live and the punning references to sexual incompetence in both plays serve to highlight the sterility and psychological harm to be caused by this failure to accept. Laurents insists that 'An end to dreams isn't an end to hope'[1] a statement which is the basic contention of the drama of confrontation. In scope, however, Miller's play passes far beyond the restrictive psychological preoccupation of *A Clearing in the Woods* and indeed approaches something of the metaphysical concern of another work whose close connection to *After the Fall* is evident in more than a mere similarity of title. *The Fall (La Chute)* by Albert Camus was first published in 1956.

Like Quentin the protagonist of *The Fall* is a very successful lawyer. Like him also he comes to realise that his fame and success derive solely from egotism. 'I have to admit it humbly . . . I was always bursting with vanity. I, I, I is the refrain of my whole life and it could be heard in everything I said.'[2] Like Quentin also he starts with a desire to defend his innocence, a process which, as Miller indicates, is usually carried on at the expense of others. 'My innocence, you see? To get that back you kill most easily.'[3] Camus makes the same point:

'People hasten to judge in order not to be judged themselves. What do you expect? The idea that comes most naturally to man, as if from his very nature, is the idea of his innocence. From this point of view, we are all like that little Frenchman at Buchenwald who insisted on registering a complaint with the clerk, himself a prisoner, who was recording his arrival. A complaint? The clerk and his comrades laughed: "Useless old man. You don't lodge complaints here." "But you see, sir," said the little Frenchman, "my case is exceptional. I am innocent!"

We are all exceptional cases. We all want to appeal against something! Each of us insists on being innocent at all costs, even if he has to accuse the whole human race and heaven itself.'[4]

Thus here too the concentration camp serves as a demonstration of man's quest for innocence at the expense of others. Just as Quentin

---

[1] Arthur Laurents, *A Clearing in the Woods* (New York, 1957), p. 169.
[2] Albert Camus, *The Fall*, trans., Stuart Gilbert (Harmondsworth, 1963), p. 37.
[3] *After the Fall*, p. 58.
[4] *The Fall*, p. 60.

realises that he has 'loved them all, all! And gave them willingly to failure and to death that I might live' (A.F. p. 127) so Camus' protagonist admits that 'I used to advertise my loyalty and I don't believe there is a single person I loved that I didn't eventually betray'.[1] Thus to both writers the central need for humanity is to abandon an 'innocence' which is real only in the context of an unreal world and which, in its concern with self, is the source of human treachery and cruelty. Confrontation—the acceptance of reality and thus responsibility and guilt—becomes the key to genuine existence. Both writers, however, come dangerously close to saying 'We are all guilty, therefore all guilt is equal, therefore we are all innocent'. For if man is by nature cruel and violent how can the individual bear any blame? A system which ascribes the same culpability to personal deception as to mass murder seems guilty of a radical over-simplification.

From Camus, perhaps, we can derive the full meaning of the Christ symbolism which coalesces in *After the Fall* for the first time in Miller's work. In former plays there had been nothing but a mere suggestion— a tree planted as a symbol of the son who had given his life in expiation in *All My Sons,* a man destroyed, partly by himself and partly by society after working for his company thirty-six years in *Death of a Salesman.* Here Quentin, referred to by Rose as 'the light of the world', clasps two light fixtures in a conscious crucifixion image. The gesture is a symbol of his final acceptance of guilt. For Camus Christ too is guilty. He bears the guilt of the survivor—the survivor of the massacre of the innocents: 'Knowing what he knew, familiar with everything about man—ah, who would have believed that crime consists less in making others die than in not dying oneself!—brought face to face day and night with his innocent crime, he found it too hard for him to hold on and continue. It was better to have done with it, not to defend himself, to die, in order not to be the only one to live.'[2] Similarly Holga had returned to the concentration camp 'because I didn't die here (A.F. p. 24), because 'survival can be hard to bear' (A.F. p. 25).

Like Quentin Camus' protagonist arrives finally at the necessity for acceptance, '. . . I realised once and for all that I was not cured, that I was still cornered and that I had to make do with it as best I could. Ended the glorious life, but ended also the frenzy and the convulsions. I had to submit and admit my guilt. I had to live in the little-ease.'[3]

[1] *Ibid.,* p. 63.
[2] *Ibid.,* p. 83.
[3] *Ibid.,* p. 80.

The 'little-ease' of which he speaks is a cell in which it is impossible either to stand or lie down. He accepts, therefore, that man's aspirations have their limits and that acceptance is the necessary conclusion of an honest self-examination.

Camus' *The Fall* is a confession rather than a novel; Miller's *After the Fall* is a confession rather than a play. The individual is, however, in both cases confessing on behalf of man. Miller and Camus both underline the failure of success to serve anything but the ego, to mean anything but a conditional belief in innocence, which, when it dissipates, leaves both protagonists alienated from their former existences. To secure a real place among mankind, like Hawthorne's characters, they have to stress the guilt which is their link with humanity. In *The Fall* Clamence keeps a stolen painting and arranges everything 'so as to make myself an accomplice'[1] while Quentin leaves a note for his wife to read 'in order to . . . somehow join the condemned'.[2]

What makes *After the Fall* finally such an unsatisfactory play is not the intrusion of personal detail but the fact that Miller fails to establish the credibility of his protagonist. The confessional form necessitates a dominant character, since the play ultimately consists of his thoughts and memories. So that Quentin's unbelievably pretentious language reveals itself not as a necessary aspect of his character but as a mark of Miller's submission to the self-indulgence which is an endemic danger in the play's form. In making his protagonist a lawyer Miller was seeking something more than lucidity, just as was Camus in *The Fall* and Osborne in *Inadmissible Evidence* (1956). The analytical probing of the confessional form calls for a combination of advocate and prosecutor able to probe objectively for an elusive truth. Miller's fault lies in an over-concern with language at the expense of conviction. Quentin's eloquence too frequently degenerates into rhetoric. The man who strikes his chest in confession may derive his satisfaction not so much for his admission of guilt as from the exquisite nature of the blow.

Miller's intention in *After the Fall* was clearly to write a 'cosmic' play—one which would encompass the most bewildering aspects of mid-twentieth-century life. It was his attempt to answer the challenge which Durrenmatt had thrown down to Brecht. Seemingly unaware of Camus' work he has attempted to demonstrate the reality of man's nature and situation as revealed by the virtually incomprehensible cruelty of the Second World War. The 'momentous enlightenment' which Quentin

---

[1] *Ibid.*, p. 107.
[2] *After the Fall*, p. 47.

experiences in the course of his self-examination is clearly one which Miller would present as valid for a world still reeling from this horrifying truth. Confrontation is here both method and theme while the love, which Camus had foreseen as the necessary end of revolt and absurdity, remains as the source of that affirmation for which Bellow had called and towards which Miller has always inclined.

Miller's latest work, *Incident at Vichy* (1964), serves merely to make the concerns of *After the Fall* more explicit. A group of men picked up by the Germans during the war sit in an outer office waiting to be called into an examination room by a professor who turns out to be an anthropologist. They anxiously cling to the hope that this is merely a document check. The nervous suspicions of Lebeau, a painter, however, together with information smuggled to them by a waiter, make it clear that they are here because they are Jews and that they are to be taken to Poland to die. LeDuc, a psychiatrist, accepts this as true not because they are Germans or Fascists but 'because they are people'.[1] He thus identifies, as Quentin had in the former play, the origin of violence as being man himself. He recognises also that it is a fact of man's nature to require a victim, 'Each man has his Jew; it is the other. And the Jews have their Jews',[2] a fact highlighted here by the prejudice shown by the detainees towards a gypsy who has been brought in with them. It is interesting to note that once again Camus had made the same point, 'Every man needs slaves as he needs fresh air'.[3]

LeDuc clashes with Von Berg, an Austrian nobleman arrested by mistake. He taunts him with the guilt of the survivor since it is clear that he will escape the purge. The taunt is neatly reversed, however, when Von Berg offers him his free pass. LeDuc accepts, 'his hands springing to cover his eyes in the awareness of his own guilt'.[4] This is essentially a repetition of *After the Fall* and LeDuc's speech, at the moment of his own treachery, could equally well have been made by Quentin after his 'momentous enlightenment'. 'I am only angry that I should have been born before the day when man has accepted his own nature; that he is *not* reasonable, that he is full of murder, that his ideals are only the little tax he pays for the right to hate and kill with a clear conscience.'[5] Like Quentin, having accepted the fact of his own

---

[1] Arthur Miller, *Incident at Vichy* (London, 1965), p. 20.
[2] *Ibid.*, p. 66.
[3] *The Fall*, p. 34.
[4] *Incident at Vichy*, p. 69.
[5] *Ibid.*, p. 65.

guilt, LeDuc accepts the responsibility and decides to live with it, while his recognition of idealism as a cover for cruelty does something belatedly to elucidate the character of Chris in *All My Sons*. *Incident at Vichy* has little or nothing to add to *After the Fall*. Its characters, if less easily identifiable as ghosts from his own past, are none the less ineffectual, tending as they do to the stereotype. Its method is as hackneyed and obvious as Katherine Anne Porter's *A Ship of Fools* (1962). Yet these two plays represent a logical extension of his early concern with guilt, innocence and cruelty and if they owe something to the metaphysical concern of Gelber and Albee they are equally evidence of Miller's own determination to establish the validity of a cerebral drama. That he should, in search of this goal, have been driven to what is virtually monologue, as in *After the Fall*, is regrettable since he clearly lacks the discipline demanded by this particular form. It is, however, perhaps evidence of the truth of Saul Bellow's comment, in a book-review of Gide, that, 'Sadly enough, the number of intelligent people whose most vital conversation is with themselves is growing'.[1]

Arthur Miller, despite his reputation as a 'social dramatist', has attained to something considerably more than a humanised social play. If his earlier work never finally breaks free of a standard railing against the pursuit of success, his consciousness that 'a play which appears merely to exist to one side of "ideas" is an aesthetic nullity'[2] does something to explain the significance of his work to a theatre obsessed with emotion and escapism. Miller's triumph lies in his refusal to evade and his distrust of resolution. To him the core of action lies in integrity. This in turn depends upon a clear perception of the reality of a naked identity forged out of choices made and not moulded to fit the illusions of a dream world. In so far as this penetrates the theatrical weaknesses of his plays it can be seen as the main inheritance which he has passed onto those dramatists who have succeeded him. His commitment to a theatre of ideas lifted him above the norm of an enervated theatre. His concern with the establishment of a dialectic having its base in a real world anticipated Albee's and even Brown's concern with the necessity of seizing the reality of the human condition as the one legitimate theme for a modern American drama free at last of the responsibility for justification or for the ritualistic destruction of social scape-goats. The line from *All My Sons* to *After the Fall* is a logical one. In successive plays Miller has probed deeper and deeper into the

[1] Tony Tanner, *Saul Bellow* (London, 1965), p. 108.
[2] *Arthur Miller's Collected Plays*, p. 9.

metaphysical life of man while simultaneously moving away from that distrust of 'rectitudinal fever' demonstrated by Ibsen towards a faith in the necessity for confrontation. This faith is in essence that outlined by James Baldwin in an early essay published in *Notes of a Native Son* (1955), 'People who shut their eyes to reality simply invite their own destruction, and anyone who insists on remaining in a state of innocence long after that innocence is dead turns himself into a monster.'[1] If the affirmation of *Death of a Salesman* is largely unconvincing and unjustified that of *After the Fall* is a genuine aspect of a dialectic which sees confrontation as the necessary prelude to a renewed faith in the 'humanist heresy' of belief in man. While in his early plays Miller was clearly moving towards the position adopted by the drama of confrontation it is equally clear that it was not until his vision had been tempered by the cold pessimism of the absurd that his belief in affirmation through confrontation could offer any truly universal meaning. For it is only in his last plays that he has attempted to define the full nature of the human situation which must be faced. He is no longer content with demonstrating that a man is limited to his own possibilities. He now demands an acceptance of the full implications of human nature and the human situation. For between *Death of a Salesman* and *After the Fall* the theatre of the absurd had defined with meticulous care the nature of a world beyond the immediate comprehension of a Willy Loman—a world more terrifying than that represented by the mechanised unconcern of success-society.

[1] James Baldwin, *Notes of a Native Son* (London, 1964), p. 165.

3

The Living Theatre

The Connection is ostensibly a play about drug addiction. It invites the audience to believe that they are seeing a number of 'junkies' hired to take part in an improvisational drama. Jaybird, the supposed author of the play, appears on stage with the producer to explain his ideas but it soon becomes apparent that the junkies are not prepared to collaborate fully and they refuse to follow the guide lines which he has laid down. While the play is in progress two photographers wander around the set apparently in order to take a motion picture of what happens. Gradually they are drawn into the web of the addicts and by the end one of them has taken dope, in common with the supposed playwright. The action of the play is concerned with this small group of people who await the arrival of the 'connection' with some heroin. Although this contact does eventually arrive there is no sense that the play has reached a climax for this is presented as merely another and accepted stage in the usual routine. One of the addicts takes an overdose of the drug and comes near to death but to be revived by two of the others. The play ends on an inconclusive note.

While the play ostensibly invites comparison with Michael Gazzo's *A Hatful of Rain* (1955) in fact such a comparison would be misleading for *The Connection* is in no sense a social play. Clearly George Wellwarth is incorrect in identifying it as a defence of drug addiction, in his book *The Theatre of Protest and Paradox*.[1] Gelber is neither lamenting the plight of the dissolute junkie nor is he calling for reform. For him the addict, in the grip of an apparently remorseless need, is an image of the human situation and his play is an analogue of the condition of man in a universe which he identifies as empty, repetitious and cold. Indeed this is emphasised by Solly, the most lucid of the junkies and the one whose perception identifies him most closely with the author. He guesses that the author had chosen this 'petty and miserable microcosm' because of its 'self-annihilating aspects'.[2]

[1] George Wellwarth, *The Theatre of Protest and Paradox* (London, 1965).
[2] Jack Gelber, *The Connection* (London, 1960), p. 127. All future references will be abbreviated to 'T.C.' and be incorporated in the text.

Gelber is indeed unnecessarily concerned with establishing that the conclusions of the play have a relevence outside of the immediately destructive world of the drug addict. For if the junkie needs his fix so, Gelber insists, does a society which sublimates its need for hope and meaning in a frenzy of meaningless activity, '. . . the people who walk the streets, the people who work every day, the people who worry so much about the next dollar, the next new coat, the chlorophyll addicts, the aspirin addicts, the vitamin addicts' (T.C. p. 22). The meaningless repetition of a nine to five existence is seen by Gelber as an equivalent of the empty repetition of a junkie's life which is lived from one fix to the next. There is none of the hipster's contempt for the 'square' to be found in the play for Gelber's point is that there is basically no difference between them. They are both 'hungry for a little hope' (T.C. p. 23), and thus both make the absurdity of their situation more absurd by their response to it. If the junkie is 'hung up' on heroin then one of the addicts identifies the basic obsessions of society as money and sex.

Gelber's particular strength lies in his ability to establish the ironies of his terms. Indeed it is the ambiguity which surrounds his use of the word 'connection' which holds the clue to his central meaning. On the surface a connection, in the argot of the addicts, is the middle man between the junkie and the supplier. In a more general sense, however, it refers to the relationships between things—the relationships which create a semblance of order out of disorder. So that if the addict waits for his connection to bring him his heroin, on a more fundamental level man waits for that which will create some sense of meaning out of an apparently arbitrary life. Kenneth Tynan is clearly right in suggesting that there are lines of force relating *The Connection* with *Waiting for Godot*[1] for both plays are at first sight concerned with the same issues and both appear to have similar frightening implications. In fact a comparison will demonstrate how closely Gelber's play follows what is in many ways its European forbear.

Waiting for Godot is also an analogue of the human situation. Its basic premise is that man's life is spent waiting for something to bring meaning to the boring tedium of a repetitious existence. As Vladimir says, '. . . one thing alone is clear. We are waiting for Godot to come . . . Or for night to fall.'[2] This is equally true of Gelber's play. The addicts are waiting for the connection to arrive or, like Leach who

[1] Kenneth Tynan, 'Preface', *The Connection*, p. 7.
[2] Samuel Beckett, *Waiting for Godot* (London, 1959), p. 80.

takes an overdose, for the darkness which will finally make that connection irrelevent. For Beckett's characters the choice is between
distraction and suicide. Estragon and Vladimir, when they are not
hiding behind their protective chatter, contemplate the feasibility of
hanging themselves. So too the nature of the addicts' distraction is such
that it presents both an escape and a flirtation with extinction. Although
Cowboy, the connection, does eventually arrive it is clear that he fills
a similar role to that of the young boy in Beckett's play. The addicts
will go on waiting again and tomorrow will be the same as today and
so on until increasing physical decay stamps out simultaneously both
the individual and the hope or anticipation which was that individual's
will to live and the source of his self-torture. The connection, in the
fuller sense recognised by Solly, however, is no more identifiable with
a particular person or philosophy than is Godot. As Solly says, 'We
are waiting. We have waited before. The connection is coming. He is
always coming. But so is education, for example. The man who will
whisper the truth in your ear. Or the one who will shout it out among
the people.' (T.C. p. 27.)

The parallels between the two plays are not limited to their basic
premise, however, for the similarity of their approach naturally leads
to a similarity of detail. The drug addicts of *The Connection* relapse
whenever possible into a sleep which protects them from the reality
of their situation. This, however, tends to exacerbate the essential
loneliness of those who remain awake. Leach, in whose apartment the
action is presumed to take place, wakes up a fellow addict so that he
can listen to the meaningless chatter which serves as his protection—
an action which recalls not only *Waiting for Godot* but also *Endgame*
(1957). When Solly objects that 'I haven't slept since the night I met
you' (T.C. p. 19) we are reminded of the parallel situation in *Waiting
for Godot* when Estragon, who wakes Vladimir because he feels lonely,
is castigated by his partner. 'I was asleep! Why will you never let me
sleep?'[1] Looking for proof of existence the junkies seek it in the
fix, 'A fix to remember, to be sad, to be happy, to be, to be' (T.C. p. 23)
while Vladimir and Estragon similarly grasp at distraction as a proof
of their existence, 'We always find something . . . to give us the
impression that we exist'.[2]

Nevertheless *The Connection* is not merely a transposition of *Waiting
for Godot* to an American locale for there is a sense in which Gelber is

[1] Samuel Beckett, *Waiting for Godot* (London, 1959), p. 19.
[2] *Ibid.*, p. 69.

aware of the possibility of transcending Beckett's deterministic absurdity. For Beckett the absurdity of the human situation makes man himself absurd *per se*. His attempts to seize dignity and to comprehend —those marks of the *gens humanus*—serve only to add self-ridicule to absurdity. Gelber, on the other hand, while recognising the validity of the absurdist's vision, granting, that is, that man is alone in an empty universe and that he is born 'astride of a grave',[1] suggests that there are two possible responses to this fact. The response which serves to make man absurd is the debilitating need for distraction which, in avoiding a confrontation with reality avoids also that positive alternative which he goes on to outline. Gelber's characters are aware of the non-existence of established absolutes. They refuse to believe in 'the big connection', the man behind the connection, thus, in a wider sense the man behind the creation of order, the god. 'I have never seen the man because there is no man.' (T.C. p. 25.) In the absence of such an absolute, however, they transfer the paraphernalia of religion to the drug addiction which becomes its substitute. When Sam has had his fix he returns to the room and announces, 'I've seen the light! Brethren, I used to be a sinner! A sinner . . . I am redeemed! From my eternal suffering I am redeemed!' (T.C. pp. 40-1).

The sense of a possible alternative to the absurdity of this reaction is embodied in the person of Solly. It is an alternative, however, which Gelber presents only tentatively and which he refuses to trace to its logical conclusion. Solly derives from his sense of the human condition what amounts to an existentialist implication—an implication, moreover, which makes freedom and subjective meaning valid concepts. 'The man is you' he says, 'You are the man. You are your own connection. It starts and stops here.' (T.C. p. 26.) It is Solly also who dismisses Jaybird who, as the author of the play, is ostensibly his creator, with what amounts to a declaration of freedom, 'Go ahead . . . it's our stage now.' (T.C. p. 24.) In spite of this realisation, however, Solly fails to project his 'enlightenment' into concrete action. Although it is repeatedly suggested that he is not 'one of the people' and that he is 'out of it' he is sensible of a counter-force which he identifies as the 'tyranny of the majority' (T.C. p. 60). To break away from the illusions accepted by those around him is to invite isolation and possible persecution. This dilemma is in fact reminiscent of Sartre's *The Flies* (1943) in which the apparent systematised order to which men subjugate themselves crumbles before the realisation of freedom. For freedom to

[1] *Ibid.*, p. 89.

be real, however, it has to be accepted and acted out. The irony which both Gelber and Sartre emphasize is that men would rather have apparent order with subjugation than the chaos of total freedom. In Sartre's play Orestes pictures the reality of his situation, 'I knew myself alone, utterly alone . . . I was like a man who's lost his shadow. And there was nothing left in heaven, no Right or Wrong, nor anyone to give me orders', but as Zeus points out, 'Your vaunted freedom isolates you from the fold; it means exile.'[1] It is this fear of 'exile' which keeps Solly amongst the passive addicts—which prevents him from acting on the realisation that 'life begins on the far side of despair'. To 'kick' the habit is to embrace the gift of freedom and as Zeus insists 'Your gift to them will be a sad one; of loneliness and shame. You will tear from their eyes the veils I had laid on them, and they will see their lives as they are'.[2] This, of course, is the 'momentous enlightenment' of the drama of confrontation and if Gelber's play does not progress from this enlightenment to the positive affirmation of *After the Fall* it does acknowledge a vision of the human situation which is more austere than that recognised by the earlier Miller. For it is through *The Connection* that the theatre of the absurd makes its most direct impact on the American theatre. Indeed it is the synthesis of the absurdist's vision and the humanist's faith which gives the drama of confrontation its particular quality of positive validity. Where the affirmative mood of *Death of a Salesman* had been largely unconvincing and unearned, the affirmation of the drama of confrontation is leavened by the cynicism of the absurd. In the words of Lorraine Hansberry's *The Sign in Sidney Brustein's Window* (1964), which also falls into this category, this is an affirmation 'seasoned, more cynical, tougher, harder to fool'.[3] Where Albee's plays, like *After the Fall*, are concerned with redemption, *The Connection* is a play about the possibility of redemption.

While Gelber accepts the validity of the absurdist's vision of the human situation, however, he rejects that response which both Camus and Beckett advance as the only genuine reaction to an empty universe —a response embodied here in the persons of two photographers apparently hired to film the play. In *Act Without Words I* Beckett had

[1] Jean-Paul Sartre, *The Flies* and *In Camera*, trans., Stuart Gilbert (London, 1946), p. 96.

[2] *Ibid.*, p. 97.

[3] Lorraine Hansberry, *The Sign in Sidney Brustein's Window* (New York, 1965), p. 141.

shown man learning to distrust the senses which led him to participate in the world. At the end of the short mime the man had ended up, as does the boy in *Endgame*, motionless and unresponsive. This is in essence the state of the two photographers at the start of the action. When one of them is addressed by an actor he replies that he is not supposed to speak. They merely observe life without participating in it. In fact in a stage direction Gelber explains that in the course of the play they are to exchange their clothing and their personalities. Clearly then he sees this quietism as an absurd denial of existence while the comments which they interject into the action—'That's the way it is. That's the way it really is' (T.C. p. 23)—serve to stress the uselessness of an enlightenment which is not converted into a positive dialectic.

The drug addicts of *The Connection* are then only an image. As Jaybird suggests he could have chosen other examples. It is apparent that Gelber sees the modern neurosis over the bomb as an ironical method of inventing purpose, for worry, like waiting, presupposes a meaningful object for concern. Waiting and worry themselves become the fix to which not only the addicts surrender. 'So you wait and worry. A fix of hope. A fix . . . to be, to be.' (T.C. p. 23.) *The Connection* rejects the popular image of the junkie as the outsider who must be rescued and brought back into society. This had been the import of *A Hatful of Rain* whose final curtain falls on the stirring sight of a wife telephoning the police who will bring with them the doctors to cure her husband's anti-social sickness. This, Jaybird confesses, is the solution which he had in mind at the start of the play. In fact in his drug-induced state he still insists on stating what has now moved beyond cliché to irony, 'I thought perhaps the doctors would take over. That's the message for tonight from me.' (T.C. p. 61.) It is apparent by this time, however, that the junkie is not an outsider, that his sickness is shared by society and that the doctors themselves are offering the same destructive oblivion as the drug pushers. As Cowboy says, '. . . the doctors would be the big connection' for it is they who 'mildly electrocute thousands of people every year' (T.C. p. 62) and carry out prefrontal lobotomies. The drug addicts and the success addicts are finally indistinguishable from each other for as Cowboy insists, 'We all pay our dues whatever we do' (T.C. p. 60). Both the junkies and society at large are hooked to an indefinable need which leads Leach to take an overdose of drugs and those outside to 'jump into the street against the lights'. (T.C. p. 60.) This headlong flight towards destruction seems to Gelber the inevitable result of an addiction to distraction. The self-annihilating aspect of the addict group is emphasised by the sterility of their society. Leach, the greedy and repulsive host, is described as an incipient homosexual who, while enjoying the excitement of procuring women, usually by bribing them with drugs, can derive no satisfaction from them. So too Cowboy confesses that he has left love behind. In so far as this group of junkies can now be accepted as a valid microcosm it presents a horrifying picture of man's fear to confront reality and the resulting impotence and meaningless death. This connection between illusion and impotence is one which Edward Albee was to accept as valid in *Who's Afraid of Virginia Woolf?*

The Connection is, I believe, the first American play to confront the essential paradox of drama and the first play effectively to adopt from the European theatre the concept that form and content are indivisible. The central paradox of drama lies in the fact that the act of presentation is also an act of limitation. Unlike a novel, which is interpreted directly by the individual, a play is interpreted not so much by the audience as by the actor and the director. Thus in presenting the play as apparent improvisation Gelber is stating the dramatist's dilemma. He clearly does not imagine, as George Wellwarth seems to think he does, that he can resolve this dilemma. Nevertheless *The Connection* is not merely a petulant complaint against his craft any more than had been Pirandello's *Six Characters in Search of an Author* which Gelber's play resembles in some respects. In it Gelber is drawing attention to a form which is both an image in itself and a challenge to the theatrical norms of the American theatre.

In each of the two acts the stage directions indicate that there is approximately thirty minutes jazz—pure jazz, improvised, as in theory is the play of which it is a part. It is this very improvisational form which carries the key to Gelber's sympathies. For jazz itself is also an image. Its improvisational form is an image of an authentic response to the human condition. More than any other form of music it is dependent for its existence on the ability of individuals to create their own meaning and harmony and to establish their own relationships with their fellow musicians. So that it is apparent that neither the introduction of jazz nor indeed the ostensible improvisational nature of the play are the result of Gelber's perverse naïvete, as Wellwarth suggests, but that rather they re-inforce the freedom of action which is the basis of Solly's enlightenment. It is for the individual to accept his freedom and not to accept dictation from a majority 'hooked' on the need for distraction.

For Gelber meaning derives from relationships deliberately created by individuals having a sense of their community with others.

The significance of the jazz image is emphasised not only by the acknowledgement in the play's first minute of 'the authenticity of that improvised art' (T.C. p. 15) but by the presence of what amounts to a prophet for this authenticity—Harry McNulty. Harry appears twice in the play. He enters at the beginning and goes through a fixed ritual of plugging in a portable phonograph, playing a Charlie Parker record, unplugging the machine at the end and then going out again—the whole performed without dialogue. The music silences the self-pitying complaints of the junkies and temporarily unites them. Whatever understanding might result from this is aborted, however, by the interruption of Jaybird who insists that they follow the guide-lines of his standardised plot. McNulty's second appearance occurs at the end of the play when Jaybird is forced to concede the freedom of his characters, 'It's all yours now' (T.C. p. 62). This serves to herald Harry's entry. The ritual is repeated and the play ends with the sound of jazz penetrating the darkness of the stage.

The conventional response of desperate commitment to religion, characterised by the Salvation Sister brought back to the apartment by Cowboy, and the compulsive anaesthesia and isolation of the addict, both defer to the man who arrives with a phonograph record of improvised jazz. The Salvation Sister, obsessed by thoughts of death, turns naturally to Solly for insight into this superior salvation which she sees as a challenge to her own faith. Solly asks, 'What makes you think I would know him?'. The Sister replies, 'Oh, he loves jazz music. I thought perhaps . . . never mind, I'm probably wrong anyway. The Lord willing, that is.' (T.C. p. 45.) She finds her religion neither proof against her loneliness nor able to grant any meaning to an existence dominated by the fact of physical disintegration. She begs to be allowed to stay but is forced out still muttering to herself the reassurance which we now see to be hollow, 'You are not alone. You are not alone. You are not alone.' (T.C. p. 48.) Similarly Jaybird, in trying drugs for the first time, discovers that far from revealing meaning to him or destroying his loneliness it serves to erect walls between himself and others. Thus a retreat into illusion is revealed as ineffectual while the play concludes on Jaybird's admission of the freedom of his characters and the sounds of improvised jazz from Harry McNulty's phonograph.

Gelber's play is in fact an attack on the established American concept of drama. The play which Jaybird had planned would have been in-

distinguishable from the social and psychological theatre of Broadway
—would in fact have been another version of Gazzo's comfortably
reassuring play. When he intervenes, as the characters are apparently
getting out of control, he does so to impose the rigidities of conventional drama, 'I had characters, with biographies for each of them.
I thought that was clear'. The questions which he fires at the junkies
serve only to emphasise his formularised concepts, 'Solly, where is
your philosophy . . . Where are your confessions? Your capsule
comments?', 'Leach, where is the plot?' Leach's reply sums up Gelber's
dissatisfaction with standardised drama, 'I flushed it down the toilet'
(T.C. p. 24). When the junkies invite Jaybird to stay on the stage and
really 'find out about things' (T.C. p. 24) they are indicating a schism
between the contrivances of the theatre and reality which is precisely
that which had motivated Pirandello. If *The Connection* is concerned
with repudiating the false logic of a desperate humanity trapped by its
own rationalism it is also dedicated to destroying the self-justifying
nature of the theatre. When Jaybird says, 'I believe it all fits together
. . . We wouldn't all be on stage if it didn't' he is expressing both a
deterministic vision of existence and an equally restrictive concept of
drama. It is left to Solly, with the same dual relevence, to reply, 'It
doesn't have to fit' (T.C. p. 62). Perhaps the best comment on the
significance of this declaration is to be found in the words of Oedipus
in Cocteau's *The Infernal Machine* (1926), 'What we want . . . is not
to fit, to breakaway. That's the sign of masterpieces and heroes.'[1]

The horror of the group of junkies lies in their ignorance, with the
exception of Solly, of the passive state into which they have betrayed
themselves—of the breach which they have allowed to open up
between themselves and reality. Granting the emptiness of their universe they invent an abstraction to which they can do obeisance and
which will reveal a new order on a plane removed from the suffering
of positive existence. Gelber is at pains to insist that the same can be
said of the audience not just in the sense that it represents the macro-
cosm to the junkies' microcosm but in the attitude with which it
approaches the theatre. Theatre, the conventional and reassuring
stereotype of modern American theatre, acts as just such a drug. Under
the guise of seeking truth the audience retreats behind its assurance of
theatrical illusion, aware that the convention of American drama is one
of reconciliation and resolution. *The Connection* is an assault on the

[1] Jean Cocteau, *Orpheus, Oedipus Rex, The Infernal Machine*, trans.,
Carl Wildman (London, 1962), p. 129.

audience not in the almost physical sense that *The Brig* was to be but in the sense of jolting it with the apparent spontaneity of parts of its dialogue, the constant interruptions for a seemingly irrelevent jazz and the refusal to follow the normal lines of dramatic progression. The pseudo-improvisational nature of the play does not break down theatrical illusion but it does tend to diminish the effect of that illusion. Tennessee Williams, in *Camino Real*, had directed his characters up and down the theatre aisles but this had had the appearance of an arbitrary theatricality whose very flamboyance was a denial of its significance. In *The Connection* Gelber succeeds, where he was later to fail with *The Apple* (1961), in establishing a direct involvement on the part of the audience which is not dependent merely on the physical traffic between stage and auditorium.

The 'shock value' of the play lies, not in the fact of its stage presentation of addicts, which had been done before, but in Gelber's blunt refusal to adopt any of the simplicities of structure and theme which had been the mark of the bulk of American drama up to this time. The eccentricities of his play function, like the famous first word of Jarry's *Ubu Roi* in 1896, to jolt the audience out of its insulated self-satisfaction.

In Europe Strindberg and Maeterlink had experimented with a 'non-linear' drama at the turn of the century while the absurdists, writing fifty years later, felt free where necessary to reject totally the logic of time and causality. While Williams had tended towards a similar non-linear form in *Camino Real* he had subverted his effect by imposing the structure of a dream. So that (with the exception of the surrealistic drama of the thirties) it is with *The Connection* that American drama turns away from what Marvin Rosenberg has called the standard 'linear pattern'.[1] With *The Connection* Gelber firmly rejects Miller's contention that a play must 'end with a climax'. Like *Waiting for Godot* his play ends on a low note with the suggestion that the full stop could have been placed anywhere along the line for the action is a demonstration of a continuing state of consciousness. The only actions of any significance are the arrival of Cowboy, which occurs half-way through the play, and the overdose of drugs taken by Leach towards the end. Cowboy's arrival, however, takes place in the interval so that there is no element of suspense while Leach's overdose does not act as the climax to the play which simply comes to an end with the prospect that the action will be repeated over and over again. As Eric Bentley has

[1] Marvin Rosenburg, 'A Metaphor for Dramatic Form', in *Directions in Modern Theatre and Drama*, p. 344.

said, however, '. . . a new form always seems formless to the con-
servative mind'.[1] The apparent formlessness of Gelber's play is illusory
for it is in fact a strictly organised unit in which no element is
extraneous to the whole. For *The Connection*, like *The Brig*, is an
expression of a state of consciousness which therefore has no climax
in the sense which Jaybird imagines essential to a play.

Jack Gelber's experimentation is not mere aestheticism for as
Pirandello proved and Ionesco has insisted, '. . . it is only when we
have pulled apart the conventional characters in our plays, only when
we have broken down a false theatrical idiom, that we can . . . try to
put it together again—its essential purity restored'.[2] Here, then, was
evidence that at last an American dramatist was prepared to search out
the fundamentals of his craft and was prepared to learn the advantage
of a drama in which form and content were not strangers unhappily
forced into the same bed. *The Connection* further serves as proof that
philosophically based drama is not necessarily precocious for Gelber's
'philosophy' arises not from abstract speculation but from an acute
awareness of the dilemma which is the human situation. As Ionesco
says, 'In so far as an artist has a personal apprehension of reality, he is
a true philosopher . . . The quality of a work of art directly depends
on how "alive" philosophy is, on the fact that it springs from life and
not from abstract thought.'[3] Gelber's play was proof too that an
American audience could become attuned to the nuances of a drama
which rejects the turgid conventionalities of Broadway and those playwrights for whom drama was all too frequently a compromise with a
society demanding reassurance and resolution.

Gelber's insistence on the need for confrontation is made with a
full awareness of the frightening implications of the absurdist's vision.
Influenced alike by Sartre and Beckett, two forces essentially anti-
thetical, he is acutely aware of the essential dilemma which confronts
modern man. While anxious to avoid facile resolution it is clear that for
all Solly's failure to act Gelber sees his perception of the need for
confrontation as a genuine one. While his failure to embrace reality
frustrates the affirmation and redemptive love, which emerge as essential
aspects of the drama of confrontation, it is clear that *The Connection* is
the first American play to admit to the full horror of the absurdist
vision while denying the validity both of illusion and quietism. Solly's

[1] *The Playwright as Thinker*, p. 182.
[2] *Notes and Counter Notes*, pp. 32-3.
[3] *Ibid.*, p. 35.

comprehension of the human situation is thus clearly greater than either Willy Loman's or Biff's while he differs from Quentin not in depth of perception but in the extent of his courage. *The Connection* thus defines for the first time the nature of that reality which Albee, Brown and the later Miller urge on their protagonists.

Gelber himself has produced nothing of any note since *The Connection* and his attempts to repeat his effects have necessarily resulted in failure. He has tended to slip back into a self-indulgent formalism which if successful in breaking down a false theatrical idiom has done little to put it together again with or without its purity restored. Nevertheless this does not detract from the value of *The Connection* for not only did this play a significant part in the development of the drama of confrontation but it also introduced a self-conscious note to American theatre which led eventually to the exciting experiment of Kenneth Brown's *The Brig*.

The Connection was first staged by *The Living Theatre*, originally a repertory group and as artistically adventurous and sound as it was economically unstable. In common with the *San Francisco Workshop* and the *Artists' Theatre* in New York it was largely responsible for introducing American audiences to the best of European drama and for providing an outlet for American dramatists turned away by Broadway and even the more fashionable off-Broadway. Its repertory included, over a period, Brecht, Auden, Picasso, Lorca, Stein, Eliot, Strindberg, Cocteau, Pirandello, William Carlos Williams and Gelber. Although eventually forced to leave America because of its chaotic financial situation, before leaving it staged a play which represented a total departure from the norms of American drama and which, ironically, fitted almost exactly the theatre demanded by Artaud and Copeau as well as that outlined but never truly enacted by Ionesco. This play, which opened in May 1963, was *The Brig*. It is significant, however, not merely because it acts as an exemplar for those theoreticians who presently dominate European experimental theatre but because it constitutes a fusion of theory with viable practice and because it represents evidence of radical experimentation hitherto unknown in America. Artaud's and Ionesco's theories were not outside the tradition of philosophical and metaphysical drama, which was their inheritance, but rather were expressions of a desire to reduce the structure of drama itself until form and theme should be synonymous until, that is, drama should cease to inform and start to re-enact. For all his theories, how-

ever, Artaud's attempts at playwriting were disastrous and certainly
Ionesco's plays never attain to the purity of his conception. *The Brig*,
therefore, represents an achievement which not only confirms a new
spirit in American drama but which further represents a direct challenge
to Europe's hegemony of dramatic experimentation.

The ostensible situation of *The Brig* is that of a Marine Corps deten-
tion centre at the foot of Mount Fujiyama in central Japan. Here the
detainees are subjected to a frightening discipline which forces them to
perform the most menial of jobs under a rigid control which commands
their every movement. Normal daily duties, such as washing and
shaving, are used as a further means of humiliation. The printed text
of the play is prefaced with a list of regulations which is in effect a
summary of the content of a play which for two hours presents the
hideous order of meaningless activity. The regulations state:

> 'No prisoner may speak at any time except to his guards.—A prisoner
> must request permission to do any and everything in the following way:
> "Sir, prisoner number — requests permission to speak, sir." He must
> speak in a loud, clear, impersonal, and unaffected tone.
> 'At each exit and entrance there is a white line. No prisoner may cross any
> white line without requesting permission to do so. . . . No prisoner will
> sit down at any time unless it is necessary for the completion of his task.
> 'Under no circumstances will a prisoner be permitted to walk from place
> to place. He must run, or if this is not practical, he must at least show
> evidence of a trot.'[1]

All these and six other 'regulations' are strictly observed throughout
the play while the prisoners, all identically dressed, are referred to only
by numbers. The play does not progress through the development of
character or through the causal connections of plot. The only logic is
that imposed by the regulations so that the stage directions, which are
minutely precise, become a complete description of activity which is
both the means and end of Brown's dramatic intention. Frequently a
stage direction accounts for as much as ten minutes of time on the stage
while the dialogue which punctuates this action operates, as Artaud
had foreseen language operating in the theatre, as a form of incantation
functioning on the level of intonation and timbre. Brown insists that
'the voices of the guards, when speaking to the prisoners, shall be of a

[1] Kenneth H. Brown, 'The Brig', *Tulane Drama Review*, VIII, iii (Spring,
1964), p. 223.

deep and authoritative tone'.[1] Such stage directions indicate the nature of the communication at which Brown is aiming. He is not concerned with an audience interested in the flow of events or held by the immediacy or virtuosity of dialogue. The communication which is relevant to him is a 'visceral contact', that is an assault immediately on the senses—an attempt to communicate through the overwhelming pressure of action and sound. It is, in fact, a realisation of Artaud's desire to achieve 'violent physical images' which 'crush and hypnotize the sensibility of the spectator'.[2] Perhaps a single example will suffice to demonstrate Brown's method and to reveal his concern with operating through the establishment of what amounts to ritual:

'All the *prisoners* run into the head in single file. Moments later they begin at the inside exit from the head to exclaim, Sir, prisoner number one requests permission to cross the white line, sir. *Eberhardt* stands at the door to the head and says, Cross, as each one finishes the statement, naturally using his own number. The *prisoners* then stop at the entrance to the compound and repeat the formality. *Cpl. Sease* is there uttering the same word, Cross, and the *prisoners* enter the compound, return their soap and towels and pick up their marine manuals, stand at attention in front of the racks, and begin to read'.[3]

As Richard Gilman points out, in talking of Beckett and Genet,[4] criticism tends to lag behind dramatic invention so that we try to interpret the new in terms of the old. Clearly even the normal terms of dramatic criticism become suspect and the modern critic is at as great a loss to understand and explain Gelber and Brown as was the nineteenth-century critic confronted with *A Dream Play*. It becomes increasingly necessary to fall back on the apparent imprecision of such words as 'visceral', 'myth' and 'ritual'. In doing so, however, it becomes obvious how closely Brown's play matches that theatre for which Ionesco had looked in vain. Ionesco has said that '. . . one could by means of set gestures, a few words and pure movement succeed in expressing pure conflict, pure drama in its essential truth, the permanently destructive and self-destructive pattern of existence itself: pure reality, non-logical and non-psychological (transcending what today is called absurd and

[1] *Ibid.*, p. 225.
[2] *The Theatre and its Double*, pp. 82, 83.
[3] *The Brig*, p. 229.
[4] 'The Drama is Coming Now', p. 31.

non-absurd)'.[1] In essence *The Brig* does just this. In abandoning concentration on plot and character and retaining only the most tenuous of linear development Brown throws attention purely on the violent pattern of action which becomes not merely an image but a re-enactment of his belief that 'the world is in a terribly degenerated state'.[2] Seeking to bring his audience into a direct relationship with 'pure reality' he adopts the method which Ionesco had suggested but which he had also thought impossible of attainment. He creates 'a new cosmos within the cosmos with its own laws and consistencies' but which can finally be 'substituted for that other world with which other people could identify themselves'.[3] The violence with which the audience is assailed does indeed generate its own logic which stems from presence in the brig. To exist here is to suffer, is to accept the reality and validity of the regulations. To survive the individual has to yield to indignity and to tolerate the arbitrary and irrational nature of punishment.

The basis of Brown's method is thus clearly that which Ionesco had identified as the logical next step for drama—a move towards myth. Indeed there is a real sense in which *The Brig* comes closer to realising his statement of possibilities than have any European attempts. 'Another kind of drama', he had suggested to be possible, 'More powerful and far richer. Drama that is not symbolist, but symbolic; not allegorical, but mythical; that springs from our everlasting anguish; drama where the invisible becomes visible, where ideas are translated into concrete images, of reality, where the problem is expressed in flesh and blood; where anguish is a living presence, an impressive witness.'[4] Myth lies in the supremacy of the archetype over the stereotype—in the validity of universal symbols. As Frye has said, 'In the archetypal phase the work of literary art is a myth, and it unites the ritual and the dream'.[5] To Ionesco however the archetypal image is an idiom 'that has been lost in our own times, when allegory and academic illustration seem to have been substituted for the living image of truth, which must be rediscovered.'[6] *The Brig* constitutes such a rediscovery. It is concerned with forcing on an audience just this 'living image of

---

[1] *Notes and Counter Notes*, p. 226.

[2] Richard Schechner, 'Interview with Kenneth Brown', *Tulane Drama Review*, VIII, iii (Spring, 1964), p. 216.

[3] *Notes and Counter Notes*, p. 226.

[4] *Ibid.*, p. 237.

[5] Northrup Frye, *Anatomy of Criticism* (Princeton, 1957), p. 118.

[6] *Notes and Counter Notes*, p. 32.

truth', which is the essence of confrontation, while avoiding the restrictive irony of the absurd.

Where Beckett fails to achieve a middle ground between the dis-
cursiveness of *Endgame* or *Waiting for Godot* and his mime plays, *The
Brig* utilises the dramatic potential of action and fuses it with a language
which serves not to subvert or adorn the action but to function as a
counterpoint. To the audience watching *The Brig* there is less sense of
a succession of meaningful phrases and sentences than of a fusion of
sound and action. In those scenes in which the stage becomes a hive of
activity individual commands and marching orders become lost as
directives but are absorbed in the totality of the scene. In fact the
relationships of those on stage are accentuated through the use of sound.
The prisoners are restricted to a self-mocking loud monotone while
their guards speak with a cynicism and sarcasm which, according to
Brown, should vary to extreme degrees according to what must be
said. While his use of incantatory sound brought him close, in some
respects, to a symbolist poet such as Rimbaud *The Brig* is far removed
from the misty imprecision which all too often could be taken as the
mark of symbolist drama. His play is equally far removed from the
'static drama' of Maeterlinck and the hazy suggestiveness of O'Neill's
sea plays which reveal something of the symbolist sensibility. Nor
indeed does it succumb to the grotesquely trite symbolism which we
associate with Tennessee Williams and also at times Arthur Miller and
even Edward Albee. Brown's play is symbolic only in the sense that
a Roman Catholic mass is symbolic. That is to say it is not a substitution but an actual re-enactment. Hence when Ionesco urges a move from
allegory to myth this is in essence the change which he is suggesting.
Thus *The Brig* circumvents that problem of communication which had
perplexed Pirandello and the theoreticians who followed him by
establishing contact at a more fundamental level, for myth and ritual
depend not upon individual experience but upon a common situation.
So that Brown's definition of the play as 'an indictment of the senses in
order to reach the soul'[1] is a better description of its method than of
its theme.

The action of *The Brig* does cling tenuously to a normal development in so far as it takes place during the course of a single day but the
series of distinct actions which constitute the play have no relationship
beyond the consistency of their setting or outside of the logic created
by the brig itself. They should rather be regarded as variations in

[1] 'Interview with Kenneth Brown', p. 214.

intensity and focus. The two acts, into which the play is divided, both start with a scene of general activity and violence and then focus for the following two scenes on the individual as the victim of specific cruelties. Where the general scenes emphasize the uniform subjugation of the prisoners the others highlight the malicious insensitivity of an authority which creates rules and forces their contravention. Nineteen is ordered to collect some shovels. When he does so he fails to perform a military about face and is called to attention by one of the guards. This necessitates his dropping the shovels which starts a chain of events which inevitably leads to a beating:

> 'Idiot. Breaking my shovels. I order you to die for
> such a crime. Die idiot.
> *Nineteen remains at a rigid position of attention.*
> *He begins weeping silently.*
> Pick up the gear and move, maggot.
> *Nineteen picks up the four shovels and runs to the white*
> *line near the freedom door.*
> Nineteen, you crossed my white line without asking me first.
> Tonight is your night, nineteen.'[1]

The depersonalising use of a number instead of a name functions here as an endemic and natural part of the play's logic in contrast to Rice's use of the same device in *The Adding Machine* (1923). By concentrating on the individual unit Brown was not merely insisting on the individual's dilemma but was sharpening a focus which in the opening scene of each act was intended to present a broad picture of the horror of collective obedience to order. Clearly, within the context of the brig there is a necessary abrogation of compassion. When twenty-six, driven mad by his situation, emits a terrifying scream those around him continue with their assigned task. They all watch the frequent beatings administered to individuals without demur. Brown himself, in an interview in the *Tulane Drama Review*, suggests that while the individuals in the brig make no move to stop the suffering of their fellow prisoners, 'The next man to him knows that it is necessary for the first man to negate a normal reaction to his suffering and loves him for it'.[2] It seems clear, however, that no such compassion is apparent in the play itself which is rather a Kafkaesque examination of one aspect of the human condition.

[1] *The Brig*, p. 237.
[2] 'Interview with Kenneth Brown', p. 218.

Ionesco has pointed out the tendency of modern critics to search for allegory in the absence of a structure and intent which they can fully comprehend. *Waiting for Godot* has been the victim of such allegorisers who have found support for all their theories in the simplicity of its situation. *The Brig* has suffered similarly and Brown, like Arthur Miller, has shown that he is not always the best guide to his own work. Pressed by interviewers he has committed himself to a restrictive and allegorical interpretation of his play which sees the guards as '. . . . the dehumanised members of society. They are the people who have been given the responsibility of caring for and leading the prisoners . . . or the lower middle class, or, in the present scheme of things, the Negro'. The chief value of the play in fact lies in its refusal to surrender to such simplicity. For above all it is a play which relies solely on generating its own validity in action which is not discussed or placed in a specific moral context. The inappropriateness of Brown's comments is perhaps best demonstrated by his attempts to elaborate on a meaning which he admits became subordinated to other interpretations as the play progressed and reached the stage. 'I found man's strongest drive is the will to power. Man does not seek to survive for the sake of surviving. Man seeks to survive to rule. Every man dreams consciously or subconsciously of being a ruler, or a leader, or a guard.'[1] Certainly the nature of power and the relationship of the strong to the weak is an endemic part of the play but there is no indication of the will to power of the prisoners whose state of mind must remain unknown to us so long as they function as mere ciphers at the hands of a malicious and arbitrary authority. It is important, therefore, for the critic to avoid the temptation of narrow allegorical interpretation for if *The Brig* can be seen as an image of a world grimly inventing its own violent order out of a need for belief it can also be seen, as Brown further suggests, as a revelation of the responsibilities of the men who lead.

While Brown's play has much in common with absurdist drama it ultimately transcends the limited scope of the absurd, just as Ionesco had suggested a ritualistic drama would do. It comes close to fulfilling Artaud's prophecy of a *theatre of cruelty*, a predominantly visual drama resting in myth and ritual, expressing itself through movement and intonation and dedicated to impelling men to see themselves as they are. It lacks the irony which is an essential part of the absurd—an irony expressed in the continuing hope of Beckett's hopeless characters and in the contrast between thought and action which is the basis of his

[1] 'Interview with Kenneth Brown', p. 218.

dramatic technique. *The Brig* is a simple statement of one aspect of the human condition. In the absence of a central protagonist there is no possibility, within the play, for the affirmative stance adopted by Miller and Albee but in the absence also of an ironic tone there is no justification for calling it nihilistic. For as Brown has pointed out the brig represents only one part of human reality. Clearly it is not a total picture for there is an acknowledged world outside the wire of the compound. To embrace that world, however, it is necessary first to accept the perverse logic of the brig itself—to accept the reality of meaninglessness and limited determinism. The only alternative is madness—a distraction from reality which Albee, too, was to explore and reject in *Who's Afraid of Virginia Woolf?* and *Tiny Alice*. Brown, like Miller, feels that to accept the validity of love and compassion necessitates the acceptance, too, of its counterforce. In his own words, 'you reach a point when you can take the reality of your life, the miserable reality as well as the joyous reality, and instead of negating the misery and overplaying the joy, you balance them out, put the joy aside, because it is there, and receive more joy by seeking the nature of the misery'. This, in fact, could be taken as the major premise of the drama of confrontation. For Miller and Albee alike both accept Brown's contention that 'the misery is as much a part of life as the joy'[1] and that the ability to face that reality is the only means to personal transcendence. Indeed confrontation is taken a stage further here than in either Gelber or Albee. For the audience itself is placed in the position of one of Albee's protagonists, assailed by an attack on its sensibilities and forced to react to the sombre reality with which it is confronted. So that confrontation is here genuinely an aspect both of content and form. Here in fact is everything that Miller's *After the Fall* had sought to convey (treachery, restriction, arbitrary suffering, the demise of love) but handled to much greater effect. It achieves all that Miller's play had set out to do and not by means of abstruse and pretentious monologue but by returning to the technique of Donne, to the technique of the metaphysical poet who could so mould language with thought that the reader was forced to follow physically the tortuousness of the poet's image. Brown achieves the same effect on the stage through the compulsive nature of his action. Perhaps there is some validity in this parallel with poetry, in fact, for Brown's work, which we have already

---

[1] 'Interview with Kenneth Brown', p. 218. It is interesting to note that the play originally included scenes set outside the brig. These, however, were dropped during production.

noted as having affinities with Rimbaud and the symbolist poets, conforms closely to what Artaud has called the poetry of the theatre and was in fact first written as a poem. Brown has said that he rewrote it for the stage because the 'only way a person can experience someone else's experience is by doing it on a stage'.[1]

Judith Malina, who first produced *The Brig* for *The Living Theatre*, has said that she considers it to be improvisational, a part of what has inevitably come to be known as a 'theatre of chance'. Although the stage directions are precise what the play really creates is an entire environment. The regulations serve to define that environment and whenever they are infringed, whether as a part of a prepared script or accidentally by an actor, then that infringement is incorporated into the action and has necessary consequences. 'Every time an actor playing a prisoner steps on a line there is an improvisation . . . There is an extraordinary amount of improvisation in *The Brig*, probably much more than in *The Connection*.'[2] It is clear, however, that the improvisation of *The Brig* is radically different from that found in Gelber's play. For Brown everything is subordinated to the rationale created by the brig itself so that where the improvisation of *The Connection* serves to highlight the division between reality and art that of *The Brig* serves to show that there need be no such division.

The significance of Brown's play can hardly be over-emphasised. In its originality of form and concept it goes not only beyond the vapid unadventurousness of standard American drama but also beyond the achievement of a European theatre whose practice does not always match its inconoclastic theory. It is, perhaps, difficult to understand why the American theatre should have proved for the most part so unrepentedly mundane until *The Connection* broke down the norms of its sterile repetitiveness. The commercial forces were, however, largely responsible and it is significant that the break-through should have come with *The Living Theatre* which staged its first production in an uptown loft for the outlay of thirty-six dollars. More radically, however, this lack of experimentation can be traced to a contentment with the theatre as it already existed. The first season of *The Lincoln Centre* demonstrated the inflated worth ascribed to American drama by those responsible for the season's repertory. When the personnel was changed, at the end of the first and largely disastrous year, Herbert

---

[1] *Ibid.*, p. 212.

[2] Richard Schechner, 'Interview with Judith Malina', *Tulane Drama Review*, VIII, iii (Spring, 1964), pp. 211-12.

Blau, who replaced Elia Kazan as Director, based the 1965 repertory on four European plays. Indeed Blau's comments, while still a Producing Director of *The Actor's Workshop of San Francisco*, serve to indicate his opinion as to the cause of the lack of experimentation in the American theatre, '. . . if there hasn't been much experiment up to now in the American theatre, it is neither the government nor the foundations which are primarily at fault. The tragic fault is the people in the American theatre—congenitally nerveless, unoriginal, browbeaten, prostituted, self-seeking, whiny and deluded.'[1]

In the context of this 'nerveless . . . prostituted' theatre the work of writers like Gelber and Brown is clearly of vital importance, going, as it does, to the root of the dramatic process itself. For as Ionesco has said, 'Every genuine creative artist makes an effort to get rid of the relics and clichés of a worn-out idiom, in order to rediscover one that is simplified, reduced to essentials and renascent, capable of expressing realities old and new, topical and timeless, alive and permanent, both particular and universal.'[2] Indeed it is possible now to see that American drama has begun to establish itself as a vital form which can draw the attention of writers seriously concerned with 'relocating' man. The metaphysical drama of recent years has attracted major American talents to a stage which has long been the poor relation in American arts. While both Robert Lowell's *The Old Glory* (1964) and Saul Bellow's *The Last Analysis* (1964) (see p. 93) failed in production their very existence demonstrates a belief in the power and validity of the dramatic mode which is largely traceable to the experimentation of a theatre closed down by the United States Internal Revenue Service and now touring disconsolately around Europe.

[1] Herbert Blau and Jules Irving, 'The Living Theatre and Larger Issues', *Tulane Drama Review*, VIII, iii (Spring, 1964), p. 197.
[2] *Notes and Counter Notes*, pp. 162-3.

4

Edward Albee

AMERICAN drama in the early sixties has been effectively dominated by one man. In three years Edward Albee took the American theatre by storm. His first play, *The Zoo Story* (1959) was greeted by *The Villager* as, 'The finest play, written by an American, that can be seen for love or money' while *Who's Afraid of Virginia Woolf?* received the New York Drama Critics Circle award for the season 1962-3. Indeed this, his first full-length play, was nominated for a Pulitzer Prize by that Committee's drama jury. The nomination was, however, rejected because, in the words of W. D. Maxwell, a member of the advisory board, 'I thought it was a filthy play'.[1]

Albee, like Gelber, has shown himself to be fully aware of the vision of the European absurdists and indeed he has adopted both their analogical method (*The Zoo Story*) and their style (*The American Dream*). At the same time, however, again in common with Gelber, he has been struck by the insufficiency of their vision. If Solly, in *The Connection*, represented merely a potential, in Albee's plays that potential is realised and confrontation is accepted as the necessary basis for a life which if absurd in origin need not be so in fact. Albee accepts Camus's suggested progression from absurdity to love and his plays, starting with *The Zoo Story* and progressing to *Tiny Alice* and *A Delicate Balance*, are directly concerned with that 'momentous enlightment' which leads to a 'real companionship, founded on truth and purged of all falsehood'. Where Gelber has become frozen in stylistic revolt Albee has refined both his method and his thought in formulating a genuine alternative both to illusion and to despair. Indeed in some senses this process of refinement has gone too far so that *Tiny Alice* is in danger of degenerating into mere esoteric theorising.

Albee's faith is essentially that which Bellow insists upon in *Henderson the Rain King*, which was published in the same year as *The Zoo Story*. Indeed it is interesting to note just how closely these two writers' philosophies match one another. To both writers the self

[1] Wendell V. Harris, 'Morality, Absurdity, and Albee', *Southwest Review*, XVIX, iii (Summer, 1964), p. 249.

is seen as a barrier between the individual and the rest of humanity. Ihab Hassan, in his book *Radical Innocence*, has pointed out that the natural progress of Bellow's heroes is from humiliation to humility[1]— a process which purges this egocentricity while establishing the need for acceptance. This progress is equally true of Albee's protagonists who similarly come to understand that genuine existence lies only through the acceptance of reality and the establishment of a true relationship between individuals. Ironically this is a lesson which both Henderson and Jerry, the protagonist of *The Zoo Story*, derive from a contact with animals. In *Henderson the Rain King* it is a lion whose unavoidable qualities teach Henderson the need for acceptance and thus love while in Albee's play the same lesson is taught by a dog.

The Zoo Story describes the life which man has created for himself as a 'solitary free passage' characterised by indifference towards others. The isolation, which is the result of this attitude towards life, is stressed by the image of the zoo which is established in the course of the play as a valid image for man who has come to accept loneliness as the norm of existence. Albee's thesis is that there is a need to make contact, to emerge from these self-imposed cages of convention and false values so that one individual consciousness may impinge on another. This act he defines as love.

The *New York Times* has called *The Zoo Story* 'a harrowing portrait of a young man alienated from the human race'. Yet ironically the play is dedicated to demonstrating that this alienated individual, a man in his late thirties called Jerry, has more sense of the urgent necessity for human contact than does society itself. Jerry has reached a moment of crisis. The purposelessness of his life has begun to evidence itself in his appearance. He is 'not poorly dressed, but carelessly'; his body 'has begun to go fat'. As Albee says, 'His fall from physical grace should not suggest debauchery; he has, to come closest to it, a great weariness'. (z.s. p. 11.) The origin of this weariness is his growing realisation of the gulf which exists between him and his fellow men. As he admits, 'I don't talk to many people—except to say like: give me a beer, or where's the john, or what time does the feature go on, or keep your hands to yourself, buddy.' (z.s. p. 17.) Jerry's isolation is complete. Not only does he know nothing of those who share his rooming house—itself in a state of dilapidation which mirrors Jerry's own decline—but he is also effectively cut off from the past. His parents are

[1] Ihab Hassan, *Radical Innocence: Studies in the Contemporary American Novel* (New Jersey, 1961), p. 291.

long dead and the two picture frames which he owns are both empty. But having undergone a sudden enlightenment, a perception of the need for real human contact, he sets out across Central Park to pass on his new-found message. There he meets Peter, the epitome of middle-class complacency.

Peter is 'neither fat nor gaunt, neither handsome nor homely'. He is, in fact, virtually non-existent. His opinions are shaped by *Time* magazine and his values are those of a society to whom status and income rank before communication. He is sitting on his bench in Central Park precisely because here no demands can be made on him. He is remote from other people. If he exists as little more than a stereotype with no individuating characteristics this is essentially how Albee sees him. The world he lives in is essentially that of the American dream. Indeed even his marriage is revealed by Jerry's relentlessly probing questions to be little more than a social contract in which the dominance of the woman has emasculated the man and thus denied the necessity even of sexual contact. In a real sense, therefore, Peter is ultimately as isolated as Jerry had been.

To Albee, rather as to Karl Jaspers, modern society has detached itself from fundamentals and has created a new system of values by which the pursuit of material wealth and technological efficiency have come to replace basic human needs. As Philip Mairet says, paraphrasing Jasper's beliefs, these new values 'console man with the feeling that he is progressing, but make him neglect or deny fundamental forces of his inner life which are then turned into forces of destruction'.[1] Jerry's function in *The Zoo Story* is literally to 'save' Peter; to bring him back into a genuine relationship with his fellow man.

Jerry attempts to establish the importance of human contact by explaining the source of his own conversion. He describes a macabre duel which he had fought with a dog. This dog had attacked him each time he had entered his rooming house. Anxious to avoid contact he had tried at first to placate it with food, feeling as he did so rather as if he were offering a sop to Cerberus. When this had failed, he explains to Peter, he had then attempted to kill it. Only when the dog was dying, however, had he suddenly realised that some sort of connection had been possible between the dog and himself—a contact which his action had aborted. It was at this point that Jerry had experienced his 'momentous enlightenment' for he had realised the absolute need for contact between human beings. As he says to Peter, who is clearly disturbed by

[1] Philip Mairet, 'Introduction', *Existentialism and Humanism*, p. 11.

the story, 'if you can't deal with people, you have to start somewhere, WITH ANIMALS'. (z.s. p. 34.) When Peter refuses to learn the lesson implicit in the parable Jerry goes on explicitly to insist on the validity of animals as an image for humanity, 'I went to the zoo to find out more about the way people exist with animals, and the way animals exist with each other, and with people too. It probably wasn't a fair test. What with everyone separated by bars from everyone else, the animals for the most part from each other, and always the people from the animals. But, if it's a zoo, that's the way it is'. (z.s. p. 39-40.)

With this insistence on the validity of the zoo as an image for human beings consciously cut off from their kind Jerry comes finally to the conclusion that only through the stimulus of violence will any permanent contact be established. Neither allegory nor direct statement has succeeded in bringing Peter face to face with what Jerry sees as the basic problem of humanity. When his right to possession of the bench is challenged Peter's indignant reply shows that all of Jerry's comments about the evil of human isolation have had no impact. 'I see no reason why I should give up this bench. I sit on this bench almost every Sunday afternoon . . . It's secluded here; there's never anyone sitting here, so I have it all to myself. (z.s. p. 41.) Jerry recognises that his defence of the bench has become not only a defence of the solitariness of the human condition but also a justification of the values of a society which, it is implied, distracts man from the real problem of human existence. Jerry's retort expresses Albee's belief that absurdity stems not from the human situation but from man's response to that situation —a response which values the achievement of success above genuine fulfilment. 'You have everything in the world you want; you've told me about your home, and your family, and your own little zoo. You have everything, and now you want this bench. Are these the things men fight for? Tell me, Peter, is this bench, this iron and this wood, is this your honor? Is this the thing in the world you'd fight for? Can you think of anything more absurd? (z.s. p. 44.) Jerry throws Peter a knife and by deliberate insults provokes the violence which ensures that he will not be able to escape the consequences. As Jerry thrusts himself onto the knife one is conscious of the fusion of sexuality and violence which has emerged as a mark of the urge to establish contact. There can be little doubt that contact has at last been established and that Peter will never be able to return to his bench of isolation, 'You won't be coming back here any more, Peter; you've been dispossessed. You've lost your bench'. (z.s. pp. 48-9.) The message which Jerry had received from the dog in violence he has now passed on to his fellow man also in violence. Like Saul Bellow's Henderson Albee seems to subscribe to the belief that truth comes 'in blows'. Both Jerry and Henderson are shaken out of their private worlds of solitude and illusion by an enlightenment forced on them by an animal. As Henderson admits, '. . . unreality! That has been my scheme for a troubled but eternal life. But now I am blasted away from this practice by the throat of the lion. His voice was like a blow at the back of my head'.[1]

The Zoo Story is thus concerned with stressing the inadequacy of illusion—an illusion which is in essence the American dream. Peter, as we have seen, is a successful man. He has an executive position, a good salary, a family—and he is totally hollow and unaware of the needs of human beings. When Jerry had asked, 'Don't you have any idea, not even the slightest, what other people *need?*' Peter's reply had equated need with physical possessions, 'Well, you don't need this bench. That's for sure'. (z.s. p. 45.) Peter's failure stems from the fact that he has never dared to confront the reality of his life—the reality which Jerry meticulously and brutally lays bare. The compromise which he has reached with his life has left him effectively emasculated and totally solitary and yet it is not until Jerry forces him to confront this reality that he becomes aware of any insufficiency. Jerry realises that to Peter he is only 'a permanent transient' in 'the greatest city in the world. Amen'. (z.s. p. 37) but step by step he brings him to an acceptance of the fact that he has come to accept his pointlessly mundane existence, in the same way that a child uses pornographic playing cards, 'as a substitute for real experience'. (z.s. p. 27.)

The Zoo Story, is concerned, then, with redemption, for Peter is not only brought into a new and more meaningful relationship with reality but is introduced to the need for that genuine human contact which is the antithesis of absurdity. It is clear that Albee would agree with Bellow's Henderson when he says that, 'it's love that makes reality reality'[2] although it is equally clear that this is a humanistic concern for fellow men and not that sexuality which serves merely to emasculate.

While Albee was content, in *The Zoo Story*, merely to sketch in the details of an absurd society, in *The American Dream,* written in the following year but not produced until 1961, he examines the alternative to confrontation. In doing so he borrows directly the techniques of the theatre of the absurd and demonstrates the vacuity of a society which

[1] *Henderson the Rain King*, p. 307.
[2] *Ibid.*, p. 286.

refuses either to accept compassion or the need to embrace reality. While *The American Dream* is not directly concerned with confrontation it is worth dwelling on it for a moment for in this play Albee clearly identifies his vision of the absurd—a vision which differs fundamentally from the deterministic absurdity of a European drama derived out of Camus. At the same time it is apparent that through this one-act satire Albee is continuing to urge the need for genuine human contact based on a clear perception of the real.

Albee's play is dedicated to revealing the inadequacy of the American Dream—that faith in the inevitability and value of success which Horatio Alger had propounded. It is, as Albee himself has said, 'an examination of the American Scene, an attack on the substitution of artificial for real values in our society, a condemnation of complacency, cruelty, emasculation and vacuity; it is a stand against the fiction that everything in this slipping land of ours is peachy-keen'.[1] The Dream itself is a young man's vision of the future. It is a belief that the here and now is unimportant or that it is merely a step towards the achievement of some ambition which equates wealth with happiness and social acceptance with fulfilment. The future holds out the assurance of success to the young and guarantees a world where everything is 'peachy-keen'. It is a philosophy which must measure worth by utility since achievement is, according to the Dream, evaluated solely by material criteria. By this utilitarian approach, however, people become as liable to obsolescence as do machines. In Albee's play Daddy has fulfilled his social function in marrying Mommy and supplying her with the money which she had coveted while she in turn has completed her function in submitting to his sexual demands. All this lies in the past, however, and all Daddy can do now is to moan plaintively, 'I just want to get everything over with' (A.D. p. 70)—a complaint which clearly threatens the substance of the Dream itself. When he does make a concession to the Dream it is in the form of lip-service paid to the validity of ambition. 'All his life, Daddy has wanted to be a United States Senator; but now . . . he's changed his mind, and for the rest of his life he's going to want to be Governor . . . it would be nearer the apartment, you know.' (A.D. p. 83.)

In a functional society the characters are identified by their function. For the most part they are ciphers whose very hollowness is a reflection

[1] Edward Albee, *The American Dream* and *The Zoo Story* (New York, 1963), pp. 53-4. References to *The American Dream* are abbreviated to 'A.D.' and corporated into the text.

of the emptiness of the values by which they live. Mommy and Daddy, the endearing terms of family relationships, are identified with casual indifference and expediency on the one hand and emasculated ineffectualness on the other. The only character identified by name is Mrs. Barker and her name is consistently ignored or forgotten. In accepting the standards of society they have lost their individuality and hence their names. Mommy, Daddy, Grandma, the Young Man and Mrs. Barker are the expressionistic realisation of a society in which the humanising aspects of pity, affection and love have given way to a cold, clinical rationalisation which substitutes commercial value for worth and 'cool disinterest' for concern with fellow man.

The traditional foundation and justification of the Dream rests in the home and the family unit. While it is surely between the members of a family that contact can be expected to be initiated Albee shows not only that this initiative is not attempted but that a false scale of values leads to a positive widening of the gap between individuals. Daddy, who is emasculated as a result of an operation, no longer has any physical contact with his wife who has long before shown her disinclination for such contact. The situation is, in fact, reminiscent of that which has pertained in Peter's family life in *The Zoo Story*.

Marriage is seen by Mommy as no more than a social contract in which she has bought wealth and security with sexuality. It is a commercial transaction. 'We were very poor! But then I married you, Daddy, and now we're very rich . . . I have a right to live off you because I married you, and because I used to let you get on top of me and bump your uglies.' (A.D. pp. 66-7.) If the word 'love' occurs in the dialogue it is in such a context as to emphasise the devaluation of its meaning. Mommy states her 'love' for Grandma but is at the same time planning to have her committed to a home. She brings to her family relationships the criteria of the world of commerce. She seeks above all 'satisfaction'. When her adopted child fails to give her this satisfaction she dismembers it and kills all its senses of compassion, love and affection. The true value of this 'satisfaction' becomes apparent, however, when Mommy greets the Young Man, whom Grandma identifies as the personification of the American Dream, with the toast, 'To satisfaction! Who says you can't get satisfaction?' (A.D. p. 126.) For although he has an attractive manner and is 'almost insultingly good-looking in a typically American way' (A.D. p. 107) it is clear that he is as impotent as Daddy. In fact it transpires that he is the brother of the child whom Mommy had mutilated and that he has suffered injuries corresponding to those inflicted by her. These injuries have left him 'incomplete' and deprived of the emotions which prompt and facilitate human contact. 'I cannot touch another person and feel love . . . I no longer have the capacity to feel anything. I have no emotions . . . I let people touch me . . . I let them draw pleasure from my groin . . . from my presence . . . from the fact of me . . . but, that is all it comes to. As I told you, I am incomplete . . . I can feel nothing . . . I am . . . but this . . . what you see' (A.D. p. 115). Thus the faith of this society is placed solely in illusion—in the Dream. The failure to confront reality prevents the establishment of any meaningful relationships. Love becomes impossible and absurdity is accepted as the norm.

The American Dream has been identified by Martin Esslin as an integral part of the theatre of the absurd. While it is true that there are several points of contact between the theatre of the absurd and Albee's work, there does, however, remain one central difference. Esslin derives his definition of the absurd from Camus and Ionesco. Camus says, '. . . in a universe that is suddenly deprived of all illusions and of light, man feels a stranger. His is an irremediable exile, because he is deprived of memories of a lost homeland as much as he lacks the hope of a promised land to come. This divorce between man and his life, the actor and his setting, truly constitutes the feeling of Absurdity'.[1] Absurdity for Camus, therefore, derives directly from the human situation. Albee's expressionistic satire is directed, however, not at the fatuity of life *per se* but rather the nullity to which a false response reduces it. Where Camus suggests that man 'deprived of all illusions . . . feels a stranger' Albee contends, on the contrary, that absurdity lies in a continued adherence to illusion. Ionesco defines the absurd as 'that which is devoid of purpose . . . Cut off from his religious, metaphysical, and transcendental roots, man is lost; all his actions become senseless, absurd, useless'.[2] To Albee a man who is cut off from his religious and transcendental roots still remains a man. Only when he cuts himself off from the reality of his situation does he lose his humanity and become absurd. Albee is not concerned with the absurdity of reality but rather the absurdity of illusion. The target for his satire is the American Dream.

Stylistically *The American Dream* accepts the European contention that absurdity is most logically portrayed by a non-rational form which reflects and extends the theme. The influence of Beckett and Ionesco

[1] *The Theatre of the Absurd*, p. xix.
[2] *Ibid.*, p. xix.

is largely restricted to style, however, for Albee insists on a potential for amelioration which would be denied by the European dramatists. His attack on 'the substitution of artificial for real values in our society' assumes the validity of these 'real values' while in the person of Grandma he demonstrates his belief in the viability of dissent. If the inauthenticity of modern life is a mark of man's desire to choose dehumanisation rather than face the true nature of the human condition he implies that this failure of courage is not inevitable. *The American Dream*, is, however, a slight work which if it successfully adapts Ionesco's style to his own vision (in particular *The Bald Prima Donna* (1950) which similarly ridicules bourgeois society) lacks the sheer intensity and originality of *The Zoo Story*.

Richard Schechner, the editor of the *Tulane Drama Review*, greeted Albee's next play, *Who's Afraid of Virginia Woolf?*, as a 'persistent escape into morbid fantasy'. Like W. D. Maxwell he found it a filthy play and indicted it for its 'morbidity and sexual perversity which are there only to titillate an impotent and homosexual theatre and audience'. More perversely he saw in the play 'an ineluctable urge to escape reality and its concomitant responsibilities by crawling back into the womb, or bathroom, or both'.[1] The vigour of this revulsion was shared, however, by other critics who similarly misapprehended Albee's intention in a play which far from endorsing illusion remorselessly peels off protective fantasies in order to reach 'the bone . . . the marrow'. (v.w. p. 213.) Indeed as Alan Schneider, the play's Broadway director, has pointed out, '. . . is Albee not rather dedicated to smashing that rosy view, shocking us with the truth of our present-day behaviour and thought, striving to purge us into *an actual confrontation with reality?*[2] (my italics).

Who's Afraid of Virginia Woolf? is indeed concerned with the purgation and ultimate destruction of illusion and was in fact at one time to have been called *The Exorcism*. If the play's present title seems at first to be little more than an incomprehensible private joke, however, it is clear that Albee's concern with confrontation does establish something more than a tenuous link between his work and that of Virginia Woolf. For while Mrs Ramsay, in *To The Lighthouse* (1927), had felt

[1] Richard Schechner, 'TDR Comment', *Tulane Drama Review*, VII, iii (Spring, 1963), pp. 8-10.
[2] Alan Schneider, 'Why so Afraid?' *Tulane Drama Review*, VII, iii (Spring, 1963), p. 11.

that 'To pursue truth with . . . lack of consideration for other people's feelings, to rend the thin veils of civilisation so wantonly, so brutally, was to her . . . an outrage of human decency'[1] on a more fundamental level she had acknowledged the inadequacy of such a reaction for with her mind 'she had always seized the fact that there is no reason, order, justice: but suffering, death, the poor. There was no treachery too base for the world to commit; she knew that. No happiness lasted; she knew that'.[2] This was the very perception which had been granted to Miller's Quentin, while, like Miller, Virginia Woolf urges confrontation as a genuine response to this perception. Mr Ramsay accepts that 'life is difficult; facts uncompromising; and the passage to that fabled land where our brightest hopes are extinguished, our frail barks founder in darkness . . . one that needs, above all, courage, truth, and the power to endure'.[3]

On the purely realistic level the play concerns George, a professor of history at a New England College, and his wife Martha. On returning from a party given by Martha's father, the president of the college, they entertain Nick, a new lecturer in the biology department, and his wife Honey. George and Martha uninhibitedly play out a personal ritual of violence and abuse which seems to stimulate them although it embarrasses their guests. As the liquor flows more freely, however, the guests are included in the games which become more brutally crude and hurtful. Martha breaks some personal taboo by mentioning their son and in the second act, spurred on by her husband's apparent indifference, attempts to commit adultery with Nick; an attempt only frustrated by his drink-induced impotence. In the third act George revenges himself by telling Martha that their son, an illusion accepted by them both as a defence against an impotent reality, has died. When Nick recognises the child as being a compensatory illusion he accepts it as a parallel to his own case. He and Honey leave while George and Martha confide to each other their fear of the reality which they must now learn to face.

In retreat from reality Albee's characters resort to Faustian distractions, passing through the varying degrees of sensuality from drunkenness to sexuality in a play whose second act is aptly entitled Walpurgisnacht. The retreat into illusion which seems to provide an alternative to a harsh existence is not, however, an attractive alternative. For Albee

[1] Virginia Woolf, *To The Lighthouse* (London, 1960), p. 54.
[2] *Ibid.*, p. 102.
[3] *Ibid.*, p. 13.

points out that far from facilitating human contact, illusions rather alienate individuals from one another and serve to emphasise their separation. Out of contact with reality they are like the mad—undeveloped. Indeed this immaturity is emphasised by the child-language which recurs throughout the play.

In a story parable which George recounts, a boy accidentally kills his parents. When he loses his mind as a result he is locked up. Finding him unable to face reality 'they jammed a needle in his arm'. (v.w. p. 96.) This is an image of contemporary life as Albee sees it. For if the needle is replaced by liquor the escape of the child becomes valid for the man, '. . . we cry, and we take our tears, and we put 'em in the ice box, in the goddam ice trays until they're all frozen and then . . . we put them . . . in our . . . drinks'. (v.w. p. 186.) Where the young boy retreats into the protection of an asylum man retreats into the closed world of illusion. 'Do you know what it is with insane people?' George asks, 'Do you? . . . the quiet ones? . . . They don't change . . . they don't grow old . . . the under-use of everything leaves them . . . quite whole.' (v.w. p. 97.) So the characters in the play itself seem to have arrested their development. In essence they are children. Honey is referred to in Dr. Seuss terms and curls up on the floor like a young child while George and Martha play sad games like 'Vicious children' with a 'manic' manner.

The play is divided into three acts, 'Fun and Games', 'Walpurgisnacht', and 'The Exorcism'—a progression which, like that of *The Zoo Story*, leads from humiliation to humility. In the first act Albee begins to probe into the pragmatic values which direct the lives of his four characters and initiates the conflict between Martha and George in which they employ as weapons those fantasies which were to have acted as an asylum. George accuses Martha of having 'moved bag and baggage into your own fantasy world'. She has, he claims 'started playing variation' on these 'distortions'. (v.w. p. 155.) Martha, searching for a weapon with which to hurt her husband, breaks their own code and mentions their son. So the substance of their illusion is used to injure rather than to unify and Martha tells Nick and Honey that 'George's biggest problem . . . about our son, about our great big son, is that deep down in the private-most-pit of his gut, he's not completely sure it's his own kid.' (v.w. p. 71.) The act ends therefore, with George's humiliation.

The second act continues the savage games as George mercilessly lays bare the true nature of his guests' relationship, just as Jerry had penetrated Peter's illusions in Albee's earlier play. With the truth revealed Honey rushes from the room to be sick while Nick retreats into the distraction of drink and sexuality which gives the act its name. This is a retreat familiar enough to George whose whole life since coming to New Carthage has consisted in a similar distraction. He confesses that, 'I'm numbed enough . . . and I don't mean by liquor, though maybe that's been part of the process—a gradual, over-the-years going to sleep of the brain cells'. (v.w. p. 155.) The final physical humiliation which Martha inflicts on him at the end of the act, however, spurs him to wake from this coma. He hurls away the book, which is the symbol of his escapism, as it had been in *The Zoo Story*, and determines to force a direct confrontation with reality.

The third act is thus concerned with the ritualistic exorcism of all illusion. While Martha confesses that she has passed her life 'in crummy, totally pointless infidelities' (v.w. p. 189) she pleads with George not to continue 'Truth or illusion, George. Doesn't it matter to you . . . at all?' (v.w. p. 204.) His answer consists in his conscious murder of their fantasy child—a rite watched with growing apprehension by Honey whose own fear of physical reality had resulted in her present sterility, 'NO! . . . I DON'T WANT ANY . . . GO 'WAY . . . I . . . don't . . . want . . . any . . . children. I'm afraid! I don't want to be hurt'. (v.w. p. 176.) George chants the Latin of the burial service as Martha repeats the detailed mythology which they have invented to give substance to their illusion. This act completes the progression from humiliation to humility for all of the characters. Thus the ending, although not definitive, does hold out the hope of 'a real companionship, founded on truth and purged of all falsehood'.

In essence the violent games which George and Martha play are the means whereby they finally attain to this simple acceptance—just as Bellow's protagonists win through to affirmation as a result of humiliation. At first the games clearly act as a substitute for sexual excitement. The mounting fury of their bitterness and invective reaches a shouting crescendo and then relaxes abruptly into tenderness. When George pulls a fake gun on Martha at the climax to one of their fights the symbolism becomes overt and is re-enforced by the conversation between them which follows:

> '*George:* You liked that, did you?
> *Martha:* Yeah . . . that was pretty good. (*Softer*) C'mon . . . give me a kiss.' (v.w. p. 58.)

Martha then tries to put George's hand on her breast but he breaks away
and aborts the action. Nevertheless their continuing violence does serve
to 'get down to the bone . . . the marrow'. If George is not altogether
conscious that their games constitute a gradual disintegration of
illusion, however, his final act of sacrifice is made with a full understanding of its implications. Indeed there is evidence that, aware of the
danger of illusion, he had previously attempted to destroy the fantasy
child:

> '*Martha:* And George tried.
> *George:* How did I try, Martha? How did I try?
> *Martha:* How did you . . . what? . . . No! No . . . he grew . . . our
> son grew . . . up;' (v.w. p. 224.)

While there is no concrete assurance that a confrontation of reality will
permanently restore their fractured relationship the closing tableau is of
Martha leaning back on George's arm as he puts his hand on her
shoulder. The language of this closing section is drastically simplified
and the whole scene provides an audible and visual confirmation of the
simple and uncomplicated state to which their relationship has returned,

> '*Martha:* . . . You had to?
> *George:* Yes.
> *Martha:* I don't know.
> *George:* It was . . . time.
> *Martha:* Was it?
> *George:* Yes. (v.w. p. 240.)

While before they had disavowed their own failure in attacking others
they now admit to their joint responsibility for sterility. Together they
accept their inability to have children, '*We* couldn't'—a confession to
which Albee adds his own comment in a stage direction, '*a hint of
communion in this*'. (v.w. p. 238.) Accepting the Faustian imagery which
Albee introduces their final redemption is in essence that which Faust
had grasped, 'Those who their lives deplore/Truth yet shall heal'.[1]

If George and Martha are capable of creating a complex mythology
rather than face their true situation then so too is the society which
they represent. It is Albee's contention that there is as great a need for
society to abandon its complete faith in these abstractions—the
American Dream, religion and science—as there had been for George
and Martha to abandon theirs.

[1] Johann Wolfgang Goethe, *Faust — Part Two*, trans., Philip Wayne
(Harmondsworth, 1959), p. 277.

To both Miller and Albee abstractions such as the American Dream are less visions of the future than alternatives to the present. Since this serves to take individuals out of their direct relationship with actuality, which is a factor of the present, it serves also to take them out of any genuine relationship with each other. Alienation thus becomes less an aspect of the human situation than a consequence of an inauthentic response to that situation. The watch-word of this 'success-society' thus becomes 'non-involvement'. Honey does not 'want to know anything' (v.w. p. 178) while her husband preserves his 'scientific detachment in the face of . . . life'. (v.w. p. 100.) Attempts at establishing contact are scornfully rejected:

'*George:* (*After a silence*) I've tried to . . . tried to reach you . . . to . . ·
Nick: (*Contemptuously*) . . . make contact?
George: Yes.
Nick: (*Still*) . . . communicate?
George: Yes. Exactly.
Nick: Aw . . . that *is* touching . . . that is . . . downright moving . . . that's what it is. (*With sudden vehemence*) UP YOURS!' (v.w. p. 116.)

In the face of this failure in society both Miller and Albee advance the same solution. As an alternative to euphemism and self-delusion Miller urges the necessity to 'take one's life in one's arms' while Albee insists on the need to face 'Virginia Woolf' however harrowing that prospect may be.

Who's Afraid of Virginia Woolf? and *After the Fall* are in essence both modern secular morality plays. The gospel which they teach, as we have seen, is the primacy of human contact based on an acceptance of reality. If Albee sees this as essentially a Christian objective in *The Zoo Story* and, indeed, *Who's Afraid of Virginia Woolf?*, in which a son is sacrificed for redemption, then Miller recognises it as an empirical truth intuitively felt by Holga and painfully and laboriously learnt by Quentin. The religious overtones which abound in all three plays serve to create a myth for this secular religion which is not so far removed from the liberal humanism of Tillich. Where Gelber's Jaybird had congratulated himself on creating 'no heroes, no martyrs, no Christs'[1] Albee creates all three. For deprived of God man is of necessity his own salvation. Following his 'sanctification' of Jerry, in *The Zoo Story*, it is not too fanciful, I believe, to note the consistency with which

[1] *The Connection*, p. 62.

George, the man who is finally responsible for the destruction of illusion, is associated with Christ. The first line of the play, which heralds George's entrance, is 'Jesus' while the act ends with the same apparent identification. Martha leaves George alone on stage with the same contemptuous expletive, 'Jesus'. This identification is repeated in the third act when Nick throws the door open and 'with great rue' shouts out 'Christ' (v.w. p. 195.) Once again this heralds George's entrance. It is clear, however, that this play lacks the precise parallels which had brought *The Zoo Story* to the verge of allegory.

Reduced to its simplest terms New Carthage is a kind of Vanity Fair in which the Worldly Wise distract the pilgrim from his true path. Modern Christian, however, is not urged to forego the pleasures of the American Dream in order to obtain the fruits of his virtue in a later world but rather to enjoy the real consolation of fellow humanity in the alienated world of the present. Failure to accept the need to confront reality is not only to deprive man of dignity but also to leave him adrift in incomprehension, in flight from the world as it really is. This is the modern hell of Albee's morality plays. The salvation of human contact is aborted by the refusal to abandon illusion. All that remains is a frustrating parody of contact in which love begets revulsion, humour begets anger and the aspirations of the two seeking contact are disastrously out of phase. 'George who is good to me, and whom I revile; who understands me, and whom I push off; who can make me laugh, and I choke it back in my throat . . . who tolerates, which is intolerable; who is kind, which is cruel; who understands, which is beyond comprehension . . .' (v.w. pp. 190-1).

Strindberg's tortured life gave to his concern with the battle of the sexes almost a manic dynamism which has only really been matched by O'Neill, whose own experience drew him to the Scandinavian's work. It would be an error, however, to see Albee as an extension of this revolt against the natural order. For to him human relationships are out of phase not because of the workings of an ineluctable destiny or because of the arbitrariness of sexual attraction (although, in *The Ballad of the Sad Café* (1963) he shows he is not blind to this) but because of the demonstrable failure of the individual to establish a genuine relationship between himself and his situation. To Albee, as to Miller, the failure of the man/woman relationship epitomises a more general failure. For it is in this relationship that fruitful contact should be most easily attained. Where O'Neill had been concerned with establishing a compromise between the individual and his situation, and where

Beckett presents a vision of that individual overwhelmed by his situation, Albee discovers genuine hope. For he sees in confrontation the first step towards a genuine affirmation, which lies not through 'pipe-dreams' or 'flight' but through a positive acceptance of human limitations.

Albee's success on Broadway with *Who's Afraid of Virginia Woolf?* presented many critics with a paradox. For while he had formerly been hailed as the leader of the off-Broadway avant-garde his success on Broadway seemed near to sacrilege. Indeed Diana Trilling saw it as proof of his basic conservatism and triviality, although where this leaves Shakespeare is not clear. Yet Albee's play was in truth something of a landmark in American drama. It is the first full-length play to accept the absurdist vision and yet to formulate a response which transcends at once both despair and casual resolution. To the abstract speculation of Pirandello and Genet—who doubt the very existence of an objective reality—he adds a moral dimension while re-instituting the 'humanist heresies' for which Tynan had called. If he abandons the style of the absurdists as demonstrably unsuited to his theme then he still retains the analogical structure of *The Zoo Story*. For while he clearly has roots in Strindberg it is equally clear that structurally his plays have more in common with Brecht and Beckett and even the later O'Neill. Like *The Good Woman of Sezuan* (first produced 1943) and *Waiting for Godot* his plays are structured on the metaphor. Albert Camus prefaces his novel, *The Plague* (1947), with a quotation from Defoe which is in essence a justification of the analogical form, 'It is as reasonable to represent one kind of imprisonment by another, as it is to represent anything that really exists by that which exists not!'[1] This is a justification which not only Albee but also Durrenmatt and Frisch would endorse, for the extended metaphor is equally the basis for their work. Indeed it is, perhaps, from these writers also that Albee derives his masterful blending of comedy and anguish.

John Gassner has called *Who's Afraid of Virginia Woolf?* 'essentially naturalistic',[2] and certainly the play has a naturalistic 'texture', that is to say we are not in Willy Loman's insubstantial house. The walls are solid; the setting is 'real'. Yet naturalism implies a concern with surface exactitude which has nothing to do with Albee's method. He himself has described the play's setting as 'womb-like' and while avoiding the

[1] Albert Camus, *The Plague*, trans., Stuart Gilbert (Harmondsworth, 1962), p. 3.

[2] *Directions in Modern Theatre and Drama*, p. 358.

simplicities of symbolism (simplicities to which he submits in his next play, *Tiny Alice*) he is not so much concerned with maintaining a precision of appearance as with seizing an essential reality. Like Brown after him he is concerned with presenting an analogue of the human situation. He himself has called his play realistic, defining the term to mean that drama which faces 'man's condition as it is'. In defining realism in these terms he is clearly also defining what he sees as the role of the dramatist in a society in which the audience is 'so preconditioned by pap as to have cut off half of its responses'. In refusing to pander to a supposed need for 'self-congratulation and reassurance'[1] Albee was not only maintaining his artistic integrity but he was demonstrating that in *Who's Afraid of Virginia Woolf?*—originally written for off-Broadway production—he had produced a play which could seemingly resolve the paradox of the avant-garde. For where *The Zoo Story* played to only moderate audiences in *The Provincetown Playhouse*, *Who's Afraid of Virginia Woolf?* proclaimed the same message from the stage of the *Billy Rose Theatre* on Broadway and, but for the squeemishness of W. D. Maxwell would have received the Pulitzer Prize it so obviously deserved.

Albee's subsequent plays have served to extend and re-enforce his insistence on the need to abandon a faith in illusion which ultimately constitutes little more than moral cowardice. *Tiny Alice*, which was received somewhat coldly by the critics, represents Albee's rejection of religion as a substitute for confrontation. Like Nigel Dennis, in *Cards of Identity*, he sees belief in an abstraction as merely an excuse for the surrender of responsibility and identity. Its origin lies not in spiritual conviction but in fear; fear of an empty universe in which man must create his own meaning and his own relationships. Where George and Martha had created an imaginary son in *Who's Afraid of Virginia Woolf?*, the protagonist of *Tiny Alice* creates what Albee would consider an imaginary son of God. Both inventions are an expression of fear of present reality.

Like T. S. Eliot's *The Cocktail Party* the plot of *Tiny Alice* is basically concerned with a conspiracy. A group of three people, a lawyer, a butler and their employer, a rich recluse called Alice, are seemingly dedicated to weaning brother Julian, the play's protagonist, away from the church. Julian, a lay-brother, is sent to Alice by his Cardinal in order to arrange the details of a two-billion dollar grant

[1] 'Which Theatre is the Absurd One?', pp. 334-5.

which she is making to the church; a donation which turns out to be the cost of his freedom. In his first interview with her she appears at first as an old woman only to throw off her disguise after a few minutes to reveal herself as an attractive young woman—a contrast between appearance and reality which is an obvious clue to his central theme in a play which he himself has described as 'a morality play about truth and illusion'.[1]

Gradually Alice wins Julian's affection and devotion but it becomes clear that she is merely a surrogate. In embracing her he comes to embrace the concept which she represents; a concept which Albee mistakenly makes concrete in the form of a model castle which dominates the stage during much of the play. This is even referred to as 'Alice' by the conspirators and is an obvious image of the concrete and diminished world which Julian is made to accept vicariously through his marriage to Miss Alice. Julian had been unable to accept fully the God created by man, 'Soft God? The servant? Gingerbread God with the raisin eyes?'. (T.A. p. 106.) In search of a real vision he becomes the ideal subject for the conspirators secular evangelism. Yet he revolts against the limited, 'tiny', world, bereft of comforting abstractions, with which they confront him. Having lived an empty life in which the denial of intimate human contact has been a sworn article of faith he feels that continued belief in God is the only means to self-justification, 'I have . . . have . . . given up everything to gain everything, for the sake of my faith and my peace.' (T.A. p. 167.) When Alice urges him to 'accept what's real' (T.A. p. 167) he refuses. Left with no other alternative the conspirators shoot Julian and leave him to discover the truth of their precepts as he faces death.

In *The Zoo Story* Albee was prepared to point the way to a secular religion in which man pre-empted the divine function. In *Tiny Alice* he once again creates a saint for his religion; a saint this time whose message cannot be confused with support for christian mythology. Julian dies finally accepting a diminished universe and accepting a martyrdom which has nothing to do with Christ. He rejects the abstract in favour of the concretely human. Dying in a mock crucifixion he finally confesses his faith in Alice, as opposed to some diffuse and distant God. As R. W. B. Lewis says of the novelist Ignazio Silone's faith, he understands now that 'The first sign of manhood is a shedding of abstractions in an effort to press toward 'an intimate opening on to

[1] Thomas B. Markus, 'Tiny Alice and Tragic Catharsis', *Educational Theatre Journal*, XVII, p. 230.

the reality of others'.[1] This is essentially a description of the process which lies at the heart of Albee's own philosophy. Julian, then, comes finally to accept his error; to accept that the six years which he had spent in an asylum because of a loss of faith were in fact six years of sanity, 'I cannot have so misunderstood my life; I cannot have . . . was I sane *then?* Those *years?* My time in the *asylum?* WAS THAT WHEN I WAS RATIONAL? THEN?' (T.A. pp. 168-9.) At the end of the play the church is compromised and Julian is finally reconciled to his humanity and to reality. For to Albee belief in an afterlife devalues the present and thus undermines the necessity for human contact in an empty but real world. If he were to formulate the central article of faith for his secular religion it would surely be close to that of Martin Buber as expressed by the Rev. James Richmond, 'Genuine religion means being converted to this life and this world'.[2]

Here, for virtually the first time, therefore, Albee attempts a clearer exposition of his views on the 'consolation' of religion, linking it, seemingly, with a blind faith in science or the American dream as but another inauthentic response to life. Illusion and reality, he suggests have become confused. As the lawyer says, with what Albee rather preciously describes as 'a small smile', 'It is what we believe, therefore what we know. Is that not right? Faith is knowledge?' (T.A. p. 165.) Clearly a world in which faith and knowledge are accepted as synonymous is inimical to a playwright who insists on the need for a courageous confrontation of reality. As Silone says, 'In no century have words been so perverted from their natural purpose of putting man in touch with man as they are today. To speak and to deceive . . . have become almost synonymous'.[3] It is clear, therefore, why Albee feels that language has to be underpinned by a structure of imagery which facilitates communication on a more fundamental level. It is precisely Albee's failure to master this process in *Tiny Alice*, however, which detracts from the play's effectiveness. He lacks Chekhov's skill at making the symbol an endemic part of the play. Like Tennessee Williams he seems here to have developed a tendency towards strewing his stage with any number of highly significant objects. The result, however, is less to generate genuine dramatic effect than it is to simulate the appearance of a 42nd Street junk store (dried-up fountain

[1] R. W. B. Lewis, *The Picaresque Saint* (London, 1960), p. 151.
[2] Rev. James Richmond, *Martin Buber* (Nottingham, 1966), p. 13. The text of a lecture delivered at Nottingham University on March 17, 1966.
[3] *The Picaresque Saint*, p. 155.

from *Camino Real,* anatomical charts from *Summer and Smoke* and now a phrenological head and model castle from *Tiny Alice*).

Tiny Alice is not an easy play to understand and in many ways Albee has lost his command of the dramatic medium itself. When asked about its complexities, however, he has replied that, 'the play is not supposed to be terribly easily apprehensible. It's meant to contain things that audiences must take out of the theatre with them and think about.' But perhaps there is more than an element of truth in the answer that he offered to a bewildered John Gielgud shortly before the latter was due to play the part of Julian on Broadway, 'I know you want to know what the play is about, John, but I don't know yet, so I can't say.'[1]

Unfortunately Albee's next play, *Malcolm* (1966), evidences the same opacity. Based on Purdy's surrealistic novel the play, in the words of the *New Yorker* review, '. . . limped out of the Shubert last week after lingering for seven performances.' The same review found the play 'filled with stilted dialogue, pseudo-profundity, and wearisome vulgarity'[2] while Robert Brustein, writing in *The New Republic,* identified what he saw as a trend in Albee's work whereby his plays 'get more abstract and incoherent until he is finally reduced, as here, to a nervous plucking at broken strings.'[3] Certainly Albee has chosen to adapt a novel whose complexities are, perhaps, not particularly suited to the dramatic medium. Purdy's picaresque indictment of the contemporary world is phrased in the kind of oblique and stylised terms which do not translate well into a form which is so much more demanding of the audience. Nevertheless if he has not entirely succeeded in finding a viable dramatic equivalent for Purdy's unique vision he has continued his commitment to experimentation while producing a play which expands his personal vision of modern society as sketched in *The American Dream.*

Malcolm is an expression of Albee's sense of alienation from the empty and bizarre world of modern society. It is his vision of a society whose principle gods are money, sex and perjured art and in which everything and everybody is for sale. Malcolm himself is an innocent exposed to and eventually destroyed by the corruption of this society

---

[1] R. S. Stewart, 'John Gielgud and Edward Albee Talk About the Theatre', *Atlantic Monthly,* 215, iv (April, 1965), pp. 67-8.

[2] Anon., 'Innocent Astray', *New Yorker,* January 22, 1966, p. 74.

[3] Robert Brustein, 'Albee's Allegory of Innocence', *The New Republic,* January 29, 1966, p. 36.

to which, 'Innocence has the appearance of stupidity'. (M. p. 9.) This modern *Billy Budd* sees the destruction of innocence, however, not as a natural corollary of a disciplined society but rather as a by-product of a frenzied hedonism. Malcolm dies of sexual hyperaesthesia—that destructive sexuality which Albee had identified as a substitute for genuine fulfilment in *Who's Afraid of Virginia Woolf?*

At the beginning of the play Malcolm, like Peter in *The Zoo Story*, is seated on a bench—a retreat which is an expression both of his innocence and of his failure of nerve. Where Peter had been 'saved' by Jerry, however, Malcolm never really understands the forces which destroy him. His education, like that of Lemuel Pitkin in Nathaniel West's *A Cool Million*, consists of a series of encounters which gradually destroy him. By degrees he begins to accept the logic of this alien world and to become more remote from a simpler existence which remains for him little more than a vague memory of a genuine familial relationship.

At the end of the play, crucified by a world which understands nothing but exploitation, he returns to another existence; the latest in Albee's lengthening line of saints all of whom have given their lives for a world which steadfastly refuses to understand what they are on about. There is, however, a new note in this play. For although the need for love is stressed by its notable absence from this wretched world, Albee provides us with no one within the play who recognises the significance of this. He has moved, it seems, from sounding the warning bell to sounding the knell of a lost world. For after this Second Coming, a miracle recognised by no one, there lies only the apocalypse—a sobering thought for those who watch Malcolm rise on his golden bench and can only remark, 'he didn't have the stuff . . . that's all'. (M. p. 138.)

Having abused the innocent who had come among them they are left with only an image of him—a painting, itself produced for profit, and now an apt substitute for a purity which can only survive in this ersatz and therefore unthreatening form.

With his latest play, *A Delicate Balance* (1966), however, Albee takes a step back from the near-despair of *Malcolm*. Once more he goes about his self-appointed task of dissecting the quiet inhumanity of a fading civilisation. He continues his indictment of a society which has to rely on illusion to survive and which is incapable of realising that the inevitable result of this is a loss of identity and 'the gradual . . . demise of intensity, the private preoccupations, the substitutions'.[1]

[1] Edward Albee, *A Delicate Balance* (New York, 1966), p. 82.

A Delicate Balance is set in the affluent suburban home of Agnes and Tobias whose comfortable complacency is only slightly disturbed by the presence of Claire, an alcoholic relation. The action is concerned with the effect on this elderly couple of a visit by their friends, Harry and Edna, who arrive unexpectedly saying that they have experienced 'the terror'. Whatever the nature of the terror the visit serves to upset the delicate balance of middle-class temporising. The characters are made to confront the gulf which has opened up between reality and illusion in their lives and to define their own stance in relation to it. Ultimately, however, the clearest analysis of what Albee calls 'the regulated great gray life' is made by the alcoholic Claire. She expresses what can surely be taken as Albee's own conviction about the America of which he has been so critical, 'We're not a communal nation . . . giving but not sharing, outgoing but not friendly . . . We submerge our truths and have our sun-sets on untroubled waters . . . We live with our truths on the grassy bottom, and we examined all . . . the implications like we had a life for nothing else . . . We better develop gills.'[1] As we have seen Albee has already expressed his sense of the urgency of this metamorphosis in *Malcolm. A Delicate Balance* is merely his latest essay on the need for confrontation.

The relative success of this play on Broadway may be due in part, however, to the fact that the terms in which Albee is here continuing his analysis are more readily available to an audience which found the stylised allegory of *Tiny Alice* and the surrealistic insights of *Malcolm* difficult to grasp. It is certainly not a sign that Albee has finally capitulated to the pressures for re-assurance which he has always castigated in the American theatre. Indeed it is clear that without the radical approach of an Albee the American theatre would be in danger of stagnating once again. For if he is capable of grotesque misjudgement, as in *Tiny Alice* and *Malcolm*, then he is also capable of the achievement of *The Zoo Story* and *Who's Afraid of Virginia Woolf?*, while his commitment to continued experimentation makes him the chief hope for a developing drama.

[1] *Ibid.*, p. 93.

5

The New Surrealism

In 1959 Allan Kaprow coined the word 'happening' to describe a form of 'theatrical' experimentation which had much in common with the vivid surrealistic sketches of the nineteen-twenties and thirties. In the same year James Purdy published *Malcolm* (on which Albee was to base his play) and William Burroughs published *The Naked Lunch*—both novels surrealistic in style. This revival of surrealism in America which may have owed something to Henry Miller's fascination with the French surrealists,[1] has been eagerly accepted by an American theatre anxious now to extend its frontiers and suddenly conscious of the iconoclastic theories of Artaud (*The Theatre and its Double* was published in America in 1958) and Cocteau.

Surrealism has its roots in Freud's theory of the unconscious, particularly as expressed in *The Interpretation of Dreams* (1900). The original surrealists conceived of the unconscious as the source of truth and acknowledged the superior reality of the dream. The 'new surrealism' evidenced in contemporary American literature, however, places less emphasis on the autonomy of the unconscious than on a faith in the need to accept the irrational and the fantastic as valid means of revelation. Two of Albee's most recent plays have tended towards this oblique approach although they, like Saul Bellow's *The Last Analysis*, have retained a more stable internal logic than had Cocteau's or Cummings' dramas. For all the extension of theatrical experimentation evidenced both by Bellow and by the creators of 'happenings', however, confrontation remains both the purpose and indeed the justification for the contemporary dramatist. With André Breton they would agree that 'What is admirable in the fantastic is that it becomes real.'[2]

Saul Bellow's proximity to the concerns of contemporary American drama has been noted throughout and perhaps it was inevitable that he would eventually turn his talents to a stage with which he was clearly

---

[1] Henry Miller has in fact written a surrealistic play, *Just Wild about Harry: a melo-melo in seven scenes* (London, 1964).
[2] *Directions in Modern Theatre and Drama*, p. 111.

in sympathy. *The Last Analysis* was begun in 1959 and produced in 1964 at the *Belasco Theatre*. It was withdrawn after a short run and extensively revised before publication. Although a poor play it bears examination in the context of a self-conscious theatre anxious to break away from Broadway naturalism while retaining a sense of moral purpose.

The Last Analysis is ostensibly a satire on the American obsession with psycho-analysis but its real concern is with the need for confrontation. Philip Bummidge, a comedian whose popularity has waned, finds himself afflicted with Humanitis—a disease which impends 'when the human condition is suddenly too much for you'.[1] Convinced of the power of Freudian analysis he delves into his own past, co-opting everyone who passes to help him towards his eventual objective—spiritual re-birth. With the aid of these assistants, who include an ex-Bunny from the Playboy Club, an ex-rat catcher and a technician, he devises a closed-circuit television demonstration for the benefit of a distinguished gathering of psychiatrists. His do-it-yourself analysis, which leads him, like Albee's protagonists, to a mock crucifixion, is ecstatically received not only by the psychiatrists but also by the television impressario whom his shiftless relatives have persuaded to watch the performance. Tearing up cheques for a million dollars, however, Bummidge presses ahead with his plans for founding a theatre of the soul in which individuals are to be taught to face the reality of their lives.

While Bellow clearly satirises what he calls 'the peculiarly literal and solemn manner in which Americans dedicate themselves to programs, fancies, or brainstorms'[2] it is equally clear that beneath the grotesque absurdity of his protagonist's scheme there is a solid residuum of genuine perception. The choice which Bellow sees as confronting the individual, in *The Last Analysis*, is equally that which Albee had identified in all his plays; the choice between distraction and confrontation. As Bummidge laments, 'I wanted to lead you out of the realms of projections into the light of sanity. But you prefer the institutionalised psychosis of business'. (L.A. p. 36.) In the face of the cynicism and desperate inhumanity of those who surround him he presses on with his exotic plans, convinced, like Quentin and George before him, that

---

[1] Saul Bellow, *The Last Analysis* (New York, 1965), p. 41. All further references to this play are abbreviated to 'L.A.' and incorporated into the text.

[2] *Ibid.*, 'Author's note', p. vii.

though 'conditions may be impossible . . . there is nothing else for me to do but face those real conditions'. (L.A. p. 74.)

The comic fantasy of his analysis is in essence a justification of Bellow's surrealistic style. As Bummidge's wife and cousin agree, 'Everybody waiting, waiting, waiting for emotional truth . . . And can recognise it only in absurd form'. (L.A. pp. 105-6.) This is not, however, an acceptance of the absurdist's nihilism for as Bellow has said, 'it's about time everyone recognised that romantic despair . . . is absurdly portentous, not metaphysically "absurd".'[1] It is rather an acceptance of the surrealist's faith in the efficacy of fantasy and conscious theatricalism. Indeed the Bummidge Institute of Nonsense, which its founder wishes to establish on the site of a theatre turned butcher's shop, is an expression of this faith in the purgative power of drama. In fact Bummidge's description of his analytical method is equally a description of Bellow's and Albee's dramatic method, 'I formed my own method. I learned to obtain self-knowledge by . . . dragging repressed material into the open by sheer force of drama.' (L.A. p. 74.)

The disease of humanitis, which corresponds with O'Neill's 'pipe-dreams' and Beckett's nihilism as what Bellow calls 'An emotional disorder of our relation to the human condition' (L.A. p. 77), is caused, according to Bummidge, by the 'Pagliacci gangrene'. This, in essence, is that self-isolation which Albee had attacked in The Zoo Story. 'Cut off by self-pity. Passivity. Fear. Masochistic rage' (L.A. p. 78) man retreats into 'Delusion. Intoxication. Ecstacy. And Comedy.' (L.A. p. 71.) Here we can see Bellow's reason for making his protagonist a comedian for an essential element in Bummidge's 're-birth' is his ritualistic re-discovery of genuine comedy. He suggests that we are living in an era of 'sick' humour. Comedy has become devalued—an apologia for the unthinkable. As he says, 'When lampshades are made of human skin, we see that fun is very big in hell . . . Farce follows horror into darkness'. (L.A. p. 96.) To Bummidge the true subject for comedy becomes 'we fumblers and bumblers, we cranks and creeps and cripples . . . sick with every personal vice, rattled, proud, spoiled, and distracted' (L.A. p. 97). Thus comedy becomes, what it is for Albee, no longer a respite from reality but a weapon to cut through cowardly distraction. This, in fact, is how it functions in The Last

[1] Saul Bellow, 'The Writer as Moralist', Atlantic Monthly (March, 1963), p. 61.

Analysis. The mad lucidity of Philip Bummidge desperately in search of personal transcendence remains extremely funny. For although endorsing the substance of his revelation Bellow avoids the sombre pretension of *Tiny Alice* by retaining a sense of perspective and irony. Bummidge's preposterous flight of fancy, which leads him to enact a mock crucifixion, stapled to a wall, is finally deflated when he forgets his words, 'Forgive them, Father, for, for . . . What comes next?' (L.A. p. 64). While the autodidact may have perceived the necessary relationship between the individual and his situation Bellow sees no necessity for sanctifying him. Neither does he endorse, as does Miller, the solemn portentousness of a self-analysis which finally smacks of egotism, for the play ends as Bummidge dons a toga and announces that 'I am ready for the sublime'. (L.A. p. 118.)

Bummidge stands out from those around him not only by virtue of his monomaniacal concern with his gospel of redemption, however, but also by virtue of his moral sensitivity. The other characters in the play are all intent on capitalising on human relationships. All subscribe to the values of success society and fail to understand the implications of the old comedian's quest. His cousin and sister, respectively his lawyer and agent, see in Bummidge's obsession a potentially marketable commodity, as do his son and mistress. Indeed the play might justifiably have been called *Life Among the Machiavellians*—a title which Bellow had once considered for *The Adventures of Augie March* (1953). For to Madge and Winkleman, who own a decaying old people's home threatened with closure because of cases of malnutrition, people can be categorised, as Bellow had noted earlier, according to 'whether they screwed or were screwed'.[1] Thus Bummidge's earnest commitment is contrasted with society's urgent pursuit of money—a pursuit which Bellow has compared with the quest for genuine fulfilment. In fact Tommy Wilhelm, an earlier Bellow protagonist, can be seen as a prototype for Bummidge. Like the old comedian he too turns to pseudo-analysis as an escape from a world dominated by materialism, 'money! Holy money! Beautiful money! . . . that's what it was. The world's business. If only he could find a way out of it'.[2] The way out for Wilhelm, as earlier for Augie March, lies through a positive acceptance of his life which is not merely stoicism but rather a full realisation that 'It is better to die what you are than to live a stranger forever'.[3]

[1] Saul Bellow, *The Adventures of Augie March* (London, 1954), p. 73.
[2] Saul Bellow, *Seize the Day* (New York, 1956), p. 36.
[3] Op. cit., p. 485.

Bummidge, too, achieves the same positive affirmation of reality, transcending the destructive and irrelevant materialism which is represented, in particular, by Fiddleman, the impressario who offers to buy him for a million dollars. Contrasted with the apparent sanity of his voracious relatives Bummidge's insanity becomes progressively more attractive, while his plan for the redemption of 'the poor, the sad, the bored and tedius of the earth' (L.A. p. 118) becomes all the more credible for his own rejection of the pursuit of success. Thus the danger identified by Bellow, as by Albee, is the threat implied by this increasing materialism. For, as Bellow himself warned in an article written in 1959, as 'technology extends the promise of an increase of wealth we had better be aware of a poverty of the soul as terrible as that of the body'. For an improvement in material conditions brought about 'merely by the increase of goods and comforts deprives' man 'of the sense of reality'.[1] While Bummidge achieves a reconciliation with life itself, therefore, he greets society with the thunderous 'no!' which Fiedler has urged as the necessary response of the true artist.

Like most of Bellow's protagonists, then, Bummidge has to release himself from the influence of those who would impose on him and whose values threaten his own selfhood. Augie March, Asa Leventhal and Moses Herzog all suffer from this same manipulation which, together with the total impact of mass activity, threatens to stamp out their individuality. But Bellow has insisted that 'We are called upon to preserve our humanity in circumstances of rapid change and movement' and this is the purpose of the unsparing self-examination which each of his protagonists face. For as Bellow says, 'I do not see what else we can do than refuse to be condemned with a time or a place. We are not born to be condemned but to live.'[2] Tony Tanner, in his monograph on Bellow, sees this affirmation of the human spirit in contrast to a misdirected society as distinctly Russian for 'The European novel rarely envisages so naked a confrontation.'[3] It is clear, however, that this confrontation is equally accepted as crucial by the contemporary American dramatist, as indeed it is by Bellow the novelist. Indeed it becomes not only the fundamental need of man in general but also the chief function of the artist. So that when Bellow comments

[1] Tony Tanner, *Saul Bellow* (London, 1965), p. 3.
[2] Saul Bellow, 'How I Wrote Augie March's Story', *The New York Times Book Review*, Jan. 31, 1954, p. 3.
[3] *Saul Bellow*, p. 5.

on Tolstoy that he 'says of human nature that it contains a need for truth which will never allow it to rest permanently in falsehood or unreality'[1] he is equally describing the faith of an American drama which has succeeded in transcending the fatuities of Broadway. Like Albee and Miller, Bellow avoids both empty optimism and nihilism alike. His protagonists, however, all of whom lack grandeur and mastery, intuitively sense the need to establish a genuine relationship between themselves and their situation, and the need to affirm the fact that 'the spirit of man must preserve itself'. (L.A. p. 96.) Since this redemptive affirmation invariably follows a period of desperation, and, in the case of Tommy Wilhelm and Philip Bummidge, material failure, it is clear that the one pre-requisite is a divestment of wealth. So that as he had earlier suggested that wealth deprives one of a sense of reality he now insists that Henderson should abandon his possessions, Wilhelm his last seven hundred dollars and Bummidge all his money before they can achieve this final redemption. To Bellow too, it seems, the rich man is to be excluded from the ranks of the faithful.

Talking to Harvey Breit about *The Adventures of Augie March*, in 1953, Bellow suggested that a concern with form suggests a disregard of genuine reality. So, he added, 'I kicked over the traces, wrote catch-as-catch-can, picaresque. I took my chance.'[2] *The Last Analysis* is his attempt to apply the same logic to drama. Indeed in an article in *Atlantic Monthly*, in 1963, he defended the surrealistic method as a device to force a genuine receptiveness on his audience. 'Clarification, deepening, illumination are moral aims even when the means seem to readers anarchic . . . The "wild" writings of dadaists and surrealists were intended to shock the reader into a new, more vivid wakefulness.'[3] Thus the wild fantasies of *The Last Analysis* are, to Bellow, an essential element in his concern with confrontation. For through the grotesque fantasies inspired by Philip Bummidge the necessity for a genuine confrontation of reality is brought home to an audience theoretically shaken, as Jarry's had been, into a state of sensitive receptivity. The play, like *The Brig*, is a deliberate attempt to shock the audience into actual confrontation. Unfortunately the precise nature of Bellow's 'illumination' tends to be lost in the sheer flamboyance of the

---

[1] *Ibid.*, pp. 5-6.
[2] Harvey Breit, 'Talk with Saul Bellow', *New York Times Book Review*, Sept. 20, 1953, p. 22.
[3] 'The Writer as Moralist', p. 60.

production while the mad rhetoric and comic fantasy threaten the 'clarification' which he declared as his aim. The advice, given on the inside cover of the published play, that *The Last Analysis* 'is very much a play for reading—and rereading' is finally a covert admission of its failure to operate effectively on the stage. Like Albee's *Tiny Alice* this play is demanding more of an audience than can be justified, while the sheer dimension of Bellow's imagination is not itself sufficient justification for a flamboyance which is not always the conscious instrument of ordered purpose.

Peter Brook, writing of *The Connection* in November 1960, saw its value as lying primarily in its adventurous assumption 'that man is passionately interested in man'. The stage, he continued, 'is paying us the supreme compliment of treating us all as artists, as independent creative witnesses. And the evening is as interesting as we choose to make it. It is as though we were really taken into a room of far-gone drug addicts: we could be Rimbaud and spin our fantasies from their attitudes.'[1] While it is true that the value of Gelber and Brown's work lies in its power to force an audience to a re-examination of motives and attitudes there is a danger implicit in Brook's approach—a danger no less fundamental than the destruction of art itself. For when he asserts that in twenty years *The Connection* will seem plot-ridden and contrived he is no doubt correct but when he advances as his ideal the possibility that 'we may be capable of watching a normal man in a normal state with equal interest'[2] he is saying no less than that he anticipates either the total extinction of art or the widening of its definition to that point at which it ceases to have meaning. Perhaps it would not be too mischievous to point out that this statement does not seem so far removed from that of the Marxist bureaucrat, Oelssner, who, in criticising a Brecht production, had called for 'typical figures shown in typical surroundings'.[3] The aspect of *The Connection* which seizes Brook's attention is, then, its ability to stimulate awareness and force its audience to a confrontation of the mere fact of behaviour outside of any moral context. Indeed he looks forward to a theatre which would be the counterpart of the novels of Alain Robbe-Grillet (to

[1] Peter Brook, 'From Zero to the Infinite', *The Encore Reader*, ed. Horowitz, Milne and Hale (London, 1965), p. 249.

[2] *Ibid.*, p. 249.

[3] Quoted in Martin Esslin, *Brecht, a Choice of Evils* (London, 1959), p. 154.

whom the surface is the only reality and to whom other novelists are 'speliologists')—'a theatre . . . in which *pure behaviour* can exist in its own right'.[1] In essence, however, such a 'theatre' already existed potentially in the work of John Cage, Allan Kaprow, Claes Oldenburg and, in another category, Andy Warhol. It existed, that is, in the experimental form of 'happenings' and 'camp art'.

The concentration on sensual experience which we find in the Zen-derived Beat School of the early and mid-fifties, their dissociation from a world seemingly obsessed with morality and objective success, is in part reflected in that series of experimental performances, given primarily by artists, sculptors and musicians, which, following Allan Kaprow's lead, have come to be known as 'happenings'. On 4th October 1959, in the same year, that is, that saw the first production of *The Connection* and *The Zoo Story*, Kaprow staged an event entitled *18 Happenings in 6 parts*. Although not the first of such events it was from this performance that the form derives its name. Kaprow himself is a painter and has traced out the evolution of the happening in terms of his own work. He describes how he developed from abstracts to action-collages to environments—this last being a form in which the entire gallery is filled from wall to wall with his action-collages which themselves consisted of 'great hunks of varied matter . . . flashing lights . . . ringing buzzers'.[2] The happening thus emerged as a natural extension of this in that the audience became a part of the total experience while inanimate material came to be replaced by human 'actors'.

The immediate origin of the happening, however, lay in all probability with the work of John Cage, with whom Kaprow had himself studied from 1956 to 1958. Cage is a musician who has for many years been concerned with investigating the possibilities of sound itself and that pattern which could at times be distinguished in chance which he, as a student of Zen, would know as *li*. Indeed some of the experiments which he has carried out seem to have been designed as a means to stimulate the sort of awareness and perception of reality which is associated with Zen. Here we can see that the happening is in essence another aspect of that concern with the need to confront reality which we have observed as the main concern of the contemporary American

[1] *The Encore Reader*, p. 250.

[2] Michael Kirby, *Happenings* (London, 1965), p. 45. I am heavily indebted to Mr Kirby's book which together with the special edition of the *Tulane Drama Review* (Winter, 1965) remains the most comprehensive and reliable account of these events.

dramatist. For if Albee, Miller and Bellow are concerned with urging this confrontation as fundamental to personal transcendence and meaningful existence, the creators of happenings are concerned with forcing an acute awareness of the substance of that reality. In the words of Ken Dewey, who founded the *Action Theatre Inc.* in 1965, happenings are concerned with 'provoking an explosive degree of consciousness'.[1] This consciousness is quite literally forced on the audience so that the 'visceral' contact of *The Brig* gives way at times to a physical assault. In one experiment Cage wired a chair for sound and then amplified the result so that the audience was literally shaken by the noise while on another occasion he subjected his audience to random sounds issuing from eight tape-recorders. The performance which approximates most closely to a happening was, however, that given by him in the summer of 1952 at Black Mountain College. At this the audience was seated in the middle of the hall while activities were simultaneously conducted at various points around them. Cage himself conducted a lecture against the background of piano music, sound from a gramophone and the visual distraction of a projected film, modern dance and the spontaneous antics of a dog.

The sort of experiments conducted by Cage and later by Kaprow, Oldenburg and the others hardly constitute an entirely new phenomenon, however, for if they represent a natural extension of their own work they also clearly have their roots in dadaism, that movement which flourished briefly in the period from 1916 to 1924. Socially it arose out of a protest against the meaningless destruction of war. Theatrically it served as an aspect of that revolt against naturalism which Strindberg's expressionistic plays had sparked at the turn of the century. Here too was that temporary merging of the arts which is a mark of the happening. Jill Johnson quotes George Hugnet's description of a dada performance: 'On the stage of the cabaret tin cans and keys were jangled as music . . . Serner placed a bunch of flowers at the feet of a dressmaker's dummy. Arp's poems were recited by a voice hidden in an enormous hat shaped like a sugar-loaf. Huelsenbeck roared his poems in a mighty crescendo, while Tzara beat time on a large packing case . . . or, in an exercise called "noir cacadou", they waddled about in a sack with their heads thrust in a pipe.'[2] Dada was introduced into America by Marcel Duchamp and Arthur Cravan—a

[1] Ken Dewey, 'X-ings', *Tulane Drama Review*, X, ii (Winter, 1965), p. 216.
[2] Jill Johnston, ' "Happenings" on the New York Scene', *The Encore Reader*, p. 262.

nephew of Oscar Wilde. In an exhibition of the *Grand Central Gallery* in 1917 Duchamp contributed 'La Fontaine'—a urinal which caused almost as much commotion as did the obscene speech delivered by Cravan. This exhibit was significantly revived in part at the *Museum of Modern Art* in 1961 when happenings were fully in vogue.

18 Happenings in 6 parts, which took place at the *Reuben Gallery* in 1959, defies short summary. The gallery itself had been divided into three 'rooms' by means of semi-transparent plastic sheeting. When the audience arrived its members were distributed throughout these rooms with instructions to move at certain prescribed times. The performance itself consisted of an elaborately contrived synthesis of the human and the mechanical; the visual and the audible. Movements were precisely directed by Kaprow who had previously given detailed instruction cards to his 'actors'. Impossible to summarise, the action can best be conveyed by a brief description of part of it. 'In the first room, one of the men stood with his hands on his hips for sixteen seconds then leant forward with his elbows extended like wings for five seconds. Perhaps one of the girls in the next room was standing erect for ten seconds with her left arm raised, the forearm pointing toward the floor, while another was touching her left hand to her right forearm, stepping three or four paces along one of the axes of the room, and then raising one hand to her forehead for four seconds. The electronic sounds were still heard from the four speakers. In the semi-darkness of the third room slides were being shown.' (H. p. 72.)

Kaprow's happenings differ from dada experiments in their painstaking precision as well as their compartmented form. Although the audience was subjected to a number of simultaneous stimuli these had each been meticulously planned beforehand. The effect, therefore, was in part that of a ritual but a ritual in which no logic was apparent. Kaprow has said that his works are conceived on four levels. The first, which clearly derives, through Cage, from Zen, is a concern with what he calls the direct 'suchness' of every action, 'with no more meaning than the sheer immediacy of what is going on'. (H. p. 49.) This is, in essence, the experiential theatre for which Peter Brook had apparently been calling. For in urging the contemplation of a particular sight or sound for its own sake Kaprow could be said to be breaking down that stereotyped response which leads the observer to look for symbolism or logical relationship. Nevertheless it must be doubted if this sort of trust in the intrinsic value of naked behaviour can be said to constitute art for it would seem to justify the elimination of the artist's mediation.

Alan Watts, in his book *Beat Zen Square Zen and Zen* (1959) in fact, takes issue with this rather simplistic assumption, 'Some artists may argue that they do not want their works to be distinguishable from the total universe, but if this be so they should not frame them in galleries and concert halls. Above all they should not sign them or sell them. This is as immoral as selling the moon or signing one's name to a mountain.'[1] When Brown asserts, with *The Brig*, that drama can be an analogue of life he is not agreeing with Cage that any trivial action is of itself theatre for, as Ionesco has said, the essence of drama is 'an action of universal significance'.[2] So to Brown the necessary obedience of the prisoners of the brig is more than the expedient of frightened men; it is a declaration of an aspect of the human condition. So that while in one sense the line between art and life does dissolve, the life to which Cage and Kaprow point remains a clearly perceived fragment while true art resides in totality.

While it remains only one element in the structure of Kaprow's happenings this belief in the validity of pure behaviour is seen in its most extreme form in the work of Andy Warhol, whose six-hour film of a man sleeping must represent the ultimate in a belief in the inherent value of Peter Brook's 'normal man in a normal state'. Indeed the attraction of what has come to be known as 'camp art' lies not in the intrinsic interest which a particular activity or scene holds but rather in its total dissimilarity to that which is normally accepted as being of value. Yet to say that camp is destructive of art makes no more sense than to say that dada was similarly destructive. For the dadaists were actively engaged in the revolt not only against naturalism but against the mentality which it represented. Picasso, Kandinski, Apollinaire and Modigliani were all committed to extending art beyond mere imitation. Camp is a revolt against mass taste. As the public progresses from Humphrey Bogart to Fellini so the dictum of camp insists that its adherents move the other way. It is a philosophy of perversity which by the mere fact of its expression succeeds in making its point but which in persisting becomes as drearily predictable as the process against which it is in revolt. Its weakness, like that of dada, lies in its inability to progress beyond the mere fact of revolt for as Camus has said, 'no form of art can survive on total denial alone'.[3]

[1] Alan Watts, *Beat Zen Square Zen and Zen* (San Francisco, 1959), p. 11.
[2] *Notes and Counter Notes*, p. 225.
[3] Albert Camus, *The Rebel*, trans., Anthony Bowers (London, 1963), p. 227.

The second level on which Kaprow conceives his work as operating is that of fantasy. This is true also of Robert Whitman for whom 'fantasy is an object in the physical world' (H. p. 136) and Claes Oldenburg who 'considers the imaginary event as real as the "real" one'. (H. p. 202.) André Breton, in his first Manifesto of Surrealism in 1924, wrote 'Surrealism rests on the belief in the superior reality of certain forms of association neglected hitherto; in the omnipotence of the dream, and in the disinterested play of thought.'[1] This is essentially the philosophy behind happenings for Kaprow's intention is less to present a picture of life as it is than to suggest it as it might be vaguely perceived in dreams and fantasies. In Stanislavsky's words the time has come to stage the unreal.

Historically surrealism has emerged as a reaction against the meaninglessness of dada. It propounded the supremacy of the unconscious and claimed the superior reality of the dream. The means of attaining that reality lay through 'psychic automatism', that is a form of perception outside of moral, rational and aesthetic control. Where happenings differ from *The Last Analysis* and even Jean Cocteau's *Orpheus* (1926) and E. E. Cummings' *him* (1927) is in the fact that for all their wildness these plays do retain something of a recognisable structure. So that although Kaprow claims as his third level that his happenings are an organised structure of events, that structure is for the most part largely a spatial one. Sounds and actions are connected by the environment in which they function, by tenuous association, or by the largely unconscious control which is an aspect of a single creative impulse. Such verbal matter as there is in Kaprow's first work is largely the result of a random selection of which Breton would no doubt have approved for he himself had proposed the composition of poetry out of the jumbled words of newspaper cuttings.

While happenings differ in many respects from each other they are all united by a common concentration on movement and on spectacle which allies them more clearly with the circus and vaudeville than with a cerebral theatre. Indeed Red Grooms, the author of *The Burning Building* (1959), has said that 'When I was a kid, the big influence on me was Ringling Brothers, Barnum and Bailey, and the Cavalcade of Amusement which would roll in every year for the Tennessee State Fair. After that I put on my own shoes [sic] in the back yard. *The Burning Building* . . . was an extension of my backyard theatre. I wanted to have some of the dusty danger of a big travelling show.' (H. p. 118.)

[1] *Directions in Modern Theatre and Drama*, pp. 370-1.

The Burning Building itself has more sense of continuity than Kaprow's early work. It is concerned with the antics of a 'pasty man'—the familiar white-faced clown of the circus—and a number of men dressed as firemen who alternately dance, eat a paper turkey and engage in the sort of chase familiar from Tennessee Williams' *Camino Real*. The same fascination with the excitement and vitality of the circus is detectable in Robert Whitman's use of a trapeze in *The American Moon* (1960) and of clown figures in *Water* (1963). Kaprow himself demonstrates a similar interest in technical and physical virtuosity in *The Courtyard* (1962) in which a girl stands on the top of a thirty foot tar-paper 'mountain' while another one is lowered from the height of a ten storey building. E. E. Cummings too had been fascinated by the circus and his description could be aptly applied to happenings. 'Movement is the very stuff out of which this dream is made. Or we may say that movement is the content, the subject-matter of the circus-show'.[1] 'Two facts are gradually becoming recognised', he continues, 'first, that the circus is an authentic "theatric" phenomenon, and second, that the conventional "theatre" is a box of negligible tricks'.[2] So too the happening insists on the necessity for vital and dynamic action so that movement does indeed become content rather than an aspect of style. As Claes Oldenburg has said, 'The "happening" is one or another method of using *objects in motion*, and this I take to include people, both in themselves and as agents of object motion.' (H. p. 200.) In reacting against the theatre as 'a box of negligible tricks' the creator of the happening is trying to rediscover the fundamentals of theatre itself—to examine the nature of movement and of form just as painters had attempted to rediscover the nature of colour and form. Indeed as Ionesco has pointed out, 'the development of painting, for example, has never been anything but a rediscovery of painting, its idiom and its essence. The direction taken by modern painting shows us this clearly. Since Klee, Kandinski, Mondrian, Braque and Picasso, painting has done nothing but shake off all that is not painting . . . Painters are trying to rediscover the basic fundamentals of painting, pure form, colour for its own sake.' To this he adds the comment, 'Nor is it in this case a question of aestheticism or what is nowadays rather improperly called formalism, but of the expression of reality in pictorial forms'.[3] Oldenburg, Dine and Kaprow

---

[1] Norman Friedman, *e. e. cummings* (Carbondale, 1964), p. 53.

[2] George F. Firmage, ed., *E. E. Cummings: A Miscellany* (London, 1966), p. 151.

[3] *Notes and Counter Notes*, p. 32.

clearly share the same purpose. It is equally clear, however, that the line between valid experiment and aestheticism is a difficult one to draw and that the happening, with its emphasis on detail, is in constant danger of blundering into mere introversion. When Oldenburg says that his aim 'is the perfection of the details of the events rather than any composition' (H. p. 202) one is indeed reminded of Kafka's story 'The Fist' in which the building of the Tower of Babel is brought to a halt because its purpose is forgotten in an obsessive concern with logistics.

In spite of this emphasis on the surface quality of action both Kaprow and Dine have suggested that their work has symbolic overtones. Because of the non-cerebral and largely alogical nature of a happening, however, this 'meaning' is conveyed largely by a calculated prompting of intuitive response. Perhaps the best way to illustrate this aspect of the happening is to describe Dine's *The Smiling Workman*, a thirty-second image of the individual totally absorbed in his work. Although Dine's work is less interesting for the most part than that of his contemporaries this particular 'event' (one part of a happening) demonstrates something of that vitality which is an aspect of the surrealistic method. Dine explains, 'I had a flat built. It was a three panel flat with two sides and one flat. There was a table with three jars of paint and two brushes on it, and the canvas was painted white. I came around it with one light on me. I was all in red with a big, black mouth: all my face and head were red, and I had a red smock on, down to the floor. I painted "I love what I'm doing" in orange and blue. When I got to "what I'm doing", it was going very fast, and I picked up one of the jars and drank the paint, and then I poured the other two jars of paint over my head, quickly, and dove, physically, through the canvas. The light went off.' (H. p. 185.) Ironically, as is evident from this example, the very strength of the happening, its vitality and exuberance, is often also the source of its failure. For freedom easily degenerates into unmediated licence and conscious control is all too easily sacrificed to arbitrary exhibitionism.

If the happening is dedicated to destroying the distinction between the theatre and life itself it must also clearly attempt to redefine the artist/audience relationship. This in fact it does and the distinction between audience and 'actors' is deliberately broken down. Once again Cummings had identified this as an aspect of the circus, or rather that form of circus/theatre which he saw as Coney Island, 'the essence of Coney Island's "circus-theatre" ' he had said, 'consists in *homogeneity*.

THE AUDIENCE IS THE PERFORMANCE and vice versa'.[1] So Claes Oldenburg, writing in 1965, says, 'The audience is considered an object and its behaviour as events, along with the rest. The audience is taken to differ from the players in that its possibilities are not explored as far as the players'. (H. p. 202). It is for this reason that the audience is directed, as in Kaprow's *18 Happenings in 6 parts*, to precisely designated places. Nevertheless this attempt to try to establish a real involvement on the part of the audience is for the most part a parody of genuine contact. Indeed it seems at times to be little more than the petulant complaint of artists who aspire to the seemingly more immediate rapport which they see as a mark of the theatre. The assault on the audience which they initiate, unlike Brown's subtle yet aggressive immediacy, is achieved all too often through a reliance on a crude physicality. With Cage, as we have seen, it often takes the form of disconcertingly high-pitched sounds while in Oldenburg's *World's Fair II* (1962) the standing audience was pushed back against a hardboard panel so that one spectator actually felt constrained to fight back with a knife. When in Kaprow's *A Spring Happening* (1960) the audience is pursued down a narrow passage by a power-mower then valid theory has indeed degenerated into parody. For the audience is no longer a means of discovering the possibilities of objects, as Robert Whitman had suggested it might be, but has become the butt for a truculent art which values expression above communication. Certainly it would be a misunderstanding of Artaud's theories to suggest, as Kirby does, that they form the basis of what is more correctly seen as an abuse of theatricalism than a valid extension of it. For Artaud called for an attack on the sensibility and not the physical person of the audience while his aim was always the expression of his sense of the nature of physical experience within a painful and deterministic world.

In an article in the *Tulane Drama Review* Kirby tells us that 'works have recently been conceived which, since they are to be performed without an audience—a totally original and unprecedented development in art—might be called Activities'.[2] Although it is perhaps worth noting that this form is not in fact unique—Brecht had designed plays for use without an audience—it is clearly a logical development of a form which absorbs everything into itself. It is clear, however, that with

[1] *E. E. Cummings: A Miscellany*, p. 151.

[2] Michael Kirby, 'The New Theatre', *Tulane Drama Review*, X, ii (Winter, 1965), p. 40.

this development we have moved finally from the realm of art into that of therapy.

The lasting value of surrealism lay not in the significance of plays like Picasso's *Desire Caught by the Tail*, which consists of a nonsense dialogue between a number of feet, but rather in the influence which it exerted on the drama which followed it, on the music-hall satire of Brecht and ultimately on the simplified drama of the theatre of the absurd. The happening may serve a similar purpose for it has potentially forced the theatre outside the moral world; away, that is, from the contemporary obsession with right and wrong, with guilt and innocence. Its concern, derived from Zen, with surface quality established the importance of sensibility, of the simple acceptance of reality, above intellect and conscience. In the words of a Zen poem:

'If you want to get the plain truth,
Be not concerned with right and wrong,
The conflict between right and wrong
Is the sickness of the mind.'[1]

Nevertheless while the happening triumphantly fulfils Cummings' definition of art, 'It is Art because it is *alive*',[2] it lacks the disciplined perception which alone can transmute theatricality into drama. As Ionesco has said, 'liberation can come only when there is a genuine appreciation of what has been revealed and the ability to control these revelations from the supra-conscious world. I believe there must be in a writer, and even in a dramatist, a mixture of spontaneity, unawareness and lucidity; a lucidity unafraid of what spontaneous imagination may contribute. If lucidity is required of him, *a priori*, it is as though one shut the floodgates. We must first let the torrent rush in, and only then comes choice, control, grasp comprehension.'[3] It is precisely the failure of these writers to have a 'genuine appreciation of what has been revealed', to exercise a meaningful control, which finally subverts their value to the drama. The value of the happening, therefore, lies less in the form which it has evolved, namely that of the fragmented surrealistic sketch, than in the principles from which it emerged—the rejection of the standard concerns of the theatre, the expressed need for a clearer perception of physical reality, the intensification of instinctual and intuitive response. Yet the excitingly experimental can devolve rapidly

[1] *Beat Zen Square Zen and Zen,* p. 10.
[2] *e. e. cummings,* p. 60.
[3] *Notes and Counter Notes,* p. 124.

into the merely precious. When La Monte Young conducted an experiment in California which consisted of his scraping a gong over concrete for an hour we have clearly moved out of the sphere of art and into that of mysticism or psychology. For although this no doubt served to enforce a consciousness both of the nature of hearing itself and the freedom and awareness which comes with concentration on a single stimulus this finally constitutes a sacrifice of art to science and potentially replaces the rational artist by the merely competent machine.

John Cage has defined the theatre as 'something which engages both the eye and ear' adding that 'The reason I want to make my definition . . . simple is so one could view everyday life as theatre.'[1] In so far as this is a reminder that art is created out of human experience this is a truism which may or may not be worth recalling. But clearly he is claiming for the happening that faith in 'pure behaviour' for which Peter Brook had called. While in a perverse way this concern with the sensual quality of reality is a natural culmination of Albee's and Bellow's concern with confrontation it demonstrates an almost complete failure to understand the nature of the dramatic process. Indeed when Cage himself poses the obvious question which arises from his own definition his reply, while refreshingly candid, remains almost totally mystifying, 'why have the arts when we already have it in life? A suitable answer from my point of view is that we thereby celebrate. We have a history in our culture of special occasions, and I don't see anything wrong with that, and I don't see anything wrong with doing something that's unnecessary.'[2] Necessity can never justifiably be associated with art, however, and it is surely obvious that any form of art must be subject to the mediation and control of the artist. So that if Jill Johnson's permissive definition of theatre, in *Encore*, as 'a field of action where anything may happen'[3] can be justified in the context of a genuine control it makes little sense in the context of a frequently chaotic flamboyance.

If it is yet too early to assess the achievement, if any, of the new surrealism it is clear that serious dramatists like Albee, Gelber, (The Apple), LeRoi Jones (The Toilet) and Bellow have been influenced by its concern with vitality and by its faith in the significance of a direct

[1] John Cage, Michael Kirby and Richard Schechner, 'An Interview with John Cage', *Tulane Drama Review*, X, ii (Winter, 1965), p. 50.

[2] *Ibid.*, p. 58.

[3] *The Encore Reader*, p. 260.

confrontation with simple reality. Yet it is also clear that vitality is a property of art. It cannot be taken as art itself. Indeed perhaps the best assessment of the happening is that which T. S. Eliot applied to surrealistic poetry, 'The suggestiveness of true poetry . . . is the aura round a bright clear centre. You cannot have the aura alone.'[1]

[1] *Directions in Modern Theatre and Drama*, p. 371.

Section Two
COMMITMENT

. . . good writers and artists must engage in politics only as far as it is necessary to defend oneself against it. There are plenty of accusers, prosecutors and gendarmes without them.

ANTON CHEKHOV: Daniel Aaron, *Writers on the Left*

As a writer, you have to decide that what is really important is not that the people you write about are Negroes, but that they are people, and that the suffering of any people is really universal.

JAMES BALDWIN: *The Negro in American Culture*

Intelligence in chains loses in lucidity what it gains in intensity.

ALBERT CAMUS: *The Rebel*

Some of us became convinced that through the theatre we could reach an audience larger than the sprinkling of brighteyed dogooders who read the weeklies.

JOHN DOS PASSOS: *Dos Passos and the Revolting Playwrights*

6

The Theatre of Commitment

In both England and America the violent protest of a committed theatre has for the most part given way to a drama which is more truly metaphysical than social. Nevertheless there has arisen in the United States, since 1959, a new, socially-committed theatre which in many ways harks back to the simplicities of the thirties. For the Negro playwrights of the sixties have tended all too frequently to embrace the moral absolutism of thirty years ago. Relying on the stereotype and facing social injustice with anger they have tended to create not valid drama but fantasies of revenge. They have, however, generated an enthusiasm for the theatre itself which has long been absent from the American scene. For just as Langston Hughes had founded Negro theatres in the thirties and early forties, theatres like the *Suitcase Theatre* in Harlem, the *Negro Art Theatre* in Los Angeles and the *Skyloft Players* in Chicago, so LeRoi Jones, the most violent of the new Negro dramatists, has founded the *Theatre of the Black Arts*—a Harlem theatre which later distinguished itself by becoming the headquarters of a secret Negro extremist group. (When raided in March 1966 it disgorged rifles, pistols, meat hooks and ammunition as well as revealing a target range in its basement.) Just as the proletarian theatre of the thirties had arisen against a background of profound social unrest so this revival of committed theatre had as its background that intensification of the Civil Rights struggle which started with the bus boycotts of 1956 and the 'sit-ins' of 1960.

There is a distateful arbitrariness in most categorisations and perhaps more so in one based on race. Yet the minor renaissance in committed theatre is clearly of particular interest especially in the context of a drama which has tended to move away from such an overtly social stance. Further, while these writers approach the problem from different angles they all share weaknesses which spring from the nature of their commitment. Overwhelmed by the enormity of injustice and prejudice they tend to slip back into that mixture of sentimentality and violence which had been a mark of earlier partisan theatre. Obsessed by the reality of racial barriers they stress not the uniformity of human fate but the divisions of society. In doing so they fail to establish that sense of universality which is the essence of drama and which Miller has insisted must constitute the core of a valid social drama, 'The social drama . . . is the drama of the whole man. It seeks to deal with his differences from others not *per se*, but toward the end that, if only through drama, we may know how much the same we are . . . The social drama to me is only incidentally an arraignment of society.'[1] Yet it is necessary to see this Negro drama, concerned as it is with the stresses and implications of the racial situation, in the context of past attempts to present a valid picture of the Negro on stage. For the Negro existed in the American theatre for long as little more than an object of contempt, fun or pity, and in many ways this movement of the sixties is virtually the first attempt by major talents to represent the anger, frustration and violence of a life lived in a basically hostile society.

It was not until 1920 that the Negro was even granted any kind of genuine existence in American drama. In the early American theatre the stock Negro character had been the minstrel, usually portrayed by whites with blackface. With the rise of abolitionist sentiment, however, he became the sentimental hero of plays like *Uncle Tom's Cabin* (1853). While this did something to redeem the Negro from the travesties of the minstrel era it did so merely to create another stereotype, namely that of the faithful servant whose value lay in proportion to his loyalty to his white master. The nature of such melodramas can, perhaps, best be judged from the advertisement which proclaimed on the one hand, 'a pair of full-blooded bloodhounds, trained to take part in the Drama, are used in the thrilling scene showing Eliza escaping from the Slavehunters' while on the other hand urging that 'As your clergyman will tell you, it will return you both instruction in American history and wholesale recreation'.[2] In 1859 Boucicault further strengthened the stereotype with *The Octaroon* and trod the difficult path between Northern and Southern sensibilities by making the blackguard southerner an *arriviste*. It was not until Eugene O'Neill's *Emperor Jones* (1920), however, that the Negro became the central protagonist of a drama and then this was as the protagonist of a play which stressed the deterministic nature of existence by demonstrating a Negro's inability

[1] Arthur Miller, 'On Social Plays', *A View from the Bridge* (London, 1957), p. 8.
[2] Jordan Miller, *American Dramatic Literature* (New York, 1961), pp. ii-iii.

to escape from his origins. Four years later, however, in *All God's Chillun Got Wings* (1924), he produced the first play to confront, genuinely and with sympathy, the fact of miscegenation. The importance of this play, if dramas by and about Negroes were not to be restricted to quaint folk plays, can hardly be exaggerated while its revolutionary nature can be gauged from the popular reaction as summarised by *The Provincetown*, 'The fact that it dealt with a marriage between a Negro and a white girl, and that the wife at one point in the action kisses her husband's hand, had been avidly seized upon. Ku Kluxers, Citizen Fixits and Southern Gentlewomen, most of whom did not trouble to read the play . . . were goaded into action. Facts were enlarged and distorted, and expressions of opinion from pastors in Mississippi, from Colonels of the Confederate Army, from champions of Nordic integrity in Iowa, were printed and reprinted from one end of the country to the other. A picture of Mary Blair, who was to play the wife, was syndicated hundreds of times with the caption "White Actress Kisses Negro's Hand".'[1] For all its melodramatic plot and the chilling determinism of its mood, 'We're never free—except to do what we have to do',[2] *All God's Chillun Got Wings* does penetrate below the stereotypes which had satisfied playwrights in the past. For the love/hate relationship between Jim Harris and his white wife, Ella, serves to release those subtle pressures and prejudices which if absent from the stage had proved real enough off it. Jim, anxious to prove himself in a white world, tries to pass the law examinations which will lift him out of that restricted life assigned to the Negro. Yet while himself intimidated by that world, to the extent that he repeatedly fails the examinations he knows he should be able to pass, he remains blithely unaware of his wife's antagonism. For she, like the white world in general, loves Jim only as a boy or as 'my old kind Uncle Jim who's been with us for years and years'. (p. 73.) When he persists in his efforts his wife, now in a demented condition, plans his murder just as earlier a fellow Negro infuriated by Jim's attempts to improve himself, had screamed at him, 'Tell me befo' I wrecks yo' face in! Is you a nigger or isn't you? (*Shaking him*) Is you a nigger, Nigger? Nigger, is you a Nigger?' (p. 24.) Thus O'Neill dramatised for the first time the dilemma of the Negro desperately anxious to escape the limitations of race but held back both by the bitterness of those around him and by a seemingly ineradicable prejudice rooted in the distant past. (Here

[1] Sophus Keith Winter, *Eugene O'Neill* (New York, 1961), p. 202.
[2] Eugene O'Neill, *All God's Chillun Got Wings* (London, 1925), p. 31.

once again we are touching on O'Neill's determinism.) The central conflict of the play is between Jim's wishful humanitarianism and the active commitment of those around him. While his sister declares, 'We don't deserve happiness till we've fought the fight of our race and won it!' (p. 44) he voices the hopes of a liberal humanism, 'You with your fool talk of the black race and the white race! Where does the human race get a chance to come in?' (p. 63). Yet for all his attachment to liberal sentiment the ending is at once sentimental and deterministic. For the conflict between Jim and Ella is only resolved by his failure and his preparedness to fill the role dictated by her madness. Yet O'Neill's willingness to draw the white world as on the one hand brash and inhuman, in the form of Mickey who seduces and deserts Ella, and on the other hand mad, constituted a revolutionary step in the stage representation of the Negro. For here was a Negro who was genuinely a sympathetic protagonist, one, moreover, whose chief virtue lies in his tolerance for a demented white woman.

The late twenties and the thirties produced proletarian plays in which Negroes functioned, as did workers, as exemplars of political dogma. These were for the most part poor efforts which did little to establish the Negro as a genuine human being and which while mouthing the slogans of utopian socialism failed to learn from O'Neill the necessity for genuine sympathy.

The failure of these writers to produce significant drama must raise the question of the effect of commitment on the artist. For while it is true that many of the playwrights in the twenties and thirties were attracted to the theatre merely as a means to spread their political philosophies it is equally true that some of these were men of considerable talent including John Dos Passos and Upton Sinclair. It seems, however, that in their concern with the plight of the under-priviledged they were prepared to sacrifice artistic integrity to social expediency or that at least they tended to confuse the two.

It is true that in propounding the subservience of aesthetic criteria to social or even moral ones they were asserting little more than Shaw who was always concerned with attacking hedonism and praising moral intent. Yet the fact that Shaw has signed his name to the heresy fails to make it more attractive, for while a great work of art surely reveals a moral and social dimension this rarely constitutes either its sole value or indeed the sole justification for its existence. Indeed Shaw himself has said that: 'Social questions are too sectional, too topical, too temporal to move a man to the mighty effort which is needed to produce great poetry. Prison reform may nerve Charles Reade to produce an effective and business-like prose melodrama; but it could never produce *Hamlet, Faust,* or *Peer Gynt* . . . *A Doll's House* will be as flat as ditchwater when *A Midsummer Night's Dream* will still be as fresh as paint . . .' When he adds to this, 'but it will have done more work in the world; and that is enough for the highest genius'[1] he would seem, however, to be still clinging tenaciously to a social aesthetic. Yet in his drama Shaw was concerned with far more fundamental issues; with the conflict, as he put it, between human vitality and the artificial system of morality, with the conflict between reality and illusion. The social problems which find effective voices in his drama function as elements in his concern with these conflicts rather than as political pronouncements. Unlike the 'proletarian' playwrights in America he refused to produce dramatised tracts about strikes or workers. He likewise refused to project his political faith into a system of morality which assigned vice and virtue according to class or profession. If he was capable of taunting the critics by saying that his early play, *Widowers' Houses* (produced 1892; published 1893), was 'intended to induce people to vote on the Progressive side at the next County Council election in London' he was also capable of voicing the fervent wish that his audience would 'please judge it not as a pamphlet in dialogue but as in intention a work of art as much as any comedy of Moliere's is a work of art'.[2] Of course this is the sort of cheerful contradiction which we have come to expect as an endearing if frustrating aspect of Shaw's comments on both his own work and drama in general so that it is particularly dangerous to isolate any of his remarks from the context of his works—a fact demonstrated by the gulf which frequently exists between his plays and the prefaces which accompany them. Nevertheless it is clear that he was as convinced of the need to relegate propaganda and simple-minded protest to the pamphlet as he was of the need to add a humanity and morality to aestheticism. While asserting, with due Shavian pomp, that 'the general preference of dramatists for subjects in which the conflict is between man and his apparently inevitable and eternal rather than his political and temporal circumstances, is due in the vast majority of cases to the dramatist's political ignorance' he felt constrained to add, 'and in a few cases to the comprehensiveness of his philosophy'[3] —a significant admission of the restrictiveness of political fervour.

[1] Eric Bentley, *Bernard Shaw* (London, 1950), p. 118.
[2] *Ibid.,* pp. 9-10.
[3] Bernard Shaw, *Shaw on Theatre* (New York, 1958), p. 65.

Bertolt Brecht, the other great 'social' dramatist of this century, similarly owes his greatest successes not to the dynamism of revolutionary commitment but rather to his sensitive perception of the human condition. In his best plays, in fact, his achievement is that of sensibility and compassion over a committed intellect. For he was constantly shocked and dismayed by the reaction of audiences who turned his villains into heroes and who saw resilience and doggedness where he had seen corruption and moral degeneracy (*Mother Courage*, 1939). His achievement was largely the involuntary victory of the artist over the polemicist—a victory which owed much to the vital inspiration of a sincere commitment but which was achieved in spite of the limiting tendency of that commitment. Unlike Shaw he did at times sacrifice aesthetic standards to ideological purposes while plays like *St. Joan of the Stockyards* (Written 1929-31; Produced 1959) lose much of their impact as a result of his naïve apportionment of vice and virtue. Nevertheless like Shaw, Brecht's practice transcends the austerity of his theory. While he proclaims that 'The main thing is to teach the spectator to reach a verdict'[1] and urges the destruction of empathy as a means to this end, his plays succeed largely in so far as they fail to conform to this dogma. *The Good Woman of Sezuan* and *The Caucasian Chalk Circle* (1945), two of his finest plays, while didactic in tone are less concerned with teaching a political lesson than with celebrating human nature.

Thus it seems apparent that neither Shaw nor Brecht seek to replace aesthetic judgement by the criterion of social utility. Neither, in contrast to the 'proletarian' playwrights of the thirties, do they sacrifice the universality of drama to the parochialism of 'unrewarding rage'.[2] If there is some justice in Richard Wright's comment that '*All* literature is protest' there is more justice in James Baldwin's retort that 'all protest was not literature'.[3] So that it becomes apparent that the committed writer is capable of producing valid drama only in so far as he is able to subordinate immediate social and political objectives to a concern with 'the whole man'. Those playwrights who in the nineteen-thirties saw in the stage a useful extension of the political platform failed to produce any significant drama precisely because they chose to replace the universal with the particular and the complexities of human relationships with utilitarian stereotypes. Driven to the theatre by

[1] *The Playwright as Thinker*, p. 219.
[2] James Baldwin, *Notes of a Native Son* (London, 1964), p. 37.
[3] James Baldwin, *Nobody Knows my Name* (London, 1964), p. 161.

political motives they produced necessarily simplified political homilies whose distortions, while justifiable by the ethics of political expediency, had little to do with dramatic necessity. The degeneration of didacticism into assertive propaganda resulted in plays which are of interest today solely as sociological documents. Thus the theatre of commitment differs from 'social' drama chiefly in the restrictiveness both of its premises and of its purpose. (Commitment here is taken to mean not just involvement but involvement in a specific social problem. It further implies a determination to present that problem, not objectively, but with a view to offering a potential solution. It is perhaps interesting to note that the definition of commitment offered by the O.E.D. is 'an engagement that restricts freedom of action'.)

Following the simplistic protest of the thirties the 'proletarian' theatre in America has mellowed into the social problem play. Arthur Miller, in an article 'On Social Plays' written in 1957, attacked the plays of the pre-war decade as 'special pleadings . . . further from a consideration of the whole man than much of the antisocial drama is'.[1] To him 'The social drama . . . must do more than analyse and arraign the social network of relationships. It must delve into the nature of man as he exists to discover what his needs are, so that those needs may be amplified and exteriorised in terms of social concepts'.[2] If this was a somewhat elastic definition it was because Miller was taking cognizance of his own tendency towards examining man's metaphysical rather than strictly social self. Shaw's idea of the 'problem play' was equally expansive. For him the problem play was a drama which was not 'frivolous'. His definition of 'frivolous', one imagines, varied according to his temper. With the urgencies of the Depression passing into history such direct social criticism and protest as there has been has been directed against the false values of a materialistic society rather than concerning itself with the plight of a persecuted minority. This has been equally true in England where the 'new wave', starting with Osborne's *Look Back in Anger* (1956), was greeted as a revival of social protest. The 'anger' of the title was appropriated by the critics and applied, albeit briefly, to a whole range of emerging dramatists. Here too, however, it soon became apparent that the movement was if anything apolitical and that the anger, far from constituting the wrath of the righteous, could more accurately be seen as baffled rage. In accord with Miller's definition this was a drama concerned less with man's

[1] 'On Social Plays', p. 4.
[2] *Ibid.*, p. 14.

societal relationships than with the nature of man himself. The radical simplicities of committed literature were left far behind and indeed the subject of both Osborne's and Wesker's work was the fact of living with this disillusion. In the words of Osborne's Jimmy Porter: 'I suppose people of our generation aren't able to die for good causes any longer. We had all that done for us, in the thirties and forties, when we were still kids. There aren't any good, brave causes left. If the big bang does come, and we all get killed off, it won't be in aid of the old-fashioned, grand design. It'll just be for the Brave New-nothing-very-much-thank-you.'[1] Equally in Wesker the same lament is to be heard, 'I've lost my faith and I've lost my ambition . . . I don't see things in black and white any more'.[2]

In the United States, however, with the production in 1959 of Lorraine Hansberry's *A Raisin in the Sun*, a new, socially committed theatre based on the Negro situation began to make itself felt. Her play was followed in 1962 by LeRoi Jones's *The Toilet*; in 1963 by Martin Duberman's *In White America* and in 1964 by LeRoi Jones's *Dutchman* and *The Slave*, Lorraine Hansberry's *The Sign in Sidney Brustein's Window* and James Baldwin's *Blues for Mr. Charlie*. Not since the committed theatre of the thirties had there been such a concentrated concern with a single social problem not had there been so many highly talented Negro writers turning their attention to the stage. Of the writers named above only Martin Duberman is white and indeed his play, *In White America*, is of considerable interest in a consideration of the viability of committed theatre.

The possibility of creating disciplined drama out of a subject so immediate and overwhelming as the racial situation in America or the mass murders of the *Second World War*, for example, must be in doubt. Peter Weiss's solution to the latter problem, *The Investigation*, was a series of readings taken from the Auschwitz trials and indeed it is possible that this may be the closest it is feasible to approach to drama-tisation of such a problem. Certainly the austerity of these readings, the terrifying contrast between the human voice and the enormity of its message, is in itself a part of the effect. *In White America* is Martin Duberman's attempt to apply the same technique to the 'Negro problem'. He tries to attain a similar objectivity by also turning to historical documents. In a year that saw the murder of Negro children in a Sunday-school in Birmingham, Alabama, objectivity was liable to

[1] John Osborne, *Look Back in Anger* (London, 1960), pp. 84-5.
[2] Arnold Wesker, *The Wesker Trilogy* (London, 1960), pp. 73-4.

be an elusive quality. For if the Negro was bound to confess, as does Alton Scales in Hansberry's *The Sign in Sidney Brustein's Window*, that he was 'born with *this* cause'[1] then the white was similarly bound to admit, as does Duberman, that he too was writing from a prejudiced viewpoint.[2] Duberman's documentary play does go some way towards avoiding the perils of committed theatre but it equally fails, however, to approach the level of real drama.

Baldwin has stated very succinctly the peculiar dilemma of the Negro writer influenced by dual and largely contradictory responsibilities. For, as he points out, on the one hand writing 'demands a great deal of stepping out of a social situation in order to deal with it' while on the other hand 'all the time you're out of it you can't help feeling a little guilty that you are not, as it were, on the firing line, tearing down the slums.'[3] The danger which persists for the Negro writer is thus that the isolating prejudice of society will lead him to convert this social guilt into a literature of revenge. The reality of this danger, when placed beside the failings of the 'proletarian' protest of the thirties, lends something of the air of a fundamental law to Camus' comments on the imprisoned De Sade, 'Intelligence in chains loses in lucidity what it gains in intensity . . . He did not create a philosophy, he pursued a monstrous dream of revenge.'[4]

Alfred Kazin sees in the development of the Jewish writer in America a relevant parallel for 'when the Jewish immigrants, from whom I come, arrived in this country 50, 60 years ago, there was a whole hoard of sweatshop poets . . . They worked 18, 19 hours a day; they lived horrible lives. None of this poetry that I have seen, in English, in Hebrew, or in Yiddish, is any good at all.' To these writers, embroiled in the actuality of social inequity and prejudice, he contrasts the Jewish writers of recent years, Bellow, Mailer and Malamud. In searching for a reason for the extent of their achievement he seizes on that universality which is the essence of genuine art, 'they've come to recognize their fate as being universal in the same sense, and not merely accidental or

---

[1] Lorraine Hansberry, *The Sign in Sidney Brustein's Window* (New York, 1965), p. 41.

[2] Martin Duberman, *In White America* (London, 1964), Preface.

[3] James Baldwin, Emile Capouya, Lorraine Hansberry, Nat Hentoff, Langston Hughes, Alfred Kazin, 'The Negro in American Culture', *Cross Currents*, XI, iii (Summer, 1961), pp. 205-6.

[4] Albert Camus, *The Rebel*, trans., Anthony Bower (London, 1953), pp. 32-3.

parochial.'¹ Of the playwrights considered here only Lorraine Hansberry achieves this sense of universality which succeeds in transforming the stereotype into the archetype. While Baldwin shows a similar understanding in his critical writings, 'As a writer, you have to decide that what is really important is not that the people you write about are Negroes, but that they are people, and that the suffering of any person is really universal',² he fails to apply this to his work for the theatre.

In 1956 a conference of Negro writers was held in Paris. It was billed as non-political but it rapidly became clear, as Baldwin points out, that political issues could not be that easily divorced from cultural ones for it seems that the exigencies of racial discord militate against purely aesthetic criteria. Indeed in a discussion of Negro drama which took place in America Robert Brustein and Richard Gilman were shouted down and openly called 'whitey' by LeRoi Jones and a largely hostile audience for insisting on the necessity for retaining aesthetic judgement as the only valid assessment of dramatic worth.

There is a very definite sense in which the work of playwrights like LeRoi Jones and James Baldwin can be seen, therefore, as an extension of that imperfect dialogue between the races which has left the Negro asking himself, as Hansberry does, 'is it necessary to integrate oneself into a burning house?'³ In the words of a young Negro novelist, Julian Mayfield, 'the Negro writer is being very gently nudged toward a rather vague thing called the mainstream of American literature . . . He may decide that though the music is sweet, he would rather play in another orchestra; or to place himself in the position of the black convict in *The Defiant Ones*, he may decide that he need not necessarily share the fate of his white companion, who after all proffers the hand of friendship a little late.'⁴ In the theatre the nature of this separation seems to consist in a persistent parochialism. Yet perhaps the considerable achievement of Lorraine Hansberry's second play indicates an advance in Negro drama to parallel that in Jewish literature. For the step from protest to affirmation is a logical one. Certainly the mainstream of American drama which had once been concerned with man's societal relationships is now exercised by a concern with his metaphysical situation. Nevertheless it is, perhaps, worth recalling Sartre's

¹ 'The Negro in American Culture', p. 210.
² *Ibid.*, p. 205.
³ *Ibid.*, p. 222.
⁴ *Ibid.*, p. 221.

criticism of a metaphysical concern devoid of practicality, 'Should a child die, you accused the absurdity of the world and this deaf and blind God which you had created in order to spit in his face. But the child's father, if he were a laid-off worker or unskilled labourer, accused men.'[1] The Negro writer is committed by virtue of his birth. His art is the expression of his attempt to come to terms with that commitment.

[1] Jean-Paul Sartre, *Situations*, trans., Benita Eisler (London, 1965), p. 98.

7
James Baldwin

JAMES BALDWIN's dilemma is essentially that which has always faced that artist who is also, consciously or not, committed to a specific social problem. As an artist he has constantly expressed the need to see humanity as a whole—to escape the narrow vision which can be an aspect of involvement. Born in Harlem in 1924 he left the United States in 1948, hoping to escape the social and artistic limitations of the racial situation. 'I doubted my ability to survive the fury of the colour problem here . . . I wanted to prevent myself from becoming merely a Negro, or even, merely a Negro writer!'[1] In rebellion against the degrading classifications of American society which left the Negro on the fringe of prosperity and dignity as it left him on the fringe of its cities, he adopted, as had so many before him, the immediate expediency of disaffiliation. In art he attacked the 'unrewarding rage' of *Native Son* (1940) which, to his mind, had destroyed itself in the violence of its own commitment, just as he had attacked the sentimentalising of *Uncle Tom's Cabin*. Yet the nine years which he spent in Paris served to convince him of the virtual impossibility of transcending his own experience. Indeed he came to accept that this experience constituted the core of his creative ability. In a review of the *Selected Poems* of Langston Hughes, in March 1959, he expressed an opinion which would have shocked the twenty-four year old Baldwin who had sought artistic integrity and personal refuge in France. 'Hughes' he said 'is an American Negro poet and has no choice but to be acutely aware of it. He is not the first American Negro to find the war between his social and artistic responsibilities all but irreconcilable.'[2]

The continuing battle which Baldwin has waged with the spirit of Richard Wright, a battle which started in 1949 with the publication of his essay, 'Everybody's Protest Novel', is symptomatic of that tension which he was later to see, more sympathetically, in Hughes's poetry. As evidence of this tension within his own work on the one hand he

[1] Herbert Hill, ed., *Black Voices* (London, 1964), p. 402.
[2] Maurice Charney, 'James Baldwin's Quarrel with Richard Wright', *American Quarterly*, XV, i (Spring, 1963), p. 65.

admits to a determinism not essentially different from Wright's and
admits that 'we cannot escape our origins, however hard we try'[1] while
on the other he generalises from this and seeks to find in the Negro's
experience an archetype for the human condition: 'Which of us has
overcome his past? And the past of a Negro is blood dripping down
through leaves, gouged-out eyeballs, the sex torn from its socket and
severed with a knife. But this past is not special to the Negro. This
horror is also the past, and the everlasting potential, or temptation of the
human race. If we do not know this, it seems to me, we know nothing
about ourselves, nothing about each other.'[2] He has to date written
five essays on his relationship with Wright and this shows not merely
the debt which he personally owed to the older writer but, more
relevantly, his consciousness of the stance into which he, as a Negro,
could so easily fall. In one such essay, 'Many Thousands Gone', he
identifies that tendency towards dehumanisation which he had seen as
operating in Wright's work, 'that artist is strangled who is forced to
deal with human beings solely in social terms'.[3] Here, of course, he is
on the verge of coming to grips with the central problem of commitment. For didacticism is transformed into art precisely in the moment
that the artist appreciates that, as Baldwin says, 'literature and sociology
are not one and the same'.[4] It is Baldwin's ability to maintain this
distinction in his novels which raises his work above the naïve absolutism of Wright's. This does not imply that as a novelist he abandons
faith in the validity of his own experience but that this experience is
seen in the broader context of the human condition. *Another Country*
(1961) confronts the fact of miscegenation but in doing so subordinates
it to the more fundamental problem of isolation and the desperate
failure of human communication. Superficially there are lines of force
connecting this, the best of Baldwin's novels, with *Native Son*. Indeed
Rufus, the protagonist, is driven to acts of violence and eventual self-
destruction by the same sense of suffocating rage which had seized
Bigger Thomas. Yet the injustice which sends him plummeting into
the Hudson River goes deeper than the pigment of his skin. The poor
Southern girl whom he brutally beats and who finally retreats into
insanity is a victim not only of the tormented dementia of a Negro
driven wild by prejudice but of the elemental failure of love and the

[1] *Notes of a Native Son*, p. 31.
[2] *Nobody Knows my Name*, p. 174.
[3] *Op. cit.*, p. 36.
[4] *Ibid.*, p. 24.

instinct for masochism which is the sign of self-hatred. This is not to say that colour is peripheral to the novel, however, for Baldwin repeatedly insists on the gulf which it opens between those already terrifyingly alone. The studied cynicism with which Ida, Rufus's sister, sells out to the white world is certainly a sign of the corrupting power of that world but more significantly it is proof of the ease with which the genuine is sacrificed to the expedient and the arid relationship substituted for real communion. As Vivaldi, Ida's white lover, says, 'suffering doesn't *have* a colour'.[1] While the inferior position of the Negro emphasises his suffering it is equally true that white and coloured alike betray themselves in their willingness to sacrifice the real to the dream. In *The Fire Next Time* (1963) Baldwin identifies the principle which in essence is the theme of *Another Country*. Urging the need for renewal he points out the impossibility of such so long as one 'supposes things to be constant that are not—safety, for example, or money, or power. One clings then to chimeras, by which one can only be betrayed'.[2] The solution which he advances, like that suggested by Ida in his novel, is the need to confront 'with passion the conundrum of life'.[3] It is this ability to penetrate beyond the immediacies of injustice and prejudice, then, which marks his work off from that of those writers for whom the novel is an extension of the pamphlet. Like Arthur Miller he is concerned with man rather than men and the savage perception which characterises his essays survives now with the added depth and perspective of the artist.

The writer who had lived for nine years in Paris, remote from the immediate dangers of a problem which was rapidly gathering to a head, came eventually, however, to feel guilty for his disaffiliation. The man who was later to point out the reason for white inactivity and indifference—'To act is to be committed, and to be committed is to be in danger'[4]—himself became increasingly certain of his need to return to America. As he explains in one of his essays, the time comes when 'someone asks him to explain Little Rock and he begins to feel that it would be simpler—and, corny as the words may sound, more honorable—to go to Little Rock than sit in Europe, on an American passport, trying to explain it . . .'[5] *Another Country* is the result of this return to

[1] James Baldwin, *Another Country* (London, 1965), p. 325.
[2] James Baldwin, *The Fire Next Time* (London, 1963), p. 100.
[3] *Ibid.*, p. 99.
[4] *Ibid.*, p. 20.
[5] *Black Voices*, p. 402.

the immediate pressures of the American experience while in 1958, for the first time, Baldwin visited the Southern states. It was out of this experience and at the urging of Elia Kazan, that he came to consider writing a play. *Blues for Mr. Charlie*, first produced in 1964, has for its protagonist a man who has returned to the South partly as a result of failure in the North and partly, one suspects, because here the fury which he feels can provoke an open response. It would hardly be too fanciful to see Richard Henry as an expression of Baldwin's sense of guilt for his remoteness from the front line of the battle to which he is committed. For the play is dedicated to the memory of Medgar Evers who was murdered while working in the South and is based 'very distantly indeed' on the murder of another Civil Rights worker, Emmet Till, who had been killed in Mississippi in 1955. The murderer, as in the play, had been acquitted and the frightening facts which surround the case are relevant in so far as they represent the challenge facing Baldwin. For he confesses to the fear that he would be unable to draw a valid picture of a murderer who would kill a man and then proudly recount the facts, after his trial, to a journalist. The fact that his brother, who Baldwin alleges had participated in the crime, is now a deputy sheriff in Rulesville, Mississippi, while not relevant to the play as such, does demonstrate the enormity of the crime and the extent of the injustice which he, as an artist, was concerned with transmuting not into social polemic but into valid drama. Indeed in choosing a murder as the central action of his play Baldwin was in danger of succumbing to that kind of sentimentality which Yeats has defined as uncarned emotion. Certainly the Actors' Studio's production of the play in London, in 1965, failed in large part because of its persistent efforts to sentimentalise. The parading of a coffin, while it has for long been a legitimate weapon of the revolutionary, can too easily degenerate into a substitute for the insight and perspective required of drama.

The play, then, is concerned with the murder of Richard Henry, the son of the reverend Meridian Henry—a Negro minister. Having been overwhelmed by the suffocating oppression of Harlem and having found in drugs a refuge from his own solitude he returns to the South bringing with him a fury which expresses itself in the contempt with which he confronts the white community. He refuses to accept the terms on which the precarious racial truce is based, boasts of the white women he has known in New York, and, in effect, forces the confrontation in which he is killed by Lyle Britten—a white storekeeper. Yet the play is concerned not only with the fate of an individual Negro who finds himself the victim of a Southern 'peckerwood'. For Baldwin the play 'takes place in Plaguetown, U.S.A., now. The plague is race, the plague is our concept of Christianity: and this raging plague has the power to destroy every human relationship'.[1] And here we might be forgiven for detecting echoes of Camus. For the grotesque code of honour which brings Richard and Lyle into direct confrontation is as arbitrary and irrational as that implacable plague which settled on Camus' Oran, while the two responses to this irrational suffering are typified in Baldwin's play by Meridian and Richard as they are in Camus' novel by Father Paneloux and Rieux. The one places faith in resignation or the positive power of love; the other in revolt. The parallel serves to emphasise too the crisis of faith which is the background not only to this play but also to most Negro novels and drama. As Camus' characters reject a God who can permit or even will purposeless suffering so Baldwin's characters rebel against a religion which preaches passivity and yet which can be made to endorse violence. In Camus' Oran or Baldwin's 'Plague-town U.S.A.' the white God is alien to a people subjected to irrational suffering. When Camus says, 'What I reproach Christianity with is being a doctrine of injustice'[2] he is identifying that same certainty which is felt by Lorenzo, a Negro student, when, standing in Meridian Henry's church, he says, '. . . you sit—in this—this—the house of this damn almighty God who don't care what happens to nobody, unless, of course, they're white . . . It's that damn white God that's been lynching and burning us and castrating us and raping our women and robbing us of everything that makes a man a man . . .' (B.C. p. 15.) It is in this absolute necessity for revolt that the parallel between *The Plague* (1947) and *Blues for Mr. Charlie* can be most usefully urged. Faced with the reality of the plague 'the only watchword for a man' Camus insists 'is revolt'.[3] So too, Richard dies still expressing contempt for the white world as Rufus, in jumping from the George Washington Bridge, had cried out against the force which destroyed him, '. . . *all right, you motherfucking Godalmighty bastard, I'm coming to you.*'[4] Richard is

[1] James Baldwin, *Blues for Mr. Charlie* (London, 1965), p. 10. All future references to this play will be abbreviated to 'B.C.' and incorporated into the text.

[2] Albert Camus, *Carnets 1942-1951*, trans., Philip Thody (London, 1966), p. 56.

[3] *Ibid.*, p. 33.

[4] *Another Country*, p. 70.

killed essentially because of his refusal to conform. He steps, apparently
with all the deliberateness of the conscious rebel, outside of the pattern
imposed on him. Yet the dialogue which Baldwin wages with himself,
through the person of Richard, remains finally unresolved. For where
Rieux had contained his revolt within a determination to heal, Richard's
death is a gesture of rebellion not essentially different from the 'unrewarding rage' which had led Bigger Thomas to strike out against the
white world. Baldwin has always been supremely conscious of the rage
with which the Negro confronts the white world and has insisted that
'the first problem is how to control that rage so that it won't destroy
you.'[1] The dilemma in which he finds himself in *Blues for Mr. Charlie*
is that Richard's rage is the substance of his rebellion and if it destroys
him it also constitutes his strength. For while the white world can
afford to ignore and persecute the non-violent demonstrators organised
by Meridian it cannot avoid the direct challenge represented by Richard
and if that challenge leads inevitably to his death then there is a logic
to that progression as disturbing but as direct as that which governed
Bigger Thomas's career.

Richard returns to the South harbouring a bitter hatred for the whites
which derives in part from his own experience and in part from his
awareness of Negro impotence, manifested here by his father's inability
to revenge his wife's murder. He sees the white man as responsible for
'all the crimes that ever happened in the history of the world' (B.C.
p. 31) and proposes the same radical cure which Bigger Thomas and
a thousand street-corner messiahs had proclaimed before him, 'the
only way the black man's going to *get* any power is to drive all the
white men into the sea.' (B.C. p. 31.) The same words which Milton
applied to Lucifer and Baldwin to Wright's most famous protagonist
seem equally applicable to Richard Henry for he prefers, like Lucifer,
'rather to rule in hell than serve in heaven'.[2] Yet his rage is not un-
relenting. He surrenders the gun which he has carried with him for
'a long, long time' (B.C. p. 32) to his father. He establishes a genuine
relationship with Juanita, a Negro student, and the complexion of his
immediate world changes. 'I been in pain and darkness all my life. All
my life. And this is the first time in my life I've ever felt—maybe it
isn't all like that. Maybe there's more to it than that.' (B.C. p. 83.)
Baldwin casts doubt on the validity of this new vision, however. For
Juanita is made to recall that Richard had seen their escape as desertion,

[1] 'James Baldwin's Quarrel with Richard Wright', p. 65.
[2] *Notes of a Native Son*, p. 46.

insisting that 'he wasn't going to run no more from white folks . . .
but was going to stay and be a man—a *man!*—right here.' (B.C. p. 103.)
Thus his death is charged with an ambiguity on which the play's moral
emphasis depends. Is he killed because of his rebellious contempt or
because of his growing magnanimity? Camus has said, 'We are in a
world where we have to choose between being a victim or a hangman—
and nothing else.'[1] This is essentially the dilemma with which Baldwin
wrestles in *Blues for Mr. Charlie* and the ambiguity with which
Richard's character is drawn is a sign of the truth of Camus' further
comment, 'It is not an easy choice.' For Richard's single-minded
intensity seems to be purely destructive and if he stands as a warning
that self-effacement has given way to self-assertion he also demonstrates
the victory of hatred over compassion. Yet, more significantly, his
death would seem to demonstrate the truth of that choice identified by
Camus. For in surrendering his gun he apparently declines the role of
hangman and condemns himself to the role of victim. The tension thus
created between Richard as contemptuous rebel and Richard as victim
accounts for something of the play's moral confusion. For while there
is never any doubt of the destructive power of the 'plague of race', the
play's conclusion, in which the Negroes retire for a prayer meeting
and Meridian talks darkly of a solution lying with 'the Bible and the
gun', (B.C. p. 123) remains evenly balanced between the two extremes.

The pressures which had torn at the son also threaten the father and
Baldwin continues the debate between passivity and active revolt in the
tortured self-examination of Meridian. For the man who had himself
borne his wife's murder without striking back and who had watched
the young demonstrators beaten and reviled comes, after his son's
death, to question both the virtues of non-violence and the value of
Christianity. Yet Baldwin has said of this play that it is 'one man's
attempt to bear witness to the reality and the power of light.' (B.C.
p. 11) and one must presume that for him this light consists of the
refusal of the Negro to retaliate and destroy. In a sermon which
Meridian delivers over the dead body of his son he confesses to his
fears and doubts but re-dedicates himself to a continued faith in the
power of love: 'What hope is there for a people who deny their deeds
and disown their kinsmen and who do so in the name of purity and
love, in the name of Jesus Christ? What a light, my Lord, is needed
to conquer so mighty a darkness! This darkness rules in us, and grows,
in black and white alike. I have set my face against the darkness, I will

[1] *Carnets 1942-1951*, p. 71.

not let it conquer me . . .' (B.C. p. 83). This declaration of faith is tempered, however, by a demand for a sign which can give him some hope. In *Blues for Mr. Charlie* this sign can only lie in the self-examination which leads Parnell, the white liberal, to commit himself completely to the cause of Negro rights. For if Richard's death accomplishes nothing in itself it does precipitate the crisis in which those involved are forced to examine the nature and validity of their stance. As in both Hansberry's and Jones's work the white liberals are the special targets for criticism. This is true also of Baldwin's *The Fire Next Time* in which he attacks them on the grounds that 'they could deal with the Negro as a symbol or a victim but had no sense of him as a man' for their attitudes, he claims, have little connexion 'with their perceptions of their lives, or even their knowledge.'[1] Parnell James, in *Blues for Mr. Charlie*, is the editor of the liberal local paper. In contrast to the rest of the white community he refuses to accept the values on which that society has come to rest. When Richard is killed he forces the arrest of Lyle Britten in spite of the fact that he is a close friend. Yet beneath his exterior Parnell is guilty, not of racism but of the fault which Baldwin had identified in his essay. He sees the crime in terms of abstract values. He is committed to justice and equality but not to involvement in the details of inhumanity. Meridian attacks him for his clinical approach when dealing with the Police Chief, 'for both of you . . . it was just a black boy that was dead, and that was a problem. He saw the problem one way, you saw it another way. But it wasn't a *man* that was dead, not my *son*—you held yourselves away from that!' (B.C. p. 48.) Yet more fundamentally Parnell's stance is undermined by Baldwin's insistence on its sexual origin. For his liberalism appears to have stemmed from a youthful love affair with a Negro girl, an affair which has left in its wake an obsessive concern with Negroes which in reality owes little to a humanistic impulse. In an essay called 'The Black Boy Looks at the White Boy' Baldwin has attacked that fascination with the Negro revealed by writers such as Mailer and Kerouac. For they had seen in the black world merely a confirmation of the stereotype—a sense of liberating sensuality. This, in essence, is the basis too of Parnell's fascination—a fascination which if it rationalises his support of 'blacktown' detracts from the force of his moral integrity. Indeed he admits to himself that 'you don't love them' (B.C. p. 110) and recognises the self-hatred which stems from his obsession: 'All your life you've been made sick, stunned, dizzy, oh,

[1] *The Fire Next Time*, p. 67.

Lord! driven half mad by blackness. Blackness in front of your eyes. Boys and girls, men and women—you've bowed down in front of them all! And then hated yourself. Hated yourself for debasing yourself? Out with it, Parnell . . . Black boys and girls! I've wanted my hands full of them, wanted to drown them, laughing and dancing and making love—making love—wow!—and be transformed, formed, liberated out of this grey-white envelope.' (B.C. pp. 109-10.) At the trial, which dominates the third act, Parnell betrays the Negro cause and the justice to which he had been committed by covering up a lie told by Lyle's wife. While he regrets this immediately after the trial his positive espousal of the Negro side, which climaxes the play, can hardly be taken as a sign that there is any justification for Meridian's faith. If Baldwin genuinely wishes to 'bear witness to the reality and the power of light' he would have done better to allow Parnell the integrity which alone could grant a validity to his final decision. One is left finally, then, with a contradiction which, while it may accurately reflect the contemporary dilemma of Negro and white liberal, subverts Baldwin's declared faith. For if the logic of the final scene is seemingly dedicated to the validity of passive resistance, gathering to itself the genuinely committed, the force of Richard's death and the sad reality of liberal 'commitment' would seem to deny this logic. In a genuine attempt to avoid facile resolution Baldwin allows conscious ambiguity to degenerate into moral and dramatic confusion.

Neither is the play's climax made any more acceptable by the specious nature of the language which substitutes the cliché for genuine communication. On learning that the Negroes are to stage a march Parnell asks Juanita, to whom he has confessed a sexual attraction, 'Can I join you on the march, Juanita? Can I walk with you?'. Her reply would have done little credit to the poorest Broadway drama, 'Well, we can walk in the same direction, Parnell. Come . . . let's go on on.' (B.C. pp. 123-4.) Indeed where Baldwin had confessed to a fear that he would prove unable to 'draw a valid picture of the murderer' (B.C. p. 10) it is rather his inability to draw a valid picture of the victim and his immediate society which ironically proves the source of the play's failure. For if some of the white characters tend to the stereotype they are at least drawn with a panache and a conscious irony which compensates for a lack of insight, while the precision of his satire is for the most part balanced with a perceptive humanity which grants to Lyle and his wife a reality denied to Richard and Juanita whose relationship is never convincingly established. For his inability to distinguish between rhetoric and genuine language has the effect of undermining the credibility of those Negro characters to whom he attributes a pretentious eloquence. Even a minor figure such as Pete Spivey, one of Juanita's suitors, is given the following speech which serves merely to destroy that empathy which he is clearly anxious to establish, 'You take all my attention. My deepest attention . . . I think there's a lot of love in you, Juanita. If you'll let me help you, we can give it to the world. You can't give it to the world until you find a person who can help you—love the world.' (B.C. p. 42.)

Baldwin's chief fault lies, therefore, not so much in his dehumanisation of the whites as in his sentimentalising of the Negroes. Indeed from the heroic endurance of Mother Henry, whose faith in God rests in a certainty that 'It's up to the life in you . . . *That* knows where it comes from, *that* believes in God' (B.C. p. 30) to the sad posturing of Juanita and Meridian he demonstrates his failure to abide by his own strictures. For in his own early essay, 'Everybody's Protest Novel', he had catalogued the faults of a literature which could more truly be seen as sociology. He had attacked its sentimentality and deplored the violence which such literature tended to do to language—an ironical comment on the pretentious dialogue of much of *Blues for Mr. Charlie*. He had then accused the protest novel of 'overlooking, denying, evading'[1] man's complexity, again an accusation which could be justly applied to his own treatment not only of the white townspeople but also of Juanita and indeed Richard himself. Baldwin's essay closes with his attack on the fruitless rage of Wright's *Native Son* which provoked the breach between them which was to persist until Wright's death. Yet as we have seen Richard's life is as much 'defined by his hatred'[2] as was Bigger Thomas's and if he becomes conscious of a more meaningful existence this awareness is never clearly motivated neither does it destroy the determinism which leads him to his death. So that Baldwin's play matches with disturbing precision his own definition of sterile protest literature. In the words of a *Times Literary Supplement* review *Blues for Mr. Charlie* 'is a 1930's sociological play which contains the "right" information and the "right" accusatory attitudes towards poor whites and Southern justice but lacks insights into prejudice and ability to create character beyond stereotypes.'[3]

[1] *Notes of a Native Son*, p. 21.
[2] *Ibid.*, p. 27.
[3] Anon., 'New Light on the Invisible', *The Times Literary Supplement*, Nov. 25, 1965, p. 1049.

In an earlier play, *Amen Corner*, written ten years before *Blues for Mr. Charlie* and yet to be published, Baldwin had attained to that same sense of objectivity and universality which he evidences in *Another Country*. Less squarely centred on the racial conflict it evidences something of that vital compassion which is to be found in Lorraine Hansberry's work. Margaret, the pastor of a storefront church in Harlem, like Miller's Quentin propounds the need for a love which can encompass every aspect of the human condition and still endure. 'I'm just now finding out what it means to love the Lord. It ain't all in the singing and the shouting. It ain't all in the reading of the Bible. It ain't even in runnin' all over everybody trying to get to heaven. To love the Lord is to love all his children—all of them.—And suffer and rejoice with them and never count the cost.'[1] Between this play and *Blues for Mr. Charlie*, however, came the increasing violence of the Civil Rights movement and above all the death of Medgar Evans. For as Baldwin has admitted, 'When he died, something entered into me which I cannot describe, but it was then that I resolved that nothing under heaven would prevent me from getting this play done.' (B.C. p. 11.) It is clear, then, that the war between his social and artistic responsibilities has become more intense. It is equally clear that the rage which he had felt at the death of his friend has betrayed him into the over-simplifications of a sociological literature which he had always consciously avoided.

Nevertheless something of Baldwin's failure in this play stems from his inability to master the dramatic form. Like Dos Passos in the thirties he was drawn to the theatre because it offered a platform for his views and a direct rapport between writer and audience not available to the novelist. Here he could publicly work out a compromise between the contradictory responsibilities of the Negro writer. The crude monologues of the third act of *Blues for Mr. Charlie* highlight, however, the difficulty of the novelist turned playwright. Denied the opportunity to develop character and motive at length he is easily tempted into radical simplification. Certainly Baldwin, failing to master the necessity for a revelation derived out of action, reverts to the embarassing expedient of 'freezing' the action while the truth of a character's inner struggle is made apparent through the capsule comments against which Gelber had rebelled.

Herbert Hill, in his anthology of Negro writers, *Black Voices* (1964),

[1] Thomas Thompson, 'A Burst of Negro Drama', *Life*, May 29th, 1964, p. 62B.

sees contemporary American Negro writing as characterised by an attempt to break out of racial parochialism and engage itself with those pre-occupations which have seized the attention of modern writers. Certainly both Ralph Ellison's and James Baldwin's strength lies in the fact that they have fought against the simplicities of protest fiction and that they have succeeded in establishing the Negro experience as of immediate relevance to a society concerned with the problems of identity and alienation, for Ellison shares with Baldwin a belief that 'people who want to write sociology shouldn't write novels'.[1] Baldwin's failure to approach this same level of artistic responsibility in his drama, however, is an indication both of the greater discipline demanded by drama and of his own increasing personal commitment to the Civil Rights struggle. As with Lawson, Gold and Dos Passos in the thirties his commitment to one section of humanity tends to betray his sense of the universal. Arthur Miller has pointed out that drama 'rises in stature and intensity in proportion to the weight of its application to all manner of men. It gains its weight as it deals with more and more of the whole man, not either his subjective or his social life alone.'[2] For all the ambiguous fury of *Blues for Mr. Charlie*, however, we still have Baldwin's own assurance that he recognises the need for the artist to keep a 'heart free of hatred'. In a statement which does much to explain that tension which underlies his play he describes both his perception of the ambiguity of the Negro's situation and his own sense of personal reponsibility. It is incidentally a declaration which makes clear that distinction between confrontation and commitment which is the fundamental division between the two main movements in contemporary American drama:

> 'It began to seem that one would have to hold in the mind forever two ideas which seemed to be in opposition. The first idea was acceptance, the acceptance, totally without rancour, of life as it is, and men as they are: in the light of this idea, it goes without saying that injustice is a commonplace. But this did not mean that one could be complacent, for the second idea was equal power: that one must never, in one's own life, accept these injustices as commonplace but must fight them with all one's strength. The fight begins, however, in the heart and it now had been laid to my charge to keep my own heart free of hatred and despair.'[3]

[1] *Black Voices*, p. 4.
[2] 'On Social Plays', p. 4.
[3] *Notes of a Native Son*, pp. 108-9.

8

LeRoi Jones

LeRoi Jones, poet, music critic, editor and dramatist believes passionately, like Lorraine Hansberry, in the need for commitment, 'A writer must have a point of view, or he cannot be a good writer. He must be standing somewhere in the world, or else he is not one of *us*, and his commentary is of little value.' There is an essential difference, however, between the commitment which he envisages and that propounded by Miss Hansberry. Where *Raisin in the Sun* and *The Sign in Sidney Brustein's Window* stress the need for compassion and find in love a possible source of regeneration, Jones rejects this as a pretty conceit having little relevance to the real world as seen by an oppressed minority, ' "People should love each other" sounds like Riis Park at sundown. It has very little meaning to the world at large.' In the place of compassion he stresses the need for violent action. Instead of Hansberry's emphasis on the need 'to care' he places his faith in the immediate need for 'Cutting throats!'[1]

His first play, *The Toilet*,[2] a poor effort which to date has only been published in a small-circulation magazine, establishes the pattern of a quasi-ritualistic violence inflicted on representatives of the white world which recurs in both of his later plays. First performed in 1962 by the Playwright's Unit of the Actors' Studio, it is a barely stageable homosexual fantasy in which the setting is a urinal and the theme the sexual nature of violence and the degradation of the white world. Karolis, a white homosexual is beaten up and left on the floor of the lavatory in which the entire action takes place. The play has little to recommend it and serves merely to demonstrate that even in this, his first dramatic effort, Jones was already showing evidence of the obsessions which continue to mar his work.

It is interesting to note that the young Brecht too had had no patience with the doctrine of love. Wholeheartedly committed, he believed not only that change was necessary but that in pursuit of this change

---

[1] LeRoi Jones, 'Brief Reflections on Two Hot Shots', *Kulture*, III, xii (Winter, 1963), pp. 3-5.

[2] LeRoi Jones, 'The Toilet', *Kulture*, III, ix (Spring, 1963), pp. 25-39.

violence became sanctified. Joan Dark, in his *Saint Joan of the Stock-yards*, at first a spiritualised evangeliser, is awakened to the realities of life and wholeheartedly embraces the need for violence:

> 'Therefore he who says down here that there is a God,
> And yet no God is visible,
> And being visible will not help them—
> His head should be beaten upon the paving-stones
> Till he die like a dog . . .
> . . . For
> Only violence helps, where violence reigns—and
> Only men can help where there are men.'[1]

Nevertheless Brecht was never entirely happy in his mind about this and, as Martin Esslin has pointed out, while on the one hand he saw the failure of the Paris Commune as stemming from a refusal to apply violence in its full terror he could never escape the conviction that force debases those who use it. Thus the same man who had made his heroine embrace violence was also capable of writing a poem in praise of non-violence:

> '. . . the movement of the softest water will
> Conquer in time the powerful hard stone,
> You understand: hard things are overcome . . .'[2]

Brecht had been intensely aware that in fighting fire with fire he was in danger of compromising himself but he sought to justify his attitude, and the sombre reality of the political situation in Eastern Europe, by seeing the present in the context of the future. In a poem, 'To Posterity' he stated this dilemma—a dilemma of which Jones, who is guilty of similar moral simplifications, seems largely unaware:

> 'For we know
> Even the hatred of evil
> Distorts the features,
> And anger over injustice
> Also hoarsens the voice. Alas, we
> Who wanted to prepare the ground for friendliness
> Could not ourselves be friendly . . .'[3]

[1] Eric Bentley, *Brecht: A Choice of Evils* (London, 1959), p. 220.
[2] *Ibid.*, p. 235.
[3] *Ibid.*, p. 61.

Jones's view of the future is not so sanguine, however. Like George Orwell in *1984* (1949) he would say 'If you want a picture of the future, imagine a boot stamping on a human face—forever.'[1] The fear which pervades LeRoi Jones's work is that of a loss of identity—a fear which becomes socially relevant when extended to the scale of racial assimilation. In this context violence functions, as it had in Wright's *Native Son*, as a means of discovering and forging identity. Ralph Ellison, too, who had demonstrated a similar sense of apprehension in *Invisible Man* (1952), had also seen violence as a positive act of self-definition, 'You ache with the need to convince yourself that you do exist in the real world, that you're a part of all the sound and anguish, and you strike out with your fists, you curse and you swear to make them recognise you.'[2] Thus while the mainstream of American drama has turned to a form of affirmation it is clear that the tone of Negro literature remains largely one of revolt and that Camus' aphorism, 'I *rebel*—therefore we *exist*',[3] can be taken as its basic premise. Nevertheless it soon becomes apparent that the positive act of rebellion, which had led Ellison and Wright to ascribe a purposeful function to violence, degenerates with Jones into a self-indulgent anger. For his is a sensitivity, created by the extremes of racial guilt and discrimination, which can see no middle ground between man as victim and man as rebel—no middleground, that is, between Faulkner's Joe Christmas, submitting to the knives and guns of white men and Walker Vessels, in *The Slave*, dominating the white man with his revolver. In this and in his readiness to endorse the stereotype of Negro sexuality he is close to Norman Mailer who, in 'The White Negro', had revealed a similar tendency to polarise human responses, 'One is hip or one is Square ... one is a rebel or one conforms, one is a frontiersman in the Wild West of American night life, or else a Square cell, trapped in the totalitarian tissue of American society, doomed willy-nilly to conform if one is to succeed.'[4] While the violence which emerges as the strongest mark of Jones's work does at times show something of the ambivalence which Brecht had felt, there is an element of unabashed relish in its presentation, particularly in *The Slave* and *The Toilet*, which constantly threatens to undermine its validity both as drama and polemic. Where

---

[1] George Orwell, *1984* (London, 1950), p. 268.
[2] Ralph Ellison, *Invisible Man* (Harmondsworth, 1965), p. 7.
[3] *The Rebel*, p. 28.
[4] Norman Mailer, *Advertisements for Myself* (London, 1961), p. 284.

Brecht's doctrinal harshness had been mitigated by an innate compassion the same cannot be said of Jones's work.

LeRoi Jones's fierce commitment is such that he has felt himself
bound, at times, to attack those who have apparently transcended the
immediate concerns of racial injustice. Accordingly he has been
savagely critical of what he takes to be James Baldwin's egotistical
hedonism, seeing in his work, seemingly, both the beginnings of
assimilation and intellectual precocity, '. . . the *cry*, the spavined whine
and plea of these Baldwins and Abrahams (a South African writer who
had incurred Jones's wrath through speaking of the racial struggle in
that country as a "horrible animal") is sickening beyond belief. Why
should anyone think of these men as individuals? Merely because they
are able to shriek the shriek of a fashionable international body of white
middleclass society . . . Joan of Arc of the cocktail party, is what is
being presented through the writings and postures of men like these.
As if the highest form of compliment the missionaries could receive
was to see their boys making good, On Their Own.' Where Brecht
had mistrusted emotions as a threat to intellectual perception Jones
sees Baldwin's sensitivity as an arrogant declaration of independence
which makes such commitment as appears in his work, mere patronage.
'A writer' he insists, 'is committed to what is real, and not to the
sanctity of his FEELINGS.' While this is a distinction which Kafka or
Lawrence, for example, could not have felt to be a real one it is indicative of Jones's refusal to accept a humanistic interpretation of the racial
situation. What is real is the economic and political history of the
Negro; what is fanciful is the belief that racial friction is a moral failure
which can be corrected by individual soul-searching. As he puts it:

> 'FACT: There is a racial struggle.
> FACT: Any man had better realize what it means. Why there is one.
>   It is the result of *more* than 'misunderstanding'. Money is not
>   simply something one gets for publishing novels, or selling
>   paintings.'[1]

Jones is never able to forget, and insists that his audience should never
forget, the brutal historical facts which have made the Negro in his
fiction as much an outcast from society as Burrough's addicts or
Kerouac's beats. On the death of President Kennedy he wrote a poem
which was hurriedly pasted into the current edition of *Kulture*, a
magazine of which he was a contributing editor. This poem, which

[1] 'Brief Reflections on Two Hot Shots', pp. 2-4.

expresses his sense of cynical disgust, closes with lines which in part account for his refusal to accept anything less than an all-out assault on a problem which he cannot believe will mellow under good intentions:

> From now on we will sit in nightclubs with Jewish millionaires listening to the maudlin political verse of a money narcissist.

> And this will be the payback for our desires.
> For history, like the ringing coin

> that will not bend
> when we bite it.[1]

Yet while he has actively supported Civil Rights Jones's plays boast a simple objective, for, unlike Baldwin, his vision is not of a unified society but rather of a world in which the present order is inverted. In this context his attraction to violence becomes little more than an aspect of revenge while his plays are dedicated less to urging a humanistic commitment than a revolutionary separatism.

Jones's best-known play is *Dutchman* which was the recipient of the ninth annual Obie award for the best American play produced off-Broadway. It opened at the *Cherry Lane Theatre* in New York City on March 24th, 1964. Somewhat in the style of Edward Albee's *The Zoo Story*, *Dutchman* is a parable of human relationships, but these relationships are seen strictly within the context of racial discord. In the same mode as *The Cocktail Party*, *Cards of Identity* and *Tiny Alice*, it is a play, too, which uses the form of an ordered conspiracy as structure.

The setting is a subway coach, 'In the flying underbelly of the city . . . Underground. The subway heaped in modern myth.'[2] Clay, a twenty-year-old Negro, sits in the coach staring blankly out of the window as the train rushes along. When it stops at a station a girl's face appears at the window and as the train starts off she enters the compartment and deliberately sits next to Clay. Lula is a thirty-year-old white woman and it is she who acts as the agent of the conspiracy, as Alice had done in Albee's play. The compulsion under which she acts, a compulsion which leads, again as in Albee's play, to the death of the conspiracy's victim, is explained by the play's title which refers

[1] LeRoi Jones, 'Exaugeral Address', *Kulture*, III, xii (Winter, 1963), facing p. 86.
[2] LeRoi Jones, *Dutchman* and *The Slave* (New York, 1964), p. 3. All future references to *Dutchman* will be abbreviated to 'D' and incorporated into the text.

to the myth of the Flying Dutchman. According to this myth a Dutch captain who, in a storm, had blasphemously declared that he would sail round the Cape if it took him till the Judgement Day, is taken at his word and a curse is laid on him. He is fated to continue sailing for ever with a crew of living-dead who will obey his orders but who never speak and have no will of their own. The progress of *Dutchman* has a similar determinism and it gradually becomes apparent that the drama which is enacted is a ritual with which Lula is entirely familiar and which will be repeated in the future just as surely as it has been in the past.

The play, as Jones has Lula pointedly emphasise at a later stage, is essentially about Clay's manhood. It is concerned, that is, with the sexual, moral and economic implications of Negro-white relations, with the castration and corruption of the Negro male by the white world as the dominant theme. As the setting suggests this is Jones's attempt to describe the reality which he sees as lying under the surface.

Lula deliberately seeks Clay's company, admitting to her intention in a manner which combines the patronage of the white liberal with the implication of Negro sexual attractiveness, 'I even got into this train, going some other way than mine. Walked down the aisle . . . searching you out.' (D. p. 7.) Where Baldwin had been at pains to deny this cliché of Negro sexuality, as he had the suggestion of intellectual and anthropological inferiority, LeRoi Jones appears to endorse it, seeing it as a vivid contrast to the enervated white world which threatens Negro vitality and virility alike. When Lula offers Clay an apple it marks the obvious beginning of Clay's corruption, a corruption which leads eventually to his death. Indeed it is hardly necessary for her to underline the point herself with the gratuitous information that, 'Eating apples together is always the first step.' (D. p. 11.) It is clear, however, that in a sense Clay's assimilation has already started, for Lula is able to identify the pretentious middle-class background from which he springs. Indeed it is this readiness to be assimilated which makes him an ideal victim.

Like Jerry in *The Zoo Story* Lula tries to provoke Clay into making some positive reaction, a provocation which becomes progressively more violent. She begins by criticising his clothes, '. . . why're you wearing a jacket and tie like that? Did your people ever burn witches or start revolutions over the price of tea? Boy, those narrow-shoulder clothes come from a tradition you ought to feel oppressed by . . . What right do you have wearing a three-button suit and striped tie? Your grandfather was a slave, he didn't go to Harvard.' (D. p. 18.) This incitement intensifies into an attack which is undermined only by the laughter which follows it, 'Who do you think you are now? . . . I bet you never once thought you were a black nigger.' (D. p. 19.) Clay is stunned but after his initial reaction he '*quickly tries to appreciate the humor*' (D. p. 19) and thus not lose face or be forced to abandon his stolid middle-class stance. When he fails to rise to the bait Lula relapses temporarily into accepting the implications of his stance—implications in which clearly neither she nor Jones place any faith, 'we'll pretend the people cannot see you. That is, the citizens. And that you are free of your own history. And I am free of my history.' (D. p. 21.)

In effect the attack on Clay is an expression of Jones's contempt for the assimilationist. Clay becomes the victim of his scorn precisely because he (like Baldwin, if we are to believe Jones) had adopted the values of 'a fashionable international body of white middleclass society.' He is attempting to live, as Jones unfairly suggests Baldwin does, 'free from such "ugly" things as "the racial struggle".'[1] When Lula's first attempt to break through this veneer fails she resorts, as Jerry had done in *The Zoo Story*, to a parable. She describes a party at which she predicts Clay will engage in egotistical conversation, 'You'll go around talking to young men about your mind, and to old men about your plans' (D. p. 22)—a significant vision in view of Jones's dismissal of Baldwin as an emotional and intellectual egotist 'rattling off sensitivity ratios at parties.'[2] Lula emphasises the solipsistic nature of the society which she represents and to which Clay aspires. It is a society whose preoccupation is with self-indulgent and priggish intellectual exercises shaped by the vicious dictates of fashionable conformism. She describes how they would, 'make fun of the queers . . . meet a Jewish Buddhist and flatten his conceits over some very pretentious coffee.' (D. p. 23.) When she describes the intercourse which would climax the imaginary evening it is indicative of Clay's complete acceptance of this sterile society. Yet while Clay appears wholly assimilated he remains a threat precisely because his adoption of middle-class white standards is merely a pose. Underneath there is a threat of violence. It is the strain of this sublimation which Lula detects and from which her hatred springs. For while the white society is in a state of stasis, clearly defined in relation to itself, the black world remains in a state of flux. It is just this shifting relationship which is the basis of white fear and hatred, 'Change

[1] 'Brief Reflections on Two Hot Shots', p. 4.
[2] *Ibid.*, pp. 2-3.

change change. Till, shit, I don't know you . . . you change. And things work on you till you hate them.' (D. pp. 28-9.)[1] The same contrast between the white and Negro world is made by Gelber in *The Apple* in which Ace, a Negro, sees change as an endemic part of his nature, 'You want me to be the same all the time. But change is my nature.'[1]

Lula tries to transform her vision of Clay's complete assimilation into fact. She tries to induce him to join her in a quasi-orgasmic dance which would parallel the intercourse which she had forecast. When she fails in this she reverts to the provocation of the first scene in an attempt to make him commit himself to some act understandable to the white world. Finally her jibes strike home when she taunts him with showing the passivity of an Uncle Tom, 'Uncle Thomas Wooly-Head. With old white matted mane . . . Old Tom. Let the white man hump his ol' mama, and he jes' shuffle off in the woods and hide his gentle gray head . . . You're afraid of white people. And your father was. Uncle Tom Big Lip!' (D. pp. 32-3.) Clay drags her to her seat and slaps her *'as hard as he can, across the mouth. LULA'S head bangs against the back of the seat. When she raises it again, CLAY slaps her again.'* (D. p. 33.) With this act of violence Clay asserts himself for the first time.

While up to this point he had played a passive role, reacting to Lula's lead, he now dominates the scene with the sheer force of his physical and vocal strength. He 'clubs' a drunk who tries to interfere and emits a sudden scream 'frightening the whole coach'. Suddenly the enervated Negro, whom Lula had attacked as a 'dirty white man' unleashes a tirade which silences the insistent white woman and which reveals the 'pure heart, the pumping black heart' (D. p. 34) which lies beneath the surface even of the assimilationist. In this violent mood he explains that his middle-class manner, his own poetry and the jazz which the white world hears but fails to understand serve as a means of sublimating the violence which alone would constitute sanity for the Negro, 'A whole people of neurotics, struggling to keep from being sane. And the only thing that would cure the neurosis would be your murder.' (D. p. 35.) Beneath the surface, behind the metaphors of jazz and the blues are the hard facts which divide the Negro and white worlds, the FACTS which Jones had insisted as lying at the very core of the Negro dilemma, 'Money. Power. Luxury.' (D. p. 35.) Yet for all this moment of control, in which the reality of Negro/white rela-

[1] Jack Gelber, *The Apple* (New York, n.d.), p. 60.

tions is thrown contemptuously and violently into Lula's face, Clay retreats from this position. Suddenly weary he rejects this brutality and withdraws, as Jones had accused Baldwin of doing, behind his own pose of self-absorbtion, 'Ahhh. Shit. But who needs it? I'd rather be a fool. Insane. Safe with my words, and no deaths, and clean, hard thoughts'. (D. p. 35.) In doing so he delivers himself into the control of the white world and his death follows almost immediately. He is stabbed twice by Lula. The other passengers, who fill the role of the living dead in the Dutchman legend (morally and spiritually dead in this case as well as physically moribund), throw the body out of the compartment. When this has been done Lula takes a notebook out and makes a quick note. Then another Negro boy enters the train and it is obvious that the whole procedure will be repeated for this is a process which Jones sees as an inevitable consequence of uncomplaining assimilation.

Jones's insistence on the irrevocability of history, expressed in the bitter poem which had followed Kennedy's death, is here clearly demonstrated in racial terms. Lula displays the traditional ambivalence of the slave owner. She is at the same time attracted and repelled by the man whom she describes as 'an escaped nigger' who has 'crawled through the wire and made tracks to my side'. (D. p. 29.) If miscegenation is the central fear of the southern bigot, however, it is also, to Jones, the core of the Negro's degradation. For in short his play challenges the whole proposition of integration. The question which he is asking is, 'integration into what?' Western rationalism, 'the great intellectual legacy of the white man', has in his eyes led merely to the rationalisation of repression and violence.

The lesson which the play bears for the white man is that the acceptance of 'half-white trustees late of the subject peoples' devitalised, with 'no more blues, except the very old ones,[1] and not a watermelon in sight' implies a definite threat to all the world. For when the 'great missionary heart will have triumphed, and all of those ex-coons will be stand-up Western men' (D. p. 36) then that same self-justifying rationalism will be used to reverse the roles. For the Negro the danger of assimilation has already been made clear in Clay's death. Yet for all

[1] This is another veiled attack on the white liberal. In his review of a record called, *A History of Jazz* (*Kulture*, III, ix, Spring, 1963, p. 90) he describes as *Moldy Figs* 'that breed of American liberal who says that jazz, "Real Jazz", died with the Negro's mass migration north'.

his passive conformity he had demonstrated a potential which represents Jones's own simplified solution. This potential exists as the threat of violence. For Clay could have been the violent messiah come to redeem his people not with the message of love but with the sword. It is a potential too which Lula recognises when she speaks to him with an ambiguous cynicism, 'My Christ. My Christ . . . May the people accept you as the ghost of the future. And love you, that you might not kill them when you can.' (D. pp. 20-1.) While this potential is not realised here it is in his next play, *The Slave*, which is concerned with a literal Negro revolt.

The Slave is in essence a dramatisation of what Norman Mailer has suggested as an inevitable conflict. With the emergence of the Negro he had foreseen a violent revolt against the restrictions of white conformity and against the effete antisexuality which is paradoxically the foundation of white power. 'A time of violence, new hysteria, confusion and rebellion will then be likely to replace the time of conformity.' Like Jones he saw this as creating a crucial pressure on the white liberal for if he could accept this new and violent manifestation of nonconformity and vital protest then it could become incorporated 'as a colourful figure in the tapestry'. If he could not accept this violence, however, the alternative lay, to his mind, in the collapse of liberal sentiment before the insistent facts of Negro emergence. '. . . if this is not the reality, and the economic, the social, the psychological, and finally the moral crises accompanying the rise of the Negro should prove insupportable then a time is coming when every political guidepost will be gone, and millions of liberals will be faced with political dilemmas they have so far succeeded in avoiding, and with a view of human nature they do not wish to accept.'[1]

The Slave, first presented at *St. Mark's Playhouse*, New York in December 1964, is described by Jones as a fable. As such it represents his attempt to circumvent what Pirandello, Artaud and Beckett had seen as the fundamental flaw of the theatre—the arbitrary and imprecise nature of language. In an article entitled 'Expressive Language' he enlarges on this distrust of formal language, pointing out that 'pluralistic' America is particularly susceptible to misunderstandings deriving from a dissimilarity of ethnic background. In this article, too, can be seen the origin of his compulsive use of jargon for he points out here what he sees as the 'terrifying risk' which the bourgeois Negro accepts in trying to become fluent in what he contemptuously calls 'the

[1] *Advertisement for Myself*, p. 300.

jargon of power'.[1] Yet unlike Brown he does not dispense with language or transform it into a ritualised sub-structure of intonation and timbre but relies, like Gelber and Albee, on what he calls a 'meta-language'[2]—the tangental communication of the parable. The parable which he presents here is an apocalyptic vision seen in purely racial terms. *The Slave* is in essence an extension of the conflict of *Dutchman* to what Jones clearly sees as its logical conclusion. 'Discovering racially the funds of the universe. Discovering the last image of the thing. As the sky when the moon is broken.' (s. p. 45.)

The play is both a prophecy and a warning. It is a desperate plea for the need of the individual to re-assess his stance in a situation of which the logical conclusion is racial warfare, '. . . ideas are still in the world. They need judging. I mean, they don't come in that singular or wild, that whatever they are, just because they're beautiful and brilliant . . . just because they're *right* . . . doesn't mean anything. The very rightness stinks a lotta times.' (s. p. 44.) Despite a further indulgence in his particular forte for a gratuitous violence inflicted on his white characters *The Slave* does progress considerably beyond the oversimplifications of *Dutchman*. For when Walker Vessels, who in the main body of the play is the leader of a Negro revolt, delivers a prologue dressed as a field-slave, he condemns that which 'passes as whatever thing we feel is too righteous to question, too deeply felt to deny' as 'a deadly filth' (s. p. 44)—a considerable advance over the dogmatic assumptions of *Dutchman*. For in that play, as we have seen, he was content to destroy one cliché but to replace it with another. If he attacked the deep-rooted association between black and evil he did so only to recall that the curse of corruption and death derived from a white Eve. Here, however, he is not merely concerned with the injustice of the racial situation but, ostensibly at least, also with that intellectual slavery which is an aspect of blind dogmatism. For both the white liberal, for whom Jones retains his complete contempt, and the Negro racist, who espouses much of Jones' own philosophy, are betrayed by the narrowness of their own viewpoints, both evidence a 'stupid longing not to know . . . which is automatically fulfilled . . . Automatically makes us killers or foot-dragging celebrities at the core

[1] LeRoi Jones, 'Expressive Language', *Kulture*, III, xii (Winter, 1963), p. 80.
[2] LeRoi Jones, *Dutchman* and *The Slave* (New York, 1964), p. 45. All future references to *The Slave* will be abbreviated to 's' and incorporated into the text.

of any filth.' (s. pp. 43-4.) For all his calls for objectivity, however, the sheer force of his commitment and even his hatred once again takes possession of his drama and the play fails to realise the potential suggested in the prologue.

The play's action centres around the conflict between Walker Vessels, the forty-year-old leader of a Negro rebellion, and Bradford Easley, a white university professor. Easley's wife, Grace, had formerly been married to Vessels but the increasing virulence of his campaign for the overthrow of the whites had finally driven her to leave him, taking their two daughters with her. Now, with his troops bombarding the city, he has come to their apartment.

This confrontation epitomises LeRoi Jones's conception of the cause and effect of the racial situation, for it is the failure of Easley's liberalism which has transformed the field-slave into the rebel. Unlike Lorraine Hansberry, who places no faith in political activism, Jones accuses the liberal of a political disengagement stemming from pre-war disenchantment. Faced with the brutal reality of a society which has sanctioned oppression and inequity Easley has limited his protest to generalised declarations of democratic principles. As Walker points out, 'You never did anything concrete to avoid what's going on now. Your sick liberal lip service to whatever was the least filth. Your high aesthetic disapproval of the political. Letting the sick ghosts of the thirties strangle whatever chance we had.' (s. p. 74.) Walker casts doubt not only on the effectiveness of the liberal's stance however but also on its integrity. For under the ineffectualness he suspects there to lie nothing more solid than pity and contempt. Indeed under pressure Grace slips easily into the clichés of white supremacy in an outburst which is reminiscent of *All God's Chillun Got Wings*. She calls him a 'nigger murderer' (s. p. 54) and begs him to leave before he kills 'another white person'. (s. p. 55.) Nevertheless it is the sterility of the contemporary liberal more than anything else which Walker blames for the revolt. He himself had once believed in the efficacy and significance of liberal humanism but its complete irrelevance to the practical world had driven him into violence, 'you all accuse me,' he insists 'not understanding that what you represent, you, my wife, all our old intellectual cut-throats, was something that was going to die anyway. One way or another. You'd been used too often, backed off from reality too many times.' (s. p. 75.) This dissociation from reality which disqualifies the liberal as an effective force also destroys him, in Walker's eyes, as an artist. Speaking of a liberal friend who, in revulsion from idealistic politics had claimed to hate those who wanted to change the world, he repeats what is in essence the Marxist contempt for a literature removed from the actual process of life. 'I knew that you had moved too far away from the actual meanings of life . . . into some lifeless cocoon of pretended intellectual and emotional achievement, to really be able to see the world again.' (s. pp. 75-6)—an echo, once more, of his denunciation of Baldwin. He identifies the poetry of such a man as 'Tired elliptical little descriptions of what he could see out of the window.' (s. p. 76.)

Walker himself is the realisation of that potential which had been embodied in the person of Clay, in *Dutchman*. He is no longer a poet, as Clay had been, for in the place of poetry he had discovered the 'sanity' of violence. He shuns both the egocentricity of the artist and the self-justification of the social critic. 'The aesthete came along after all the things that really formed me. It was the easiest weight to shed. And I couldn't be merely a journalist . . . a social critic. No social protest . . . right is in the act! And the act itself has some place in the world . . . it makes some place for itself.' (s. p. 75.) The intention of the rebellion which Vessels leads is a brutally simple one. When Easley points out that all that it will accomplish will be a change in the complexion of tyranny Walker insists that this is essentially his purpose. For he has no illusions that he is introducing 'love or beauty' into the world. He is fighting to seize the power which is the source of their oppression. 'The point is' he insists 'that you had your chance, darling, now these other folks have theirs.' (s. p. 73.) Yet he recognises the ugliness of the concept. Here indeed is the crux of the play, for given the failure of a liberal white world to take effective action, rebellion seems inevitable. If the whites, who hold the power, cannot be persuaded to relinquish it then the Negro is faced with only two possible alternatives. Either, like Clay, he can accept a gradual assimilation and loss of identity, or he can rebel. While Jones's contempt for docile assimilation is complete he does show here an ambivalence in his attitude which he would claim stems directly from the nature of the Negro's dilemma. Walker cannot remain neutral yet he admits to dissatisfaction with a solution which is in essence merely an inversion of the problem. Nevertheless in admitting to this dissatisfaction he cannot suppress a contentment with the fact that the onus for action now lies with his own race. When Easley taunts him with the arbitrary cruelty of his solution he agrees but traces its origin to that liberal failure which Mailer had anticipated: 'I know. I know. But what else you got, champ?

What else you got? I remember too much horseshit from the other side for you to make much sense. Too much horseshit. The cruelty of it, don't you understand, now? The complete ugly horseshit cruelty of it is that there doesn't have to be a change. It'll be up to individuals on that side, just as it was supposed to be up to individuals on this side.' (s. p. 74.)

LeRoi Jones' pose of objectivity is severely undermined, however, by the relish with which he once again describes the physical violence which Walker inflicts on the white liberal. In a stage direction, which is reminiscent of Clay's moment of supremacy in *Dutchman*, he describes the action. Walker: '*Slaps EASLEY across the face with the back of his left hand, pulling the gun out of his right and shoving it as hard as he can against EASLEY'S stomach. EASLEY slumps, and the cruelty in WALKER'S face at this moment also frightens GRACE.*' (s. p. 52.) When the professor tries to attack Walker he shoots him and watches him grovel on the floor. telling him to 'just die, quietly . . . No elegence. You just die quietly and stupidly. Like niggers do.' (s. pp. 80-1.) Once again Jones falls back on the stereotypes which he had affirmed in *Dutchman*. Easley, the white liberal, is by implication a homosexual who is no match for the Negro who has given his wife two children and who dominates the stage with his phallic gun. This use of violence as a virtual substitute for sexuality has been identified by Baldwin as a mark of a great deal of Negro literature. 'In most of the novels written by Negroes until today . . . there is a great space where sex ought to be; and what usually fills this space is violence.'[1] Baldwin traces this largely gratuitous violence to its source in rage and desperation. Yet while he regrets this inartistic bitterness which, particularly in the case of Richard Wright, could be seen to militate against didactic purpose, he is not so far removed from the sensibility which produced it as to fail to understand its genesis. 'And who has not dreamed of violence?' he asks, 'That fantastical violence which will drown in blood, wash away in blood, not only generation upon generation of horror, but which will also release one from the individual horror, carried everywhere in the heart.'[2] This, then, is in effect an accurate description of Jones's plays which are, at base, revenge fantasies—public rites of purgation in which the audience is invited to participate.

[1] *Nobody Knows my Name*, p. 154.
[2] *Ibid.*, p. 174.

Arthur Koestler, in his book *The Yogi and the Commissar* (1945),[1] makes a distinction which underlines the difference between Lorraine Hansberry and LeRoi Jones. The yogi believes in change from within while the commissar believes in change from without. Hansberry's commitment is basically to the need for a change in human values. Like Dickens she sees the final cure not so much in political action or even social agitation as in the need for compassion and understanding. From this derives the need to transcend history. To Jones there is little meaning in such a solution. Like the commissar he believes in the need for revolution and for direct political action. In this context history becomes the justification for change. The one sees salvation as lying with the saint and the other with the revolutionary. Eric Bentley, in applying this touchstone to the work of Brecht and Sartre, had rejected its severity for in that case it had indicated a difference in approach rather than an absolute divergence of intention.[2] So here Hansberry, as Bentley says of Sartre, comes to the collectivity via the individual. Yet if the yogi is an oversimplified image to apply to Hansberry's work, the commissar is a painfully precise metaphor of Jones's rebel. For the change which he seeks lies purely in outward form and is divorced from the fundamental engagement which could alone give it a moral as well as a sociological dimension. The alienation of Jones's rebel is in essence spurious. Far from dissociating himself from the corruptions of the dominant society his aim is to join it on his own terms. The change which he would force on that society is not a moral but purely a structural one. Slavery remains intact except that its victim is of a different pigmentation. Where once it had been the black woman who had been violated by the white man and who, in time, had her children taken from her now, in *The Slave*, the situation is reversed.

LeRoi Jones, like Burroughs and Kerouac, confers on his 'outsiders' a mystique which makes them in essence a privileged group. Diana Trilling, in an essay on *Who's Afraid of Virginia Woolf?* complained of the same weakness in Albee's work. She sensed 'a certain cozy sense of cultural superiority because I was "in" on Albee's idiom'.[3] Salinger's stories had provided a similar sense of exclusion to Mary McCarthy. While this seems a specious argument in the case of Albee, whose wit and idiom are not nearly as restricted as Diana Trilling implies, it is

[1] Arthur Koestler, *The Yogi and the Commissar* (London, 1945).
[2] *The Playwright as Thinker*, p. 230.
[3] Diana Trilling, *Claremont Essays* (London, 1965), p. 218.

clear that it can with justice be applied to Jones. There is a definitive structure of personal likes and dislikes which dictates the moral emphasis of his play. The white world is characterised as flaccid and dying—concerned with the Negro merely as an extension of a self-justifying and frankly anaemic liberalism. The symbols of this world are, on the one hand, the 'innocent white liberal made fierce by homo-sexuality'[1] and on the other the white woman powerfully attracted by Negro sexuality but harbouring always a deeper hatred. Even within the Negro world there are lines to be drawn—lines which in essence are not fundamentally different from those which would be accepted by a white racist, for he reserves a special contempt for those who choose to become a part of a supra-racial culture. In the terms of both of his major plays his approbation is reserved for those who remain actively aware of historical truths and the need for racial pride; alert alike to the facts of oppression and the need to maintain a separate culture and identity. Language becomes a sign of membership in this group—a gesture of rejection as powerful but ultimately as self-defeating as the jargon of a fading Beat movement. Nor are these personal biases always entirely integrated into the body of his play. His casual dismissal of all those outside of the inner circle of committed savants is less a significant aspect of either Clay's or Lula's character for example than of Jones's own prejudices. For when she speaks contemptuously of 'New Jersey' and 'long walks' and Clay condemns those who try to be 'hip' by 'popping their fingers' to a jazz they cannot understand this is merely a repetition of Jones's own contempt expressed in a prose work called 'The Screamers', '. . . Newark always had a bad reputation, I mean, everybody could pop their fingers. Was hip. Had walks. Knew all about The Apple',[2] It is clear that the language and indeed the plays themselves are seen as a weapon. They represent a declaration of disaffiliation reminiscent of Kerouac's *On The Road* (1957) and Ginsburg's 'Howl'. Yet with their rigid categorisation, their justification of the stereotype they represent a blunt weapon and an unconvincing declaration. By making the white race bear the curse which had once been the burden of the black race he has merely returned blow for blow. Baldwin's comments on the failure of the social novel are equally applicable to Jones's drama, 'The failure of the protest novel lies in its rejection of life, the human being, the denial of

---

[1] 'Brief Reflections on Two Hot Shots', p. 12.
[2] LeRoi Jones, ed., *The Moderns* (London, 1965), p. 294.

his beauty, dread, power, in its insistence that it is his categorisation alone which is real and which cannot be transcended.'[1]

It is ironical that in attacking Baldwin, as a writer more concerned with his own sensibility than with the social dilemma of the Negro, he should himself dwell so much on his own sensibility. For the subject of *Dutchman* and *The Slave* is less the actual plight of the Negro, about which we learn practically nothing, than the difficulties and dilemmas of the Negro writer. The poet, the social critic and the Negro activist are at war with one another. For while on the one hand he demands a literature of commitment, vigorously declaring itself, on the other hand he says that a poem 'can be made out of any feeling' and that a poet—someone, that is, with a 'tempered sensibility'—should be able to write about anything at all and make it into 'something really beautiful'.[2] This same duality is observable in his own work and while the plays, as we have seen, tend to be savagely tied to the Negro/white conflict, his poems frequently attain to an objectivity and universality denied his drama.

In common with most didactic writers Jones is something of an artistic pragmatist. The value of an idea or individual life is governed, he writes, by the extent to which it can be said to be 'specific and useful'.[3] From this it follows that value and effectiveness tend to be associated in his mind and emotional response becomes confused with intellectual assent. Thus while his disturbing revenge fantasies provoke a predictably ecstatic response from Negro audiences it is far from clear if this is indicative of their clear perception of his meaning or rather of their conscious participation in a public purgative rite.

Despite the obsessions which continue to undermine the value of his work LeRoi Jones is one of the few Negro playwrights who has shown an interest in and an understanding of the nature and problems of drama itself. For his part Baldwin had clearly demonstrated a failure to master the dramatic mode while Lorraine Hansberry's plays remain, stylistically, typical products of Broadway naturalism. Where she does experiment in *The Sign in Sidney Brustein's Window* this seems an arbitrary device dictated less by the logic of the dramatist than by the whim of the poet. While LeRoi Jones is in no sense an innovator, however, he does demonstrate a mastery of dramatic technique which reveals a genuine potentiality. The technique which he uses is essentially

[1] *Notes of a Native Son*, p. 28.
[2] *The Sullen Art*; interviews by David Ossman (New York, 1963), p. 79.
[3] 'Brief Reflections on Two Hot Shots'. p. 3.

that employed by Albee and before him by Durrenmatt and Brecht. The 'metalanguage' which is his attempt to transcend the barrier between individual perception and artistic intention is his endeavour to express something 'not included here'. (s. p. 45.) It is, as Easley says of Walker's previous work, in *The Slave*, 'ritual drama'. (s. p. 56.) Resting in myth and structured on the parable, as is Brecht's *The Caucasian Chalk Circle*, Durrenmatt's *The Visit* (1956) and Albee's *The Zoo Story*, his plays, and especially *Dutchman*, attempt to communicate through metaphor and hyperbole. Yet it is precisely his failure to communicate which ironically constitutes the greatest weakness of his work. For while Eric Bentley has rightly said that clarity is the first requisite of didacticism both of Jones's major plays flaunt their own kind of obscurity. The esoteric jargon of *Dutchman* combines with a mystifying and false profundity to subvert easy communication. Similarly in *The Slave* the ponderous pretension of the prologue, 'I am much older than I look . . . or maybe much younger . . . [Significant pause]' (s. p. 44), is merely a foretaste of the confusion which surrounds Grace's children who may or may not be dead and who may or may not have been killed by Walker. Yet even this speciousness does not entirely detract from drama which balances pretension with brutal power. Jones's is a talent lacking in discipline and controlled by a desperate commitment yet he is clearly aware of the real potentialities of the theatre. For if *Dutchman* lacks both the depth and control of Albee's *The Zoo Story* it does reveal an understanding not only of dramatic technique but also of the need for the modern theatre to examine the roots of its own power.

9

Lorraine Hansberry

LORRAINE HANSBERRY'S first play, *A Raisin in the Sun*, was awarded the New York Drama Critics' Prize for 1959-60. For all its sympathy, humour and humanity, however, it remains disappointing —the more so when compared with the achievement of her second play, *The Sign in Sidney Brustein's Window*. Yet it passes considerably beyond the trivial music-hall dramas of Langston Hughes and does something to capture the sad dilemma of Negro and white alike without lapsing into the bitter hatred of Richard Wright or the psychodrama of O'Neill's *All God's Chillun Got Wings*. Its weakness is essentially that of much of Broadway naturalism. It is an unhappy crossbreed of social protest and re-assuring resolution. Trying to escape the bitterness of Wright, Hansberry betrays herself into radical simplification and ill-defined affirmation. Like Saul Bellow she senses the validity of affirmation before she can justify it as a logical implication of her play's action.

A Raisin in the Sun is set in Chicago's Southside 'sometime between World War II and the present'. The Younger family live in a roach-infested building so overcrowded that they have to share the bathroom with another family while Travis the only son of Walter and Ruth Younger, has to sleep on a sofa in the living room. Yet the central factor of the play is not poverty but indignity and self-hatred. The survival of the family is dependent on their ability to accomodate themselves to the white world. Walter works as a chauffeur while his wife works as a maid. To both of them accommodation to the point of servility is required for the very right to work. James Baldwin has indicated the cost to the individual of accepting one's life on another's terms, 'one of the prices an American Negro pays—or can pay—for what is called his "acceptance" is a profound, almost ineradicable self hatred'.[1] *A Raisin in the Sun* is primarily a study of such self-hatred, emphasised here, as Baldwin saw it emphasised in an article called 'Alas, Poor Richard', by a confrontation between the enervated American Negro and the dignified self-confidence of the African.

[1] *Nobody Knows my Name*, p. 175.

There is a story by Richard Wright called 'Man of all Work' in which a Negro man dresses up as a woman in order to get work as a cook. His action emphasises what Baldwin has called 'the demoralisation of the Negro male'[1] when his position as breadwinner is necessarily usurped by the woman. It is this agony with which Walter Younger lives. He has been desexualised and his dignity has been crushed. It is this knowledge which underlies his bitter disgust and self-contempt. 'I'm thirty-five years old; I been married eleven years and I got a boy who sleeps in the living room—and all I got to give him is stories about how rich white people live'.[2] When a ten thousand dollar insurance matures on his father's death he has to watch the money pass into his mother's hands—a final blow to both his dreams and his manhood. '*You* the head of this family. You run our lives like you want to.' (R.S. p. 165.)

Richard Wright, sensing the emasculation of the Negro trapped in the physical ghetto of Chicago and the cage of self-contempt alike, had seen in violence both the Negro's attempt to re-assert himself and an expression of white oppression. Bigger Thomas, who kills, decapitates and incinerates a white woman thereby achieves a measure of self-awareness which had previously escaped him. Hansberry's play is set in the same locale. Its sense of desperation is the same. Walter Younger's emasculation is pushed to the point at which he condones his wife's attempt to secure an abortion. Yet where Wright created in Bigger Thomas a hardening of the stereotype, which was in effect a spring-board for an exegesis of communist doctrine, Hansberry, writing some twenty years later, is concerned with demonstrating human resilience. The gulf between the two writers is in part that dictated by the changing social position of the American Negro but more fundamentally it is indicative of Lorraine Hansberry's belief in the pointlessness of despair and hatred. Indeed Hansberry's play is essentially an attempt to turn Wright's novel on its head. Where he had examined the potential for violence, Hansberry sees this as a potential which once realised can only lead to stasis. Both works start with an alarm-clock ringing in the stifling atmosphere of Chicago's coloured ghetto. Yet whereas Bigger Thomas wakes up to the inexorability of his fate, Walter becomes conscious of the existence of other levels than

[1] *Ibid.*, p. 153.
[2] Lorraine Hansberry, *A Raisin in the Sun, Four Contemporary American Plays*, ed. Bennet Cerf (New York, 1961), p. 115. All future references to this play will be abbreviated to 'R.S.' and incorporated into the text.

the purely material. The sense of urgency presaged by the initial alarm is as much the key-note of Hansberry's play as it is of Wright's novel yet while the alarm functions as a threat in the latter it functions as a promise in the former.

The play's title is taken from a poem by Langston Hughes—a poem which expresses the sense of kinetic energy and tension which underlies the frustrations of the American Negro, an energy which can be turned into violence, self-destruction, despair or genuine realisation:

> What happens to a dream deferred?
> Does it dry up
> Like a raisin in the sun?
> Or fester like a sore—
> And then run?
> Does it stink like rotten meat?
> Or crust and sugar over—
> Like a syrupy sweet?
>
> Maybe it just sags
> Like a heavy load.
>
> *Or does it explode?* (R.S. p. 101.)

The dreams of the Youngers are sharpened and pointed by the indignity and self-hatred which is their racial inheritance. Walter dreams of owning a store and thus becoming independent of the system of which he is the victim, while his sister-in-law, impressed by the need for compassion, wants to become a doctor. Lena Younger, Walter's mother, however, is concerned only with the disintegration of the family. When the money arrives she places a deposit on a new house. The decision drives Walter into a despairing disaffiliation.

Walter Younger's sullen cynicism, which, like Willy Loman's confused mind, grants value only to wealth and power, is balanced by his sister-in-law's passionate belief in the feasibility of change and the need for compassion. Beneatha has a strong sense of racial pride compounded with humanistic commitment. Intensely aware of her racial origins she associates with Asagai, an African student, and steeps herself in the culture of her forbears. When Asagai gives her the nickname Alaiyo, 'one who needs more than bread', it is both an ironical comment on her intensity and an indication that Hansberry's concern is less with the poverty of the Youngers than with the need for spiritual replenishment which can only come with a return of dignity. Yet when Walter

squanders the money which was to have paid for her medical training Beneatha lapses into despair and the compassion which she had shown evaporates as had Ruth's hope and Walters's ambitions. Like Sidney Brustein in Hansberry's second play, forced to confront present reality, she slips into the cant of nihilism. She projects her personal disappointments onto a universal scale and Asagai identifies the questions which obsess her. 'What good is struggle; what good is anything? Where are we all going? And why are we bothering?' (R.S. p. 191.)

The personal and familial crises are finally resolved by the open challenge offered by the white world. Karl Lindner, whose name suggests non-American origins, is the representative of the white community into which the family had planned to move. He offers to buy the house from them at a profit. The insult is delivered with courtesy but it stings Walter into a response which simultaneously gives him back his dignity and commits him to an involvement which he had sought to escape. Thus in a sense this is a fulfilment of Asagai's prophesy. In speaking of his own political future in Africa he had said, 'They who might kill me even . . . actually replenish me!' (R.S. p. 192.)

Yet while leaving the Youngers committed to 'new levels of struggle'[1] Miss Hansberry brings about this partial resolution through something of a specious *deus ex machina*. Although she is as antipathetic towards a life printed on dollar bills as Odets had been, it is clear that the spiritual regeneration of the Younger family is ultimately contingent on a ten thousand dollar check, for it is only the money which makes it possible for them to challenge the system under which they have suffered. In making it the necessary prerequisite for their return to dignity and pride Hansberry would seem to demean the faith in human potential which she is ostensibly endorsing. Walter, again like Willy Loman, far from rejecting the system which is oppressing him wholeheartedly embraces it. He rejects the cause of social commitment and compassion and places his faith in the power of money. It is the unintentional irony of this play however that he proves to be right, 'You all want everybody to carry a flag and a spear and sing some marching songs, huh? You wanna spend your life looking into things and trying to find the right and the wrong part . . . There ain't no causes—there ain't nothing but taking in this world, and he who takes most is smartest—and it don't make a damn bit of difference how.' (R.S. p. 198.) Without the insurance check not only would the dreams

[1] Robert Nemerov, 'Introduction', *The Sign in Sidney Brustein's Window* (New York, 1965), p. xxi.

have been left to shrivel like raisins in the sun but so would Beneatha's compassion and Walter's courage. Indeed Walter's final conversion, or, as Hansberry would put it, the eventual realisation of his potential, is itself as unconvincing as Biff's similar conversion in *Death of a Salesman*. Her true declaration of faith is, however, embodied in the person of Asagai, the least convincing of the play's characters. This African revolutionary is used by Lorraine Hansberry as a point of reference—as the realisation of the dignity and commitment which exists in Walter only as potential. When Walter, returning home drunk, had leapt onto a table and shouted out the words of a defiant nationalism he had been establishing a contact with the African which served at the same time as a source of contrast and promise. Yet Asagai's self-assurance remains untested. His confident assertion of progress and redemption remains unreal precisely because we do not see him, as we do the Youngers, brought face to face with frustration.

The relationship between the American Negro and the African remains, as Baldwin had in part anticipated it would, a complex arrangement of subtle misunderstandings. Particularly in the nineteen-twenties' 'Negro Renaissance' Africa was seen as a pagan but innocent land. In a poem by Gwendolyn Bennett the sense of a corrupted present is emphasised by a romantic longing for an African past in which identity was more than a response to a hostile environment:

> I want to see lithe Negro girls,
> Etched dark against the sky
> While Sunset lingers.
>
> I want to hear the silent sands,
> Singing to the moon
> Before the Sphinx-still face . . .
>
> I want to hear the chanting
> Around a heathen fire
> Of a strange black race.
>
> I want to breathe the Lotus flow'r,
> Sighing to the stars
> With tendrils drinking at the Nile . . .
>
> I want to feel the surging
> Of my sad people's soul
> Hidden by a minstrel-smile.[1]

[1] Arna Bontemps, ed., *American Negro Poetry* (New York, 1963), p. 74.

And again the same contrast in 'No Images' by Waring Cuney:

> She does not know
> Her beauty,
> She thinks her brown body
> Has no glory.
>
> If she could dance
> Naked,
> Under the palm trees
> And see her image in the river
> She would know.
>
> But there are no palm trees
> On the street,
> And dishwater gives back no images.[1]

While this romantic view of Africa repelled both the Christian and the communist whose approach to that continent was coloured by their own ideology, it was a view which seems to have seized the imagination of many writers. It is certainly clear that *A Raisin in the Sun* accepts unquestioningly the validity of Cuney's symbol. Asagai has no validity outside of this convention. If Hansberry mocks the naïvete with which Beneatha tries to adopt African modes of dress and general culture she leaves unchallenged the assumption that those values stem from a purer source. Yet Asagai's vitality and enthusiasm spring from his own dreams which differ in kind from Walter's only in magnitude and in the fact that they are never put to the test. We see Walter balance his manhood against a dream of success but Asagai remains nothing but an oracle whose declarations make sense only to those who are faithful to the stereotype African of Bennett and Cuney, rich in wisdom and standing, like the noble savage, as a reminder of primal innocence. Asagai's declaration of the inevitability of change built on courage and compassion, a declaration which clearly represents Lorraine Hansberry's own faith, remains as unconvincing as do the circumstances of Walter's change of heart, 'things will happen, slowly and swiftly. At times it will seem that nothing changes at all . . . and then again . . . the sudden dramatic events which make history leap into the future. And then quiet again . . . And I even will have moments when I wonder if the quiet was not better than all that death and hatred. But . . . I will not wonder long.' (R.S. pp. 191-2.)

[1] *Ibid.*, pp. 98-99.

Lorraine Hansberry dedicates her second and last play, *The Sign in Sidney Brustein's Window* to 'the committed everywhere' and in doing so expresses not only her own personal philosophy but also her conception of the purpose of art. From her play, however, it becomes apparent that commitment does not mean for her exactly what it had for Brecht or even Rice and Odets, neither does it mean that intransigent alignment with sectional interests which undermines the drama of LeRoi Jones. The commitment of which she speaks is one to life rather than death, hope rather than despair and to human potential rather than human failure. Her enemy is thus neither the rich industrialist nor the racial bigot but rather the indifferent and the self-deceived. In terms of art her enemy is Camus and the theatre of the absurd so that *The Sign in Sidney Brustein's Window* is as much a statement of artistic responsibilities as of social inadequacies. Indeed in many ways it is a dramatic equivalent of Tynan's assault on Ionesco for while he was working, like Brecht, from a Marxist premise, Hansberry's rejection of the absurd is based on a similar desire (already noted in the drama of confrontation of which this play is essentially a part) to re-constitute the humanist heresy of belief in man.

The Sidney Brustein of the title is a liberal who fluctuates between the two poles of liberalism; Thoreauesque dissociation and enthusiastic political involvement. The play effectively spells out the inadequacies and ultimately the futility of both these extremes. In essence Sidney Brustein is but another of the American heroes in search of primal innocence waging a holy war and deeply wounding those around him. As we have noted Baldwin has said that, 'People who shut their eyes to reality simply invite their own destruction, and anyone who insists on remaining in a state of innocence long after that innocence is dead turns himself into a monster.'[1] In effect this is a savagely accurate picture of Sidney Brustein, as indeed it is of Miller's Quentin. For Sidney, in clutching naïvely at what he imagines to be innocence becomes insensitive, blind alike to the crumbling of his marriage and the halting despair of his sister-in-law. His relationship with his wife, Iris, is strained because he refuses to recognise the reality of the world but chooses rather to remould it, and her, to suit his own personal vision. On the one hand he tends to lapse into a romantic dream of man as innocent and free spirit suitably removed from the conventional corruption of the city. In this mood he takes Huck Finn as an archetype of noble dissociation and sees Iris as a mountain nymph. On the other

[1] *Notes of a Native Son*, p. 165.

hand he throws himself with naïve faith into political activism. There is
a bitter desperation in Iris's demand to know which role she should
play—Margaret Mead or Barbara Allen—for her life is lived as a
counterpart to her husband's and his sudden and impractical enthus-
iasms throw an increasing strain on their relationship. The crisis
between Sidney and his wife is ultimately a crisis of Sidney's liberalism.
For Iris rebels against the sterility of a life which gravitates around
idealistic dreams and facile crusades—a life of philosophical speculation
and meaningless activity entirely lacking in a commitment which means
anything more than an irresponsible game and which achieves nothing
more than the exchange of one corruption for another.

At the beginning of the play Sidney, who has just admitted to the
failure of one of his impractical schemes, is prevailed upon to use a
newspaper which he has bought to support a reform candidate in a
local election. He accepts the campaign as a further diversion and the
sign which he puts in his window (a sign pledging support for the
reform candidate) is less evidence of his faith in the possibility of
change than of a self-justifying sense of the righteousness of protest.
He tells Mavis, his sister-in-law, that to change one politician for
another 'is to participate in some expression of the people's about the
way things are'.[1] The act of protest is sufficient and when his candidate
is elected he is genuinely amazed for, Hansberry suggests, Sidney's
liberalism is the exercise of conscience without attendant responsibility.
Indeed he remains blithely unaware, until informed by his wife, that
he has secured the election of a candidate who has sold out to the
machine, for his vision of the world is still founded on the absolutes
of former decades. It takes the professional cynicism of a playwright
friend to point out that ' "the good guys" and "the bad guys" went
out with World War Two'. (s.b. p. 59.)

Lorraine Hansberry's portrait of bewildered liberalism, however, far
from constituting an attack on liberals, as Richard Gilman suggests in
his review of the play, lies at the very centre of a drama which is
essentially concerned with the plight of the individual in a society in
which commitment is considered passé. In an article in *The New York
Sunday Times* she describes her sense of this dilemma and sees it as
the crux of her play:

[1] Lorraine Hansberry, *The Sign in Sidney Brustein's Window* (New York,
1965), p. 60. All future references to this play will be abbreviated to 's.b.'
and incorporated into the text.

'Few things are more natural than that the tortures of the *engagé* should attract me thematically. Being 34 years old at this writing means that I am of the generation which grew up in the swirl and dash of the Sartre-Camus debate of the post-war years. The silhouette of the Western intellectual poised in hesitation before the flames of involvement was an accurate symbolism of some of my closest friends, some of whom crossed each other leaping in and out, for instance, of the Communist Party. Others searched, as agonizingly, for the ultimate justification of their lives in the abstractions flowing out of London and Paris. Still others were contorted into seeking a meaningful repudiation of *all* justifications of anything and had, accordingly, turned to Zen, action painting or even just Jack Kerouac . . . It is the climate and mood of such intellectuals . . . which constitute the core of a play called *The Sign in Sidney Brustein's Window.*'[1]

Lorraine Hansberry is acutely aware of the temper of the decade in which she is writing. In the 1930's theatres had been created for a popular and vital social drama in which there had been no apparent conflict between the demands of drama and those of the practical idealist. The theatre of the fifties, however, was dominated by the absurd to which social concern was at best irrelevant and at worst a symptom of man's self-destructive optimism. When Sidney rages, in the second act, against a world in which anger and passion have been transmuted into neurosis and anaesthetised unconcern he is voicing equally the bewilderment of his age: 'Yes, by all means hand me the chloroform of my passions; the sweetening of my conscience; the balm of my glands. Oh blessed age! That has provided that I need never live again in the full temper of my rage . . . Wrath has become a poisoned gastric juice in the intestine. One does not *smite* evil any more: one holds one's gut, thus—and takes a pill.' (S.B. p. 96.)

If Hansberry is critical of liberalism which is nothing more than naïve self-expression she is equally critical of disinterest which masquerades under the guise of liberal tolerance. Iris epitomises this attitude which constitutes the other side of the liberal coin. It takes Mavis to point out the implications of this moral disengagement. When Iris takes as her maxim, 'Live and let live, that's all' Mavis retorts, 'That's just a shoddy little way of trying to avoid responsibility in the world.' (S.B. p. 57.) This desire for non-involvement is further emphasised, rather too pointedly, by Iris's surname, Parodus, an

[1] 'Introduction', *The Sign in Sidney Brustein's Window*, pp. xv-xvi.

implication which Mavis again underlines. Parodus, as she points out, is the Greek word for chorus, '. . . the chorus is always there, commenting . . . watching and being.' (S.B. p. 103.) Iris's form of moral dissociation makes no distinctions between Sidney's naïve absolutism and a commitment which is more fundamental. When Alton, a Negro friend of theirs, is offended by what he takes to be prejudice on their part Iris attacks him, assuming that his commitment is of the same nature as Sidney's. 'You and the causes all the time. It's phoney as hell! . . . The country is full of people who dropped it when they could'. (S.B. pp. 40-1.) Hansberry's laconic stage direction appended to this speech identifies the author's attitude. She describes the substance of the speech as 'Pragmatic bohemia'. (S.B. p. 41.)

Lorraine Hansberry's involvement with the plight of the Negro is subsumed here in a more general concern. The human failure which is evidenced in the hardening of prejudice in racial matters becomes for her indicative of a more fundamental failure which underlies alike the capricious enthusiasm of Sidney Brustein and the disaffiliation of Iris. The commitment which she urges, and in which all the play's characters fail, is a devotion to humanity which goes beyond a desire for political and moral freedoms. Gloria Parodus, Iris's sister, becomes the focus of Miss Hansberry's call for compassion—a compassion which, like that identified by Albee and Miller, does not shy away from reality but which rejects complacency and despair alike.

Gloria Parodus, like Wally O'Hara, the corrupt politician, has accepted the need for compromise—that, 'If you want to survive you've got to swing the way the world swings' (S.B. p. 138). At the age of nineteen she had come to the city from the country and had become a 'high fashion whore'. (S.B. p. 50.) After seven years and three attempted suicides she sees a chance to save herself. Alton Scales, Sidney's Negro friend, proposes to her and she decides to accept. When Alton discovers that she is a call-girl, however, his own racial past combines with physical disgust. Gloria becomes for him a commodity and a commodity, moreover, which has been used by white men. In revulsion against this past he sacrifices compassion to pride, 'I don't want white man's leavings, Sidney. I couldn't *marry* her'. (S.B. p. 102.) When Sydney underlines the racial nature of Alton's failure his concession is equally an admission of the fatuity of an intellectual commitment unsupported by emotional engagement, 'I know it—(*Touching his head*) here!' (S.B. p. 102.) His liberalism thus stands revealed as an irrelevant pose and the expansive humanity of his principles is subverted by an inability to transform it into political action. This gulf between intellectual commitment and a genuine involvement rooted in passion lies at the very heart both of this play and later of Baldwin's *Blues for Mr. Charlie*. The extent of this gulf is demonstrated by the fact that Gloria is failed not only by Alton but equally by Sidney, Iris and Mavis as well. When Mavis hears of the proposed marriage she is horrified. While aware of the therapeutic value to her sister the idea of miscegenation seems worse to her than prostitution. Unaware that Gloria's last chance has been destroyed she mouths the empty slogans of conservatism which seem now only slightly more obscene than those of a hypocritical liberalism, 'Look, the world's not ready . . . You have to think about children . . . You can't expect people to change that fast.' (s.b. p. 110.) When Sidney replies it is, as Hansberry points out, 'more with wonder than assertion' for he is on the edge of a new perception which does not coalesce until after Gloria's death, 'Mavis, the world is about to crack right down the middle. We've gotta change—or fall in the crack'. (s.b. p. 110.)

Yet for all this partial enlightenment Sidney is too wrapped up in his own disillusionment to offer any help or consolation to Gloria. Having been forced to confront the true nature of his liberalism he lapses into despair and trades absurdist aphorisms with David, his playwright neighbour, while his sister-in-law's own despair deepens into suicide. Although Hansberry feels herself at odds with some of the implications of Miller's *After the Fall* (She has Sidney mock that sense of universal guilt which Miller had derived from Camus—'We are all guilty, therefore all guilt is equal. Therefore none are innocent, therefore—none are guilty.' [s.b. p. 132]) this scene is reminiscent of that in which Quentin watches Maggie's attempted suicide. For Sidney's drunken nihilism is as surely an attempt to deny the reality of his guilt as was Quentin's refusal to accept the sleeping pills from his wife's hand. Both are offered the opportunity of accepting responsibility in the act of accepting the need for compassion, and both fail. So that Sidney is finally as lacking in individual compassion as Iris whose vaunted tolerance had concealed an ignorance of the desperation which was her sister's life. 'I happen to have a sister who is a fancy call girl . . . And I say so what? . . . it's her life so—who's to say'—a speech on which Hansberry makes her own comment in the stage directions, '(*Having done with responsibility, she shrugs with confidence*)' (s.b. pp. 50-1.) If Quentin comes to an understanding of himself and the nature of human relationships through his experience with Maggie, Gloria's death brings Sidney to a similar understanding. This, together with his realisation of the true nature of his liberalism, constitutes that moment of 'momentous enlightenment' which Albee and Miller had been concerned with portraying. Where the latter revelation appears to him, as it had to Quentin, as 'the fall of man', the death of his sister-in-law teaches him the absolute need to renew love and compassion. Like Quentin therefore, he comes to accept that commitment means responsibility and that freedom is circumscribed by a knowledge of the ineluctable connection between action and consequence.

The sign which hangs in Sidney Brustein's window is not an ironical comment on the impossibility of achieving anything in what Iris sees as this 'dirty world'. It represents the public face of a man whose vision of the world is radically simplified and who, until brought to the point of confrontation, has failed to understand what Hansberry conceives as the nature of commitment. The sign becomes, as Iris puts it, like spit in his face—a significant phrase carrying, as it does, overtones of *An Enemy of the People* and *All My Sons.*

Lorraine Hansberry believes and believes passionately in the possibility of change (witness her commentary to *A Question of Colour* 1964) but she insists that that change has to be fundamental. Like Albee's Martha, in *Who's Afraid of Virginia Woolf?* and Julian in *Tiny Alice*, both Iris and Gloria sense the inadequacy of intellectual abstractions and sexuality alike. Both of them reach a crisis in their lives at which they come to realise that their greatest need is for compassion—a sense of genuine and intimate contact between human beings. So that Lorraine Hansberry's enemy is not prejudice itself nor even the corrupt nature of politics or human relationships but rather anyone who denies the relevance and even the possibility of meaningful change. This places her on a collision course with her conception of contemporary art for she sees this as being concerned with chaos, decay and death and it is her basic assumption that 'decay is *not* the deepest damn thing going ... Death is too damn easy. Chaos is easier.' (s.b. p. 33.)

The Sign in Sidney Brustein's Window constitutes one of the most complete disavowals of absurdist drama which has yet been made. In its concern with the nature and purpose of art it goes beyond the introspection of *The Connection* and even the self-conscious dramas of Pirandello. Clearly Sidney's attack on the callow prophesies of Golding and Beckett represents the credo of a dramatist who believes passionately in the validity of insurgence and the redeemable nature of man. The play is the voice of social protest, no longer touched with the embarrassing simplicity of the thirties but rather redolent with the cutting sophistication which Albee had introduced into the American theatre. It is a protest not, like *A Raisin in the Sun*, against the suffocating actuality of existence inside a coloured skin but against a defeatism ingrained in post-war man and finding expression in modern literature. Lorraine Hansberry is in rebellion against a vision of man which destroys hope and which asserts, as does Golding, that moral regression is as inevitable as physical and mental advance. She is in rebellion, that is, against a vision of 'The savage soul of man from whence sprang, in the first place, the Lord of the Flies, Beezlebub himself! Man, dark gutted creatures of ancestral—cannibalism and mysterious all-consuming eeevil!' (S.B. p. 59.) To Hansberry this solipsistic drama does not present a true picture of the world but insists on universalising what is essentially individual insufficiency or social victimisation. The avant-garde dramatist, who, perhaps significantly inhabits the upper regions of the Brustein's apartment building, is a homosexual. (Sidney's comment that, 'he worships prostitutes. He says they are the only *real* women' (S.B. p. 56) is a reference to Genet and *The Balcony* 1953.) Although Richard Gilman, in his review of the play, accuses Miss Hansberry of an attack on homosexuals, this is to misunderstand her point which is once again that made by Tynan in his attack on Ionesco —that personal vision is of interest but that it cannot be taken as being of universal significance. As Sidney says to David, '. . . you have now written fourteen plays about not caring, about the isolation of the soul of man, the alienation of the human spirit, the desolation of all love, all possible communication. When what you really want to say is that you are ravaged by a society that will not sanctify your particular sexuality! (S.B. p. 66). It is this perception which saves Lorraine Hansberry from that fault which undermines the drama of LeRoi Jones and which Baldwin had seen as destroying the effectiveness of Richard Wright. She avoids the temptation to transmute racial bitterness into universal anguish and enervating fatalism, granting an ambivalence to her characters which would have been foreign to Wright and which stems from her passionately held faith in human potential. Mavis Parodus's racial prejudice does not nullify her genuine humanity neither does Alton Scales' colour justify his brutality. Miss Hansberry weds an understanding of historical causality to a genuine belief in the possibility of change—a faith which necessarily rejects art formed out of despair and finding its genesis in individual suffering. Writing in *Mademoiselle* five years earlier she had anticipated this confrontation:

> 'In the next ten years I hope that serious American art will rediscover the world around it, that our finest painters and writers will dismiss the vogue of unmodified despair in order to pick up the heritage of a nobler art. In spite of some awe-inspiring talents involved in recent writing, the appointment of sinister universality to Ego in settings of timeless torture has been a virtual abdication of the meaning of history, which has been resplendent with what may most certainly be called progress. I hope American creative artists will look again and see that Ego, like everything else, exists in time and context.'[1]

While denying nothing of the agony which the absurdists identify, like Albee and Miller she refuses to accept the resultant nihilism. Despite the similarity between her work and that of Miller and Albee, who both stressed the need to establish genuine contact between isolated individuals, it is clear that she identifies Albee in particular with the absurd—to the extent of parodying one of his plays:

> 'Oh, who's afraid of Absurdity! Absurdity! Absurdity!
> Who's afraid of Absurdity!
> Not we, not we, not we!' (s.b. p. 133.)

She continues this parody by making Sidney mock the standard premises of the absurd, 'Zarathustra has spoken—and God is dead? . . . "Progess" is an illusion and the only reality is—nothing?' (s.b. pp. 31-2) or in Gloria's words, 'Things as they are are as they are and have been and will be that way because they got that way because things were as they were in the first place'. (s.b. p. 131.) Her complete revulsion from the absurd is summed up finally in the words which she gives to David, as the successful dramatist of the nineteen-sixties, 'Any profession of concern with decency is the most indecent of all human affectations.' (s.b. p. 133.) To Hansberry, therefore, 'it is the debate which is, for all human purposes, beside the point. The *debate* which is absurd. The "why" of why we are here is an intrigue for adolescents; the "how" is what must command the living.' (s.b. p. 82.) Thus her attack on the absurd is not the conventional Marxist complaint that it fails to concern itself with the social situation or that it lacks real contact with the proletariat. What she attacks is its lack of humanity. When Mavis explains what she had expected of art it is clear

[1] 'Introduction', *The Sign in Sidney Brustein's Window*, p. lx.

that in her emphasis on the need for compassion and hope she is speaking for Hansberry herself. 'I was taught to believe that—creativity and great intelligence ought to make one expansive and understanding. That if ordinary people, among whom I have the sense at least to count myself, could not expect understanding from artists . . . then where indeed might we look for it at all—in this quite dreadful world.' (s.b. p. 64.) If this seems too much like a philistine cry for affirmative theatre at any cost James Baldwin had cast a similar doubt on the value of intellectual narcissim when he said of Sartre and Camus, 'It has always seemed to me that ideas were somewhat more real to them than people'.[1] Neither was Hansberry unaware of how dangerously close, especially in America, she was coming to advocating a theatre of candied resolution. As she had said in her article in *Mademoiselle*, 'Nor is this a call, Heaven forbid, to happy endings or clichés of affirmation. For the supreme test of technical skill and creative imagination is the depth of art it requires to render the infinite varieties of the human spirit—which invariably hangs between despair and joy.'[2]

If she rejects despair and the naïvete of political activism alike Lorraine Hansberry is finally left with a belief in compassion which allies her not only with Albee and Miller but also with Arnold Wesker who had also tried to balance political disillusion with human resilience. Like the drama of confrontation, of which they are essentially a part, they do not deny the validity of the absurdist's view of the world but find grounds for hope in the ability of individual men to discover strength in confronting reality and hope in the fact of compassion. As Sarah says, in Wesker's *Chicken Soup with Barley* (1958), 'Philosophy? You want philosophy? Nothing means anything! There! Philosophy! I know! So? Nothing! despair—die then! Will that be achievement? To die? . . . So what if it all means nothing? When you know *that* you can start again . . . We got through, didn't we? We got scars but we got through . . . You've got to care, you've got to care or you'll die.'[3] Sidney's rebuttal of his wife's disengagement is couched in the same terms, both playwrights calling for the re-institution of passion, '*I care!* I care about it all. It takes too much energy *not* to care.' (s.b. p. 66.)

So too in his play *I'm Talking about Jerusalem* (1960) Wesker confronts the same problem in a way which establishes a clear connection

---

[1] *Nobody Knows My Name*, p. 151.
[2] *Op. cit.*, p. lx.
[3] *Ibid.*, pp. 222-3.

between his work and Hansberry's. Ronny Kahn, still believing in the simplistic operation of ideals, is made to confront the reality of his own failure—a failure which is essentially that of Sidney Brustein, namely an inability to temper commitment with humanity. As his brother-in-law insists, 'I know your kind, you go around the world crooning about brotherhood and yet you can't even see a sordid love affair through to the end.' Ronnie, in admitting the truth of this is made to confront his failure, '. . . you're right, There isn't anything I've seen through to the end . . . Isn't that curious? I say all the right things, I think all the right things, but somewhere, some bloody where I fail as a human being.'[1] Yet, as with Sidney Brustein, it is precisely this confrontation, this moment of 'momentous enlightenment' which enables him to discover a sense of affirmation. He sinks to his knees 'in utter despair' but then in a quasi-ritualistic movement, which recalls a moment earlier in the play when a young child had played a game called, 'Look, I'm alive', he rises to his feet, still uncertain yet capable of making an affirmation based on the supremacy of hope over despair, 'We—must—be—bloody—mad—to cry!'[2] Hansberry moulds the same faith out of her characters' despair and disillusionment with a similar belief in the need to end self-pity, 'Yes . . . weep now, darling, weep. Let us both weep. That is the first thing: to let ourselves feel again . . . Then, tomorrow, we shall make something strong of this sorrow.' (s.b. p. 143.) The need to temper idealism with humanity, a need recognised by Ibsen and O'Neill, becomes a central tenet of the drama of confrontation but it is a compassion built on the perception of a world which Iris identifies as 'dirty', a world in which 'vision don't work'.[3]

Inherent in Lorraine Hansberry's vision, therefore, is the assumption that the artist has a duty to respond to the agonised cry of mankind with something more than nihilism. Compassion becomes not merely a theme but the essential *modus vivendi* of the artist himself. When Sidney is finally jolted into taking a genuine and positive stance against the cynical defeatism of Wally O'Hara his declaration of intent expresses essentially Lorraine Hansberry's own conviction that the artist cannot help but be committed, '. . . you have forced me to take a position. Finally—the one thing I never wanted to do. Just not being for you

[1] Arnold Wesker, *The Wesker Trilogy* (London, 1960), pp. 76-7.
[2] Arnold Wesker, *The Wesker Trilogy* (London, 1960), p. 224.
[3] *Ibid.*, p. 222.

is not enough . . . I have been forced to learn I have to be *against* you'. (s.b. p. 141.) The essence of this commitment lies not in facile dreams of political revolution, however, but in a more fundamental belief in redemption—the belief, in Sidney's words, that 'death is waste and love is sweet . . . and that flowers smell good and that I hurt terribly today and that hurt is desperation and desperation is—energy and energy can *move* things.' (s.b. p. 142.) It is a commitment leavened but not subverted by the cynicism of the absurd, 'seasoned, more cynical, tougher, harder to fool—and therefore less likely to quit.' (s.b. p. 141.)

Lorraine Hansberry's greatest achievement lies in her ability to avoid what Saunders Redding has called 'The obligations imposed by race on the average . . . talented Negro'.[1] The obligation to limit one's scope to the immediate but parochial injustices of racial intolerance has for long sapped the creative energy of the Negro writer. Having paid her debt to this tradition with the poor *A Raisin in the Sun*, however, Hansberry achieves a significant break-through with *The Sign in Sidney Brustein's Window* which is clearly in the mainstream of contemporary drama. The Negro is no longer seen as the victim of a savage social situation but becomes an endemic part of a society desperately search-ing for a valid response to the human condition. Lorraine Hansberry's death at the age of thirty-four has robbed the theatre of the one Negro dramatist who has demonstrated her ability to transcend parochialism and social bitterness. As she has said in an article called 'The Negro in the American Theatre', 'while an excessively poignant Porgy was being instilled in generations of Americans, his true-life counterpart was ravaged by longings that were, and are, in no way alien to those of the rest of mankind, and that bear within them the stuff of truly great art. He is waiting yet for those of us who will but look more carefully into his eyes, and listen more intently to his soliloquies.'[2] Regrettably this remains as true in 1966 as it was in 1960 when Hansberry wrote it.

Camus has said that it 'would be impossible to over-emphasise the passionate affirmation that underlies the act of revolt and which dis-tinguishes it from resentment. Rebellion, though apparently negative since it creates nothing, is profoundly positive in that it reveals the part of a man which must always be defended.'[3] It is clear that neither James Baldwin nor LeRoi Jones succeed in attaining to this affirmation

[1] *Black Voices*, p. 4.
[2] *American Playwrights on Drama*, pp. 166-7.
[3] *The Rebel*, p. 25.

for their protest never progresses beyond 'resentment'. Lorraine Hansberry's commitment, however, transcends the merely parochial for her rebellion is directed less against intransigent racialism than against the sterility of the absurd and the inconsequence of a theatre founded on distraction. Like Miller, Gelber, Albee and Bellow she clearly sees the dramatist's function as consisting in a compassionate statement of the need for human contact in an unattractive world. Indeed her faith in the need to face reality effectively bridges the gap between confrontation and commitment.

Antonin Artaud in 1938 wrote that 'If people are out of the habit of going to the theatre, if we have all finally come to think of theatre as an inferior art, a means of popular distraction . . . it is because we have learned too well what the theatre has been, namely, falsehood and illusion.'[1] Mary McCarthy, writing of the American theatre twenty years later, could with justice apply the same comment. In the following eight years, however, the complexion of American drama has genuinely changed. Perhaps, as Bellow's Henderson says when finally brought into confrontation with reality, 'the sleep is burst'.[2]

[1] *The Theatre and its Double*, p. 76.
[2] *Henderson the Rain King*, p. 328.

BIBLIOGRAPHY

FOR THE sake of convenience the plays under consideration in this book are considered under 'Primary Sources' while other works, referred to in footnotes, are collected under 'Secondary Sources'. All other works to which I am indebted are to be found in the third section.

PRIMARY SOURCES

Dates shown are those of the edition consulted. For the date of original publications, see text.

Albee, Edward. *The American Dream* and *The Zoo Story*. New York, 1963·
——. *Who's Afraid of Virginia Woolf?*. New York, 1963.
——. *Tiny Alice*. New York, 1965.
——. *Malcolm*. New York, 1966.
——. *A Delicate Balance*. New York, 1966.
Baldwin, James. *Blues for Mr. Charlie*. London, 1965.
Bellow, Saul. *The Last Analysis*. New York, 1965.
Brown, Kenneth H. 'The Brig', *Tulane Drama Review*, VIII, iii (Spring, 1964), pp. 222-59.
Gelber, Jack. *The Connection*. London, 1961.
Hansberry, Lorraine. *A Raisin in the Sun*, in *Four Contemporary American Plays* . . ., ed. Bennet Cerf, pp. 101-205.
——. *The Sign in Sidney Brustein's Window*. New York, 1965.
Jones, LeRoi. 'The Toilet', *Kulture*, III, ix (Spring, 1963), 25-39.
——. *Dutchman* and *The Slave*. New York, 1964.
Miller, Arthur. *Arthur Miller's Collected Plays*. New York, 1957.
——. 'After the Fall', *The Saturday Evening Post*, Feb. 1, 1964, pp. 34-59.
——. *After the Fall*. London, 1965.
——. *Incident at Vichy*. New York, 1966.

SECONDARY SOURCES

Abel, Lionel. *Metatheatre*. New York, 1963.
Albee, Edward. 'Which Theatre is the Absurd One?' in *Directions in Modern Theatre and Drama* by John Gassner. New York, 1965, pp. 329-36.
Anon. 'New Light on the Invisible', *The Times Literary Supplement*, Nov. 25, 1965, pp. 1046-9.

Anon. 'Innocent Astray', *New Yorker*, Jan. 22, 1966, p. 74.

Artaud, Antonin. *The Theatre and its Double* . . ., trans. Mary Caroline Richards. New York, 1958.

Baldwin, James, Emile Capouya, Lorraine Hansberry, Nat Hentoff, Langston Hughes, Alfred Kazin. 'The Negro in American Culture', *Cross Currents*, XI, iii (Summer, 1961), pp. 205-24.

Baldwin, James. *The Fire Next Time*. London, 1963.

———. *Notes of a Native Son*. London, 1964.

———. *Nobody Knows My Name*. London, 1964.

———. *Another Country*. London, 1965.

Beckett, Samuel. *Waiting for Godot*. London, 1959.

Bellow, Saul. *The Adventures of Auggie March*. London, 1954.

———. *Seize the Day*. New York, 1956.

———. *Henderson the Rain King*. London, 1959.

———. 'How I wrote Auggie March's Story', *The New York Times Book Review*, Jan. 31, 1954, pp. 3, 17.

———. 'The Writer as Moralist', *Atlantic Monthly* (March, 1963), pp. 58-62.

Bentley, Eric. *Bernard Shaw*. London, 1950.

———. *The Playwright as Thinker*. New York, 1955.

Blackham, H. J. *Six Existentialist Thinkers*. London, 1953.

Blau, Herbert, Jules Irving. 'The Living Theatre and Larger Issues', *Tulane Drama Review*, VIII, iii (Spring, 1964), pp. 194-9.

Bontemps, Arna, ed. *American Negro Poetry*. New York, 1963.

Brecht, Bertolt. *Brecht on Theatre* . . ., trans. John Willett. London, 1964.

Breit, Harvey. 'Talk with Saul Bellow', *The New York Times Book Review*, Sept. 20, 1953, p. 22.

Brook, Peter. 'From Zero to the Infinite', *The Encore Reader* . . ., ed. Horowitz, Milne and Hale. London, 1965.

Browne E. Martin. 'Introduction', *Right you are !* (*If you Think So*), *All for the Best*, *Henry IV*, by Luigi Pirandello. Harmondsworth, 1962.

Brustein, Robert. *The Theatre of Revolt*. Boston, 1965.

———. 'Albee's Allegory of Innocence', *The New Republic*, Jan. 29, 1966, pp. 34, 36.

Camus, Albert. *The Rebel* . . ., trans. Anthony Bower. London, 1953.

———. *The Collected Fiction of Albert Camus* . . ., trans. Stuart Gilbert and Justin O'Brian, London, 1963.

———. *Caligula* and *Cross Purpose* . . ., trans. Stuart Gilbert. Harmondsworth, 1965.

———. *Carnets 1942-1951* . . ., trans. Philip Thody. London, 1966.

Cage, John, Michael Kirby and Richard Schechner. 'An Interview with John Cage', *Tulane Drama Review*, X, ii (Winter, 1965), pp. 50-72.

Cerf, Bennet, ed. *Four Contemporary American Plays*. New York, 1961.

Charney, Maurice. 'James Baldwin's Quarrel with Richard Wright', *American Quarterly*, XV, i (Spring, 1963), pp. 65-75.

Cocteau, Jean. *Orpheus, Oedipus Rex, The Infernal Machine . . .*, trans. Carl Wildman. London, 1962.

Copeau, Jacques. 'Once again: Style', trans. Leonard C. Pronko. *Tulane Drama Review*, VII, iv (Summer, 1963), pp. 180-91.

Cummings, E. E. *A Miscellany . . .*, ed. George Firmage. London, 1966.

Dewey, Ken. 'X-ings', *Tulane Drama Review*, X, ii (Winter, 1965), pp. 216-23.

Duberman, Martin. *In White America*. London, 1964.

Ellison, Ralph. *Invisible Man*. Harmondsworth, 1965.

Esslin, Martin. *Brecht: A Choice of Evils*. London, 1959.

———. *The Theatre of the Absurd*. New York, 1961.

Firmage, George J. Ed. *E. E. Cummings: A Miscellany*. London, 1966.

Frenz, Horst. Ed. *American Playwrights on Drama*. New York, 1965.

Friedman, Norman. *e. e. cummings*. Carbondale, 1964.

Frye, Northrup. *Anatomy of Criticism*. Princeton, 1957.

Gassner, John. *Directions in Modern Theatre and Drama*. New York, 1965.

Gilman, Richard. 'The Drama is Coming Now', *Tulane Drama Review*, VII, iv (Summer, 1963), pp. 27-42.

Goethe, Johann Wolfgang. *Faust: Part II . . .*, trans. Philip Wayne. Harmondsworth, 1959.

Guiton, Margaret, and Germaine Brée. *An Age of Fiction*. London, 1958.

Hansberry, Lorraine. *A Matter of Colour*. Harmondsworth, 1965.

Hassan, Ihab. *Radical Innocence: Studies in the Contemporary American Novel*. Princeton, 1961.

Harris, Wendell V. 'Morality, Absurdity and Albee', *Southwest Review*, XLIX, iii, pp. 249-56.

Hewes, Henry. 'The Family that Stayed Separate', *The Saturday Review*, 49, Oct. 8, 1966, p. 90.

Hill, Herbert. *Black Voices*. London, 1964.

Ibsen, Henrik. *Four Great Plays by Ibsen . . .*, R. Farquarson Sharp. New York, 1959.

Ionesco, Eugene. *Notes and Counter Notes . . .*, trans. Donald Watson. London, 1964.

Johnston, Jill. ' "Happenings" on the New York Scene', *The Encore Reader . . .*, ed. Horowitz, Milne and Hale. London, 1965.

Jones, LeRoi. 'A History of Jazz: The New York Scene', rev., *Kulture*, III, ix (Spring, 1963), p. 90.

———, 'Brief Reflections on Two Hot Shots', *Kulture*, III, xii (Winter, 1963), pp. 2-5.

———. 'Expressive Language', *Kulture*, III, xii (Winter, 1963), pp. 77-81.

———. 'Exaugeral Address', *Kulture*, III, xii (Winter, 1963), facing p. 86.

———. ed. *The Moderns*. London, 1965.

Kirby, Michael. *Happenings*. London, 1965.

———. 'The New Theatre', *Tulane Drama Review*, X, ii (Winter, 1965), pp. 23-43.

Koestler, Arthur. *The Yogi and the Commissar*. London, 1945.

Krutch, Joseph Wood. *The American Drama since 1918*. New York, 1957.

Laurents, Arthur. *A Clearing in the Woods*. New York, 1957.

Lewis, R. W. B. *The Picaresque Saint*. London, 1960.

Lorca, Federico Garcia. *Three Tragedies . . .*, trans. James Graham-Lujan and Richard L. O'Connell. Harmondsworth, 1961.

Machiz, Herbert, ed. *Artists' Theatre: Four Plays*. New York, 1960.

Mailer, Norman. *Advertisements for Myself*. London, 1961.

Markus, Thomas B. '*Tiny Alice* and Tragic Catharis', *Educational Theatre Journal*, XVII, pp. 225-33.

McCarthy, Mary. *Sights and Spectacles 1937-1958*. London, 1959.

Miller, Arthur. 'On Social Plays', in *A View from the Bridge*. London, 1957, pp. 1-17.

———. 'A Foreword by the Author', *The Saturday Evening Post*, Feb. 1, 1964, pp. 32-3.

———. 'Interview with T. G. Rosenthall', *The B.B.C. Third Programme*, Feb. 2, 1966.

Miller, Henry. *Just Wild about Harry: a melo-melo in seven Scenes*. London, 1964.

Miller, Jordan. *American Dramatic Literature*. New York, 1961.

Nemerov, Robert. 'Introduction', *The Sign in Sidney Brustein's Window*, by Lorraine Hansberry, New York, 1965.

O'Neill, Eugene. *All God's Chillun Got Wings*. London, 1925.

———. *The Plays of Eugene O'Neill*, 3 vols. New York, 1954.

———. *Long Day's Journey into Night*. New Haven, 1956.

Orwell, George. *1984*. London, 1965.

Osborne, John. *Look Back in Anger*. London, 1960.

Ossman, David, interviews. *The Sullen Art*. New York, 1963.

Pirandello, Luigi. *Six Characters in Search of an Author . . .*, trans. Frederick May. London, 1954.

———. *Right You Are! (If You Think So), All for the Best, Henry IV . . .*, trans. and with an introduction by E. Martin Browne. Harmondsworth, 1962.

Rosenberg, Marvin. 'A Metaphor for Dramatic Form', in *Directions in Modern Theatre and Drama*, by John Gassner. New York, 1965, pp. 341-51.

Sartre, Jean-Paul. *Existentialism and Humanism . . .*, trans. Philip Mairet. London, 1948.

——. *Lucifer and the Lord . . .*, trans. Kitty Black. London, 1952.

——. *The Flies* and *In Camera . . .*, trans. Stuart Gilbert. London, 1946.

——. *Situations . . .*, trans. Benita Eisler. London, 1965.

Schechner, Richard. 'T.D.R. Comment', *Tulane Drama Review*, VII, iii (Spring, 1963), pp. 7-10.

——. 'Interview with Judith Malina', *Tulane Drama Review*, VIII, iii (Spring, 1964), pp. 207-12.

——. 'Interview with Kenneth Brown', *Tulane Drama Review*, VIII, iii (Spring, 1964), pp. 212-19.

Schneider, Alan. 'Why So Afraid?', *Tulane Drama Review*, VII, iii (Spring, 1963), p. 11.

Shaw, Bernard. *Shaw on Theatre*. New York, 1958.

Steinbeck, John. *The Grapes of Wrath*. New York, 1958.

Stewart, R. S. 'John Gielgud and Edward Albee Talk about the Theatre', *Atlantic Monthly*, 215, iv (April, 1965), pp. 61-8.

Tanner, Tony. *Saul Bellow*. London, 1965.

Thompson, Thomas. 'A Burst of Negro Drama', *Life*, May 29, 1964, pp. 62A-70.

Trilling, Diana. *Claremont Essays*. London, 1965.

Tynan, Kenneth. 'Preface', *The Connection*, by Jack Gelber. London, 1960.

——. 'Ionesco, man of Destiny?', *The Observer*, June 22, 1958.

Watts, Alan. *Beat Zen Square Zen and Zen*. San Francisco, 1959.

Wellwarth, George. *The Theatre of Protest and Paradox*. London, 1965.

Wesker, Arnold. *The Wesker Trilogy*. London, 1960.

Williams, Tennessee. *Orpheus Descending*. London, 1958.

——. *The Night of the Iguana*. London, 1963.

Winter, Sophus Keith. *Eugene O'Neill*. New York, 1961.

Woolf, Virginia. *To The Lighthouse*. London, 1960.

OTHER WORKS CONSULTED

Adler, Jacob H. '*Night of the Iguana:* A New Tennessee Williams?' *Ramparts* (November, 1962), pp. 69-74.

Albee, Edward. *The Sandbox and The Death of Bessie Smith*. New York, 1963.

———. *The Ballad of the Sad Café*. London, 1965.

Beckett, Samuel. *Endgame*. London, 1964.

Bone, Robert. *The Negro Novel in America*, revised edition. New Haven, 1965.

Booth, John E. 'Albee and Schneider Observe: "Something's Stirring",' *Theatre Arts* (March, 1961), pp. 22-4.

Brecht, Bertolt. *The Caucasian Chalk Circle . . .*, trans. James and Tonia Stern with W. H. Auden. London, 1965.

Cole, Toby. *Playwrights on Playwriting*. London, 1960.

Corrigan, Robert W. *Theatre in the Twentieth Century*. New York, 1963.

Falk, Signi L. *Tennessee Williams*. New York, 1961.

Finkelstein, Sidney. *Existentialism and Alienation in American Literature*, New York, 1965.

Hagopian, John V. 'Arthur Miller: The Salesman's Two Cases', *Modern Drama* (September, 1963), pp. 117-25.

Hansberry, Lorraine. 'Me Tink Me Hear Sounds in De Night', *Theatre Arts* (October, 1961), pp. 9-11.

Huftel, Sheila. *Arthur Miller: The Burning Glass*. London, 1965.

Ibsen, Henrik. *Last Plays of Henrik Ibsen . . .*, trans. Arvid Paulson. New York, 1962.

Ionesco, Eugene. *Plays . . .*, trans. Derek Prouse and Donald Watson, 7 vols. London, 1958-1965.

Keating, Edward M. 'Mildew on the Old Magnolia', *Ramparts* (November, 1962), pp. 69-74.

Leech, Clifford. *O'Neill*. London, 1963.

Lewis, Allan. 'Fun and Games of Edward Albee', *Educational Theatre Journal* (March, 1964), pp. 29-39

Lumley, Frederick. *Trends in Twentieth Century Drama*. London, 1956.

McAnany, Emile G. 'The Tragic Commitment: Some Notes of Arthur Miller', *Modern Drama* (May, 1962), pp. 11-20.

Miller, Arthur. 'The Shadows of the Gods', *Harper's Magazine*, CCXVII (August, 1958), pp. 35-43.

———. Gore Vidal, et al., '*Death of a Salesman:* a Symposium', *Tulane Drama Review*, II (May, 1958), pp. 63-9.

Miller, Jordan. 'Myth and the American Dream: O'Neill to Albee', *Modern Drama* (September, 1964), pp. 190-8.

Richardson, Jack. *The Prodigal*. New York, 1960.

Schisgal, Murray. *The Typists and The Tiger*. London, 1964.

Silberman, Charles E. *Crisis in Black and White.* London, 1965.

Stowe, Harriet Beecher. *Uncle Tom's Cabin; or, Life Among the Lowly.* London, 1884.

Straumann, Heinrich. *American Literature in the Twentieth Century.* London, 1962.

Strindberg, August. *Seven Plays by August Strindberg* . . ., trans. Arvid Paulson. New York, 1960.

Welland, Dennis. *Arthur Miller.* London, 1961.

Wells, Arvin. 'The Living and the Dead in *All My Sons*', *Modern Drama* (May, 1964), pp. 46-51.

Wright, Richard. *Uncle Tom's Children.* New York, 1963.

——. *Native Son.* New York, 1964.

INDEX